Would the World Be Better without the UN?

Would the World Be Better without the UN?

Thomas G. Weiss

polity

The right of Thomas G. Weiss to be identified as Author of this Work has been asserted in accordance with the UK Copyright, Designs and Patents Act 1988.

First published in 2018 by Polity Press
Reprinted 2018 (twice)

Polity Press
65 Bridge Street
Cambridge CB2 1UR, UK

Polity Press
101 Station Landing, Suite 300
Medford, MA 02155, USA

ISBN-13: 978-1-5095-1725-1
ISBN-13: 978-1-5095-1726-8 (pb)

A catalogue record for this book is available from the British Library.

Library of Congress Cataloging-in-Publication Data

Names: Weiss, Thomas G. (Thomas George), 1946- author.
Title: Would the world be better without the UN? / Thomas G. Weiss.
Description: Cambridge, UK ; Malden, MA, USA : Polity Press, [2018] |
   Includes bibliographical references and index.
Identifiers: LCCN 2017019714 (print) | LCCN 2017043448 (ebook) | ISBN
   9781509517282 (Mobi) | ISBN 9781509517299 (Epub) | ISBN 9781509517251 |
   ISBN 9781509517268 (pbk.)
Subjects: LCSH: United Nations. | Security, International--International
   cooperation. | Peace-building--International cooperation. | Human
   rights--International cooperation. | Poverty--International cooperation. |
   Environmental quality--International cooperation.
Classification: LCC JZ4984.5 (ebook) | LCC JZ4984.5 .W4595 2018 (print) | DDC
   341.23--dc23
LC record available at https://lccn.loc.gov/2017019714

Typeset in 10.5 on 12pt Sabon by
Servis Filmsetting Ltd, Stockport, Cheshire
Printed and bound in Great Britain by Clays Ltd, Elcograf S.p.A.

For further information on Polity, visit our website: politybooks.com

CONTENTS

CONTENTS

ABOUT THE AUTHOR

Thomas G. Weiss is Presidential Professor of Political Science at The City University of New York's Graduate Center and Director Emeritus (2001–14) of the Ralph Bunche Institute for International Studies who was named 2016 Andrew Carnegie Fellow. Past president of the International Studies Association (2009–10) and recipient of its "IO Distinguished Scholar Award 2016," he also directed the United Nations Intellectual History Project (1999–2010) and was research professor at SOAS, University of London (2012–15), chair of the Academic Council on the UN System (2006–9), editor of *Global Governance*, research director of the International Commission on Intervention and State Sovereignty, research professor at Brown University's Watson Institute for International Studies, executive director of the Academic Council on the UN System and of the International Peace Academy, a member of the UN secretariat, and a consultant to public and private agencies. He has written extensively about multilateral approaches to international peace and security, humanitarian action, and sustainable development. His most recent single-authored volumes include *Humanitarianism Intervention: Ideas in Action* (2016); *What's Wrong with the United Nations and How to Fix It* (2016); *Governing the World? Addressing "Problems without Passports"* (2014); *Global Governance: Why? What? Whither?* (2013); *Humanitarian Business* (2013); and *Thinking about Global Governance: Why People and Ideas Matter* (2011).

ACKNOWLEDGMENTS

I begin with my profound gratitude to the Carnegie Corporation of New York, which named me a 2016 Andrew Carnegie Fellow. The generous support provided two years for the kind of research and reflection that I hope is present on every page in this book. Vartan Gregorian was my boss at Brown University and as a consultant to the corporation when he first arrived in New York. But he has become far more than that over the years, inspiring me to push myself and my thoughts about the past, present, and future of multilateralism and the United Nations. Most charitable foundations and governments invest in institutions rather than individuals and in soundbites rather than research. The Carnegie Corporation under his stewardship has gone against that conventional grain, and so other fellows and I have been the beneficiaries. This book would not have appeared as it has, or as quickly, without the foundation's generosity of spirit and vision.

The most congenial and productive of my professional homes has, since 1998, been The City University of New York's Graduate Center. Former president William Kelly hired me when he was provost and consistently and enthusiastically supported my professional activities as well as tolerated my sense of humor. Current president Chase Robinson has continued to build the distinction of the Graduate Center and nominated me to be a Carnegie Fellow, which has made possible a wonderfully rich last two years.

I have benefited over the years from a number of wonderful intellects and helping hands among my advanced graduate students. This volume reflects research by Paul Celentano, who helped fill in some of the holes that existed after I formulated the book outline. Danielle Zach, as she has over the last decade, abandoned her own work as a post-doc to apply a sharp mind and eye to the raw manuscript, improving substantially its structure and content. This book simply would not have been as timely or persuasive without Paul's and Danielle's able helping hands.

This volume marks the culmination of career-long efforts, and I repeat a bit of what I wrote in a 2011 collection of essays.[1] What has united, or perhaps haunted, my work over the years is what many would deem a curious conviction – namely, that community interests should hold sway but are invariably shortchanged, nationally or internationally. Long before the "America First" of Donald Trump in the United States, the country's welfare had often been sacrificed on the altar of individualism; but globally those of the commons are typically and tragically trampled by great powers as well as by tin-pot dictators and megalomaniacs. Yet, I have remained steadfast in believing that multilateral cooperation is a way not only to attenuate American and big-power arrogance but also to solve many, albeit not all, thorny problems that defy national boundaries.

My analyses of contemporary world politics might very well "depress Dr Pangloss," the character in Voltaire's *Candide* who believes that all is for the best in this best of all possible worlds. The gaps are enormous between what happens in the world polis and what is on the books – spelled out in the UN Charter and hundreds of international treaties, as well as in public statements by politicians, pundits, prime ministers, princes, and presidents. Surely, ours cannot be the best of all possible worlds. I remain persuaded that good people and good ideas can make a difference to the quality of both human life and international society.

That optimism needs to be asserted amidst the disturbing populist and inward-looking politics in the West and elsewhere that accompanies the most gut-wrenching humanitarian disaster in recent memory. Our collective conscience apparently was beyond shocking, as a half-million Syrians died in real time, including children suffocating from chemical weapons. That said, the bottom line for my last lecture would also resemble that from my first: I'm an inveterate optimist who believes that it is better sometimes to be wrong, rather than a pessimist and always right.

A career in any business, let alone the academy, involves heavy debts accumulated from both deliberate and unintended encounters with too many smart people to mention; but a few nonetheless stand out whose names I would like to register at the outset because much of what follows in these pages draws on collaborative work over the years. I have drawn on joint products and so would like to indicate clearly up front my debt to a number of individuals. I cite our main joint work here and will not repeat them in subsequent chapters, nor will I refer readers to my three previous Polity Press books.[2]

This book asks an honest question: "Would the World Be Better without the UN?" The answer is "no," a response that draws on four and a half decades of close encounters of a different (not "third") kind. I begin with my dear friend and mentor Leon Gordenker, whose own scholarship and unpretentious demeanor have always provided a beacon; as I pulled together the outline and elaborated the manuscript, I became even more fully aware of the extent to which I am indebted to him. Over the years, my remedial education about the world organization has continued through collaboration with David P. Forsythe and Roger A. Coate (and later Kelly-Kate Pease) on eight editions of our UN textbook.[3] I have learned much from Sam Daws on two editions of a major handbook about the world body.[4] And, on the related topic of global governance and its relationship to the UN, I have always taken away more than I contributed from collaborations with Craig Murphy, Ramesh Thakur, and Rorden Wilkinson.[5]

I would like to draw attention to my collaboration between 1999 and 2010 with Tatiana Carayannis, Louis Emmerij, and Richard Jolly in the United Nations Intellectual History Project (UNIHP), a long overdue effort to document the world organization's ideational contribution to economic and social development. The sixteen volumes and oral history are now widely cited, and I am especially pleased with our three "synthesis" volumes whose conclusions penetrate the analysis here.[6] Collaboration with Dan Plesch on the UN's wartime history filled another knowledge gap.[7] And research with Stephen Browne helped me return to the development vineyards with the Future UN Development System Project (FUNDS).[8]

My preoccupation with the humanitarian struggle to protect and help people caught in the cross-hairs of armed violence was formed in collaboration with Larry Minear in directing the Humanitarianism & War Project. Gareth Evans, Michael Ignatieff, and Ramesh Thakur were especially appreciated colleagues during the International Commission on Intervention and State Sovereignty (ICISS), which resulted in *The Responsibility to Protect* (R2P) and an accompanying research volume.[9] Peter Hoffman went from my classroom to ICISS to helping to introduce me to the theory of new wars and of new humanitarianisms in two books.[10] Finally, Michael Barnett and I worked together on two volumes that seek to re-examine humanitarian shibboleths and rethink standard operating procedures and principles.[11]

I am deeply grateful that former UN secretary-general Kofi Annan agreed to grace these pages with a foreword. I have known and admired this gracious and dedicated man for the last three decades. The world definitely would be a less kind and safe place without him.

I end by dedicating this volume to the next generation, and more especially to my grandchildren Amara, Kieran, and Grace. They and their peers worldwide deserve a safer and more just planet; and a better United Nations could help make that wish a reality.

TGW

New York, July 2017

FOREWORD

The United Nations was born from the ashes of war almost three-quarters of a century ago. Against that backdrop of unimaginable suffering and collapse in basic values, courageous politicians and citizens sought new institutional ways to deal with the life-threatening challenges of the day, and the future.

Ironically, today, as the number of threats has multiplied, the political mood has inexplicably turned inward, seeking to build walls rather than tear them down. Instead of being more central to global problem-solving, in the current climate of nationalism, the UN's value-based framework and institutions are not only not accepted by everyone but actively under attack.

In a bold and original way, Thomas G. Weiss uses a counterfactual approach to examine what the United Nations does, what would happen if it ceased to exist, and what can be done to improve it. He does not shy away from lamenting the obvious shortcomings and failures of member states and international civil servants; but he also provides a timely reminder of the crucial normative and operational work undertaken by the world organization. He points out that we can await new unspeakable disasters to prove the need for better intergovernmental organizations and undoubtedly be rewarded with unimaginable calamities. Or we can make fitter for purpose the ones that we have.

My own decade at the helm of the UN leads me to salute this book because it helps us to understand the crucial importance of the world organization in tackling the considerable challenges facing the world today. Tom Weiss has engagingly and honestly asked a very tough question found in the book's title, *Would the World Be Better without the UN?* His negative reply is an indispensable guide for anyone worried about the future of the planet and of the United Nations.

Kofi A. Annan
Geneva, July 2017

ABBREVIATIONS

APMBC	Anti-Personnel Mine Ban Convention
AU	African Union
BWC	Biological Weapons Convention
CAR	Central African Republic
CCW	Convention on Certain Conventional Weapons
CEDAW	Convention on the Elimination of All Forms of Discrimination Against Women
CFCs	chlorofluorocarbons
CHR	Commission on Human Rights
CIA	Central Intelligence Agency
CIEC	Conference on International Economic Cooperation
COP	Conference of Parties
CWC	Chemical Weapons Convention
DAC	Development Assistance Committee (OECD)
DaO	Delivering as One
DHA	Department of Humanitarian Affairs
DPKO	Department of Peacekeeping Operations
DRC	Democratic Republic of the Congo
ECOSOC	Economic and Social Council
ECOWAS	Economic Community of West African States
EOSG	Executive Office of the Secretary-General
EPTA	Expanded Programme of Technical Assistance
ERC	Emergency Relief Coordinator
EU	European Union
FAO	Food and Agriculture Organization
FUNDS	Future United Nations Development System Project
G-7	Group of 7
G-20	Group of 20
G-77	Group of 77

GATT	General Agreement on Tariffs and Trade
GCC	Gulf Cooperation Council
GDI	Gender-Related Development Index
GDP	gross domestic product
GEM	Gender Empowerment Measure
GHGs	greenhouse gases
GNI	gross national income
GNP	gross national product
GWOT	global war on terrorism
HDI	Human Development Index
HFC	hydrofluorocarbons
HIPPO	High-Level Independent Panel on Peace Operations
HIV/AIDS	human immunodeficiency virus infection/acquired immune deficiency syndrome
HLP	High-Level Panel on Threats, Challenges and Change
HPG	Humanitarian Policy Group
HPI	Human Poverty Index
HRC	Human Rights Council
IAEA	International Atomic Energy Agency
IASC	Inter-Agency Standing Committee
ICC	International Criminal Court
ICCPR	International Covenant on Civil and Political Rights
ICESCR	International Covenant on Economic, Social and Cultural Rights
ICISS	International Commission on Intervention and State Sovereignty
ICJ	International Court of Justice
ICRC	International Committee of the Red Cross
ICTR	International Criminal Tribunal for Rwanda
ICTY	International Criminal Tribunal for the Former Yugoslavia
IDA	International Development Association
IDP	internally displaced person
IFAD	International Fund for Agricultural Development
ILO	International Labour Organization
IMF	International Monetary Fund
INSTRAW	International Research and Training Institute for the Advancement of Women
INTERFET	International Force for East Timor
IOM	International Organization for Migration
IPCC	Intergovernmental Panel on Climate Change
ISEP	International Smallpox Eradication Program
ISG	International Support Group/Iraq Survey Group

ISIL	Islamic State of Iraq and the Levant
ITU	International Telecommunication Union
JCPOA	Joint Comprehensive Plan of Action
JIU	Joint Inspection Unit
KFOR	Kosovo Force
LGBT	lesbian, gay, bi-sexual, and transgender
MDG	Millennium Development Goal
MSF	Médecins Sans Frontières [Doctors without Borders]
NAM	Non-Aligned Movement
NATO	North Atlantic Treaty Organization
NGO	nongovernmental organization
NIEO	new international economic order
NPT	Treaty on the Non-Proliferation of Nuclear Weapons
OAS	Organization of American States
OCHA	Office for the Coordination of Humanitarian Affairs
ODA	official development assistance
ODI	Overseas Development Institute
OECD	Organisation for Economic Co-operation and Development
OHCHR	Office of the High Commissioner for Human Rights
OIOS	Office of International Oversight Services
ONUCA	United Nations Observer Group in Central America
OPCW	Organisation for the Prohibition of Chemical Weapons
OPEC	Organization of the Petroleum Exporting Countries
OSCE	Organization for Security and Cooperation in Europe
OWG	open working group
P-5	permanent five [members of the Security Council]
PAHO	Pan American Health Organization
PBC	Peacebuilding Commission
PBF	Peacebuilding Fund
PBSO	Peacebuilding Support Office
QCPR	quadrennial comprehensive policy review
R2P	responsibility to protect
RC	resident coordinator
RSG	representative of the secretary-general
SARS	severe acute respiratory syndrome
SDG	Sustainable Development Goal
SMG	Senior Management Group
SNA	system of national accounts
SOPs	standard operating procedures
SSDS	System of Social and Demographic Statistics
SUNFED	Special United Nations Fund for Economic Development
TNCs	transnational corporations

UDHR	Universal Declaration of Human Rights
UNAMIR	United Nations Assistance Mission for Rwanda
UNCTAD	United Nations Conference on Trade and Development
UNDOF	United Nations Disengagement Observer Force
UNDP	United Nations Development Programme
UNDS	United Nations development system
UNEF	United Nations Emergency Force
UNEP	United Nations Environment Programme
UNEPS	United Nations Emergency Peace Service
UNESCO	United Nations Educational, Scientific and Cultural Organization
UNFCCC	United Nations Framework Convention on Climate Change
UNFPA	United Nations Population Fund
UNHCR	[Office of the] UN High Commissioner for Refugees
UNICEF	United Nations Children's Fund
UNIFEM	United Nations Development Fund for Women
UNIHP	United Nations Intellectual History Project
UNMIK	United Nations Interim Administration Mission in Kosovo
UNMOVIC	United Nations Monitoring, Verification and Inspection Commission
UNOCI	United Nations Operation in Côte d'Ivoire
UNRRA	United Nations Relief and Rehabilitation Administration
UNSCOM	United Nations Special Commission
UNSO	United Nations Statistical Office
UNTAET	United Nations Transitional Administration in East Timor
UNWCC	United Nations War Crimes Commission
UPR	Universal Periodic Review
UPU	Universal Postal Union
WEP	World Employment Programme [ILO]
WFP	World Food Programme
WHA	World Health Assembly
WHO	World Health Organization
WMD	weapons of mass destruction
WMO	World Meteorological Organization
WTO	World Trade Organization

INTRODUCTION

A tourist navigating the security barriers separating New York City from the iconic UN headquarters on First Avenue innocently asks, "How many people work here?" The tour guide snidely replies, "About half." Yet that widespread impression about an inept bureaucracy and its politicized deliberations is often met with another trope: "If the UN did not exist, we would have to reinvent it."[1]

Where might we find ourselves in the early twenty-first century had the United Nations not been created at the end of World War II in 1945? After all, the planet totters on the brink of succumbing to a host of life-threatening disasters as preparations begin to mark the seventy-fifth anniversary in 2020 of the founding of the United Nations. Former secretary general Kofi Annan labeled these menaces "problems without passports,"[2] which range from proliferation of weapons of mass destruction (WMD) to pandemics, from terrorism to climate change, from mass atrocities to debilitating poverty. At the same time, few would dispute that the world body and the UN system have helped keep the lid on conflict cauldrons, eliminated smallpox, delivered life-saving assistance in war zones, and spawned useful development ideas and projects.

In pondering whether the UN is a wasteful drain on global resources or, despite its failings, essential to global order, I draw on illustrations of its achievements and shortcomings from the three substantive pillars of activities: international peace and security; human rights and humanitarian action; and sustainable development. While counterfactuals are sometimes dismissed as academic contrivances, they can serve to focus the mind – here, they demonstrate the pluses and minuses of multilateral cooperation. Two "what ifs?" anchor this book: One, where would the contemporary world be without the

1

United Nations? Two, where could it be had the UN performed better?

My conclusion is that, while the world organization that we have leaves much to be desired, it has made substantial contributions. Indeed, it has become such an embedded part of today's world order that it is taken for granted. "We are barely conscious of the continuing stabilizing role it plays in setting the broad parameters for the conduct of international relations," Australia's former prime minister Kevin Rudd points out. "If the UN one day disappears, or more likely just slides into neglect, it is only then that we would become fully aware of the gaping hole this would leave in what remained of the post-war order."[3]

I write these lines in the wake of Donald Trump's contested election as the forty-fifth US president, a man seemingly intent on destroying the rules-based international order of which the United Nations is a keystone, and which the United States has long championed and sustained. With his denigrations of other highly successful multilateral experiments – the North Atlantic Treaty Organization (NATO) and the European Union (EU) are "obsolete" – the universal UN may be an even easier target. Indeed, one of his opening salvos from the Oval Office was the announcement of two possible executive orders, one calling for a review of ongoing and pending multilateral treaties and another for halting funding to any UN organizations that recognize Palestine as a state.

That myopia makes this book's argument more not less compelling. The world is, as Richard Haass tells us, "in disarray," which requires an altered approach to sovereignty and multilateralism. New forces, challenges, and actors indeed require what he calls a "World Order 2.0."[4] However, there is a desperate need to reinvigorate and update rather than jettison the universal organization that was essential to the current operating system.

After briefly introducing the two broad-brushed counterfactuals that anchor my argument, this introduction probes the broad notion of asking "what if?" It ends with a roadmap for the book.

Counterfactual #1: The World without the UN and its Ideas and Operations?

One way of considering the UN's impact is to imagine where the globe might be without a world body, or with one set up to act solely as an arena for discussions, with no autonomous capacity for generat-

2

ing ideas, norms, and principles or for helping to test or implement them. It would be a markedly different organization even from the beleaguered one that we have. It would have a minimum of staff, presumably composed exclusively of ex-diplomats or facilitators in bringing groups with differences together and helping to resolve them but with few ideas or initiatives of their own. It would be a strange international institution, although not altogether different from the type that extreme critics put forward as what they think preferable. Such a stripped-down UN would be more limited even than its defunct predecessor, the League of Nations.

In this counterfactual world, what might have happened to the ideas that the UN in its existing form has spawned and brought to fruition? And what might have happened to operational experiments to test these ideas or simply to improve human welfare or keep the peace?

First, in the arena of international peace and security, the invention of peacekeeping and the effort to create breathing room for negotiations would be absent or present in a watered-down form; also missing would be the formal and informal settings that are available when belligerents become fatigued enough to talk. The 100,000 soldiers, 10,000 police, and 10,000 civilians currently serving worldwide in peace operations – 80 percent of them in Africa – would also be absent from the international landscape, along with the monitoring capacities of the International Atomic Energy Agency (IAEA), which were essential for the practicability of the Iran nuclear "deal."

Second, what might be lost in a world without the United Nations is perhaps even more clearly suggested in considering human rights and humanitarian action. Even a world focused solely on economic efficiency and free markets would be under public pressure to invent an institutional capacity to foster some rights and to "twist arms." The UN, however, embraces a wide range of contested human rights not because of efficiency or political necessity but because of the vision and humanity of its founders. Human rights remain on many agendas because of the continuing concerns that are reflected in the Charter and the Universal Declaration of Human Rights as well as in a host of other UN treaties, covenants, conventions, and declarations.

Such vision and idealism are also reflected in the mandates and work of the UN's specialized agencies, funds, and programs – for instance, the UN Educational, Scientific and Cultural Organization (UNESCO), the World Health Organization (WHO), the Food and Agriculture Organization (FAO), and the International Labour Organization (ILO), as well as the UN Children's Fund (UNICEF), the UN Development Programme (UNDP), and the World Food Programme (WFP). They are also at the core of the offices of the UN High Commissioner for Refugees (UNHCR) and UN High Commissioner for Human Rights (OHCHR). The rights of minorities and indigenous peoples as well as the prevention of torture and genocide figure in many UN job descriptions. Because their mandates put human values ahead of economic concerns and market efficiency, they often clash with the interests of governments and markets, and they call for more political and financial support than governments are prepared to provide. In terms of action, who would have guided the relief directed to victims of the 2004 tsunami or to the half of Syria's population who fled repression inside and outside the country?

Third, in the economic arena, the need for rules and regulations to facilitate international trade and other economic transactions in the global market would have generated a more limited range of institutions, not so different from the Organisation for Economic Co-operation and Development (OECD). If the world organization did not exist, it would have been invented, if not in 1945 then about 1960, with the rush of decolonization, or in the 1970s, with the floating of the dollar and the surge in oil prices. A series of ad hoc meetings to cope with wide-ranging issues of such vital economic importance to wealthier countries would rapidly have been exposed as inadequate and something on a more permanent basis would have been created. Cynics might comment that this would be little different from the former General Agreement on Tariffs and Trade (GATT) or the present World Trade Organization (WTO), which have commanded support from developed countries but less enthusiasm and more hostility from the Global South.

However, the WTO alone at present employs some 600 staff, approaching the peak of the entire League of Nations when it disbanded with World War II. Most WTO staff members are economists and lawyers, many engaged in producing research and statistical reports in areas in which the UN is also engaged. But the UN tries to create policy ideas to confront extraordinary situations, whereas the WTO takes the rules of the game as fixed and tries to interpret and enforce them. However, facilitating negotiations rather than contributing substantively – including questioning the fairness of the rules of the game and who sits at the gaming table as well as whether it is level – is hardly a viable or acceptable aspiration for a universal institution, now or in the future.

Some of what the UN does in other areas would also be required and thus need to be re-created; two examples are helpful – the UN's work in global public goods and climate change. Rule-setting and regulation would be needed for health, food, and agriculture, weather and meteorology, civil aviation, and maritime law. Economists prescribe international public goods for individual countries and their populations and for the efficient functioning of markets. At the same time, they are beyond the capacity of the global market because individual countries lack the incentive and capacity to provide them. To ensure their provision, many specialist UN organizations would need to be reinvented if they did not exist. Indeed, many actually predated the current generation of post-World War II entities. The Pan American Sanitary Bureau, founded in 1902, transformed into the Latin American arm of the WHO in 1948, and renamed the Pan American Health Organization (PAHO), and mid-nineteenth-century organizations such as the Universal Postal Union (UPU) and International Telecommunication Union (ITU, although "T" earlier was "telegraph") continue to provide essential services as part of the UN system. And the world body's emphasis on the human environment since the Stockholm conference in 1972 and on the human influence on climate since the establishment of the Intergovernmental Panel on Climate Change (IPCC) in 1987 by the World Meteorological Organization (WMO) and the UN Environment Programme (UNEP) has placed this issue squarely on the public policy agenda, including the Paris Agreement in 2015.

Would the world really be a better place without the UN? If the San Francisco Conference on International Organization had not created the United Nations, undoubtedly other institutions would have been established to help fill the void. That such fictional alternatives would have been more effective and made more significant contributions is not obvious, at least to this author. The counterfactual in our hand is certainly as persuasive as two or several hypotheticals in the bush. That is the first justification for this book.

Counterfactual #2: The World with a More Creative and Effective UN?

The United Nations often fails; and it achieves far less than the visions of its founders would lead us to expect. Part of the reason for UN failures to achieve goals is that these are too visionary, or at least go far beyond where most governments are prepared to go. Another reason is the insufficient resources that governments provide. The old adage that states get the international organizations that they deserve continues to ring true. However, another explanation consists both of the waste and inefficiency resulting from weak personnel, who accomplish less and with less imagination than they might, and of the overlap and competition among the UN's various moving parts. The UN's organizational chart refers to a "system," which implies coherence and cohesion. In reality that system has more in common with feudalism than with a modern organization. Frequent use also is made of the term "family," which is apt because, like many such units, the UN's is dysfunctional.

An informed exploration of this second counterfactual suggests possible steps toward a more creative and effective United Nations, which is not only desirable *but also* feasible. Former UN deputy secretary-general Mark Malloch Brown stated: "[T]he call for reform is likely to grow steadily ... the question remains when not if."[5] The last seven decades demonstrate growth by accretion, with more and more moving parts with less and less synergy, as well as higher transaction costs related to coordination for both host governments and UN staff. The results have been too few.

The overlapping jurisdictions of various UN bodies, the lack of coordination among their activities, and the absence of centralized financing for the system as a whole make ferocious turf battles more attractive than sensible collaboration. The UN's various organizations too often work at cross-purposes instead of in a mutually reinforcing fashion. The system's entities relentlessly pursue cut-throat fundraising to finance their expanding mandates, stake out territory, and pursue mission creep. Fundamental change, coherence, and integration are not in the bureaucracy's interest; inertia and competition are.

Consolidation is anathema as officials rationalize complexity and react to incentives from donors to go their own way. Individual organizations focus on substantive areas often located in a different city from other relevant UN partners and with separate budgets, governing boards, organizational cultures, and independent executive heads. An almost universal chorus sings an atonal tune praising decentralization and autonomy; and the General Assembly and the Economic and Social Council (ECOSOC) chambers provide the main concert halls for this cacophony.

Recalling the UN's lofty ideals and significant achievements is no defense for its ineffectiveness. Nor is it a reason for suggesting that the world organization could not have done far better in formulating ideas as well as in ensuring their practical follow-up. "What ifs?" apply to both the ideational and the operational aspects of peace and security as well as human rights, but perhaps it is easier to illustrate here quickly what the world organization could and should have been in the economic and social arena.

First, the United Nations could and should have been more efficient and effective had recruitment and promotion followed the principles of a dedicated international civil service haltingly begun by the League of Nations but spelled out by Dag Hammarskjöld. They should have been independent of governments and with their own identity, ideals, and interests.[6]

Second, far more work could and should have been done on the conditions to create stability in weak, failing, fragile, and conflict-prone states. Even if international inequities were reduced, more robust efforts are required to address inequalities within countries. The Peacebuilding Commission (PBC) is an encouraging experiment because sustaining peace has emerged as a priority, but here too performance is dismaying – for instance, all six of the original target countries are back at war or close to it. UN operations continue in all developing countries rather than in the least well-placed and poorest ones where the UN system has a comparative advantage and can provide an incomparable range of services.

Third, better promotion of UN ideas, norms, and principles could and should have helped foster its work. The UN should have pursued far greater outreach for its cutting-edge ideas, for which it has a distinct voice. Such work outside the box of neoclassical economic orthodoxy should have included the encouragement of multidisci-plinary efforts in which economic issues interact with human rights, human security, and human development. For instance, the UN could have engaged in debate, publicly and privately, over the weaknesses of the Bretton Woods dogma and the Washington Consensus. Even many who are unconvinced that these approaches are broadly correct now recognize that some of the UN's past work often led to crucial new insights into the inadequacy of conventional approaches.

Fourth, more creative work could and should have been done on issues of political economy for which the international system has failed. Economic weaknesses in how the global system limits opportunities for the least developed countries is one such area; others include inadequate progress toward the goals of sustainable development and environmental protection; the presence of bias in aid allocations; the lack of coherence in the global trade system and failure to practice public commitments to an open international eco-nomic system; and lack of incentives for measures of disarmament and development.

7

Fifth, more sustained attention could and should have been given to measures to achieve a more egalitarian international system and to pursue national policies that combine redistribution with growth. It may sound hopelessly naïve to utter the acronym "NIEO" (the 1970s call for a "new international economic order"), but the sentiments motivating that clarion call for a more just distribution of global wealth and the benefits of growth can hardly be ignored, as the populist backlash in the June 2016 "Brexit" and November 2016 US presidential votes indicated. With inequalities evident at all levels within and among countries, the glaring and growing gaps in power and income are aberrant and the subject of widespread and growing commentary and disgruntlement.

Counterfactuals in the following pages include proposals that never materialized but still make sense, such as Trygve Lie's 1947 rapid intervention brigade and Kofi Annan's 1997 consolidation of UN humanitarian entities. They also include the need to reverse sensible designs that went astray, such as the UNDP as a dedicated central funding organization instead of a supposed coordinator also competing with specialized agencies to execute projects.

That these alternatives would have been sensible, possible, and beneficial is clear, at least to this author. Such counterfactuals are worth pursuing as a thought exercise to make the United Nations fitter for purpose in the next decades of the twenty-first century. That is the second justification for this book.

Counterfactuals, the Briefest of Introductions

The scholarly world of social science is filled with in-depth counterfactuals that aim to be scientific and set up testable hypotheses. While counterfactual reasoning is regarded with skepticism by many observers, and especially by positivists, it is useful and indeed unavoidable when one wishes to draw cause-and-effect conclusions. While historians are appalled about exploring "what might have been" – "an idle parlor game" according to E. H. Carr[7] – such reasoning is actually a *sine qua non* of learning lessons from history. Moreover, as James Fearon points out, social scientists routinely engage in them and thus "should be methodologically aware of what they are doing and should make their counterfactual arguments as explicit and defensible as they can."[8] Moreover, without counterfactual thinking and analysis – through which we may imagine the world as it could have been in order to envision the world as it should be – we are left with a deterministic view of reality in which our past missteps are, perforce, bound to echo into the future.

Much scholarly debate revolves around methodology. The most robust research designs rely on controlled experiments with subjects randomly assigned to variable treatment conditions that investigators can manipulate to determine the causal impact of particular factors.[9] Such experiments, of course, are impossible in historical research; we simply cannot study multiple iterations of some phenomenon under variable conditions to determine what factors were relevant in producing an outcome. The confluence of attendant circumstances in any given historical instance never repeats itself exactly. Therefore, we must look to other approaches.

The term "counterfactual" suggests a subjective conditional in which the antecedent is known or supposed, for the purposes of the argument, to be false. That is, a historical fact is altered or omitted for the purposes of judging the effect resulting from altering that single antecedent.[10] A provocative illustration of what I hope this book can accomplish is Alan Weisman's *The World without Us*,[11] which describes the physical world were humans suddenly to vanish. The world without the UN would undoubtedly be less dramatic to imagine than Weisman's visions of New York's Park Avenue collapsing, as groundwater eroded the railroad tracks leading to Grand Central Station, and the world being set ablaze as nuclear plants went, well, nuclear.

My aim is considerably less highfalutin and more modest than scientifically testable propositions, but nonetheless straightforward. This book investigates honestly the proposition, held by many, that the United Nations has made a trivial or non-existent or even negative contribution to world order since 1945. I probe illustrations from the last seven decades when the UN has made a generally acknowledged positive contribution. In doing so, I hope to push the reader to entertain seriously the proposition that we should feel indifferent about the existence of the world body – that is, we could take it or leave it. It is crucial to portray a clear-eyed description of the more difficult world that we would have without the multilateral institutions that have grown up as part of the UN system. In trying to imagine their absence from the world stage, the value-added of multilateralism will become explicit along with the consequences for a world without the United Nations. Warts and all, it would be implausible to argue that international society would have turned out much the same or be better today without UN ideas and operations since 1945.

The second counterfactual focuses on removing at least some of the warts. It is less of a stretch of the imagination insofar as it examines how a better supported, equipped, and staffed world organization could and should have made more of a difference. There may be a host of political and economic explanations for having fallen short or having outright failed in numerous instances; but here too it would be difficult to maintain that a better performance is irrelevant. Thus, my second series of counterfactuals provides an equally clear-eyed analysis of the implications of the UN's major problems. The goal is to think about a coherent agenda for transformational change. In brief, my approach is more heuristic than scientific. Nonetheless, it reveals, in startling detail, the essential stakes and abiding consequences of decisions to establish the current generation of international organizations.

There are many categories of counterfactuals, but the most important for the purposes of this book is what Philip Tetlock and Aaron Belkin call a "mental simulation of counterfactual worlds." This type of reasoning involves imagining and working through the detailed implications of another outcome in order to determine if this eventuality would lead to a different conclusion. Perhaps the best way to summarize this approach is with a less cumbersome expression – "thought experiment." While we do not have the counterfactual knowledge of what would have happened had there been no active UN in the world or norms and operations, the *acquis* of the historical record is useful to weigh before tossing aside multilateralism's contributions.

My hope is that this approach to the international political phenomena surrounding the United Nations respects a number of conditions that help prevent taking us too far afield from reality and thereby risking the integrity of the argument. Neither of my two counterfactuals qualifies as hopelessly speculative or self-evidently true. The first condition is clarity in the specification of variables. That is, it must be made clear what variables are under study and how they are defined. There must also be logical consistency. Despite the fact that counterfactual reasoning involves the invention of circumstances to test the impact of an alteration, occurrence, or non-occurrence of particular events, the principles connecting antecedents and consequences must remain plausible and tenable. Finally, there must be a degree of historical consistency in the counterfactual. In other words, proposed antecedents must require the alteration of as few well-established facts as possible. Moreover, counterfactuals should not presuppose unreasonable knowledge on the part of actors, given the time and circumstances in which they were acting.

I have done my best to respect these conditions in exploring the repercussions of many instances for a world without the United Nations, as well as with a better one. The aim is not to overstate the centrality of the UN but, rather, to tease out the implications of the absence of an essential contributor to peace and security, human rights, and development; it also is key to appreciate the potential of a more robust United Nations at a moment when the value of multilateral institutions has come under fire – in the United States, to be sure, but elsewhere as well. The hope is that the world organization's champions and skeptics alike will be obliged to take my propositions seriously and that the community of UN historians will also engage.

About This Book

The argument unfolds in three main parts. The "Building Blocks" (players and problems) in Part I provide the way to organize the stories that are recounted about the three main pillars of UN activities – international peace and security; human rights and humanitarian action; and sustainable development. Chapter 1 parses the main actors across "three" dimensions of the United Nations: the First UN (member states), the Second UN (international secretariats), and the Third UN (civil society, the private sector, the media, commissions, consultants, and individuals). Chapter 2 explores "Four UN Ailments," namely sacrosanct state sovereignty; North–South theatrics; atomization; and lackluster leadership. There is no attempt to sugarcoat or trivialize the shortcomings of either the major players or the world organization itself. These problems constitute common threads that explain unsatisfactory outcomes or possibly better counterfactual outcomes in the remainder of the book. Readers encounter the three UNs from chapter 1 throughout the text, although the explicit emphasis here is on the member states and staff; the Third UN requires another volume. Readers also confront the four ailments from chapter 2 throughout the book.

Part II consists of instances in which UN ideas (or norms, principles, standards) and operational efforts have made a substantial and often crucial difference to world order. That is, this part explores the question: "The World without the UN and its Ideas and Operations?" It unpacks examples of ideas and operations that made singular contributions within each pillar of activities. Thus, chapter 3 contains an examination of "A More Violent World with Diminished International Peace and Security?"; chapter 4 of "A More

Repressive and Unkind World with Diminished Human Rights and Humanitarian Action?"; and chapter 5 of "A More Impoverished and Polluted World with Diminished Development?" I have chosen with some care three examples of ideas and three of operations in each chapter. Some illustrations are undoubtedly well known, others less so; but the essence is to provide solid evidence of a wide variety of activities that show how the United Nations has made a difference.

Part III shifts gears and teases out how an alternatively configured UN system could have made a greater contribution in a number of specific ways. This third part analyzes examples in which the UN failed – or perhaps made matters worse – but where a more effective world body could and should have made a real difference. Each illustration has basic information; however, the emphasis is not on specific details but, rather, on why a complete or partial failure could have been avoided. That is, Part III asks readers to consider the possibility of "The World with a More Creative and Effective UN?" It explores illustrations of ideas and operations under similar substantive rubrics of "A Less Violent World with Enhanced International Peace and Security?" in chapter 6; "A Less Repressive and Unkind World with Enhanced Human Rights and Humanitarian Action?" in chapter 7; and "A Less Impoverished and Polluted World with Enhanced Sustainable Development?" in chapter 8.

The result is a persuasive dual challenge: To skeptics, or even enemies, Part II asks: "Are you serious, would the planet have been better off without the UN's efforts in [you choose the topic]?" And then, to card-carrying members of the UN fan club, Part III asks: "Are you serious, was this performance in [you choose the topic] really all we can expect from multilateralism?" Truth in packaging is found in punctuation: a question mark in the book's title should tempt readers from both the Heritage Foundation and the UN Foundation; the same punctuation in the title of Part II and its three component chapters are rhetorical questions; and the interrogatory punctuation throughout Part III indicates available affirmative answers but ones that require action.

Chapter 9 contains a clarion call without any question mark: "Let's Be Serious – The UN We Want (and Need) for the World We Want." There is still time. The objective of the empirically grounded thought experiments is to shake up both ardent opponents and proponents to realize that the world without the world organization is neither plausible nor desirable. A world with a more creative and effective UN is both.

12

Part I

Building Blocks

Part I sets out the main actors and problems around which are organized the illustrations in Parts II and III regarding the three main categories of UN activities – international peace and security; human rights and humanitarian action; and sustainable development. The players are briefly spelled out in chapter 1: member states; international secretariats; and other stakeholders (civil society, the private sector, the media, commissions, consultants, and individuals). Chapter 2 parses four major ailments of the United Nations: unreconstructed state sovereignty; North–South theatrics; atomization; and lackluster leadership.

The shortcomings of the major players and the world body's organizational dynamics reappear as explanations for unsatisfactory outcomes as well as components for possible and more satisfactory outcomes. Readers encounter the three UNs from chapter 1 and the four problems from chapter 2 throughout these pages.

1

"THREE" UNITED NATIONS

This first chapter unpacks the UN's most important actors. The world organization is, first and foremost, an intergovernmental organization; and so a major explanatory factor behind the UN's minuses is the extent to which member states paralyze decision making and impede action. That the governments of its almost 200 member states are part of the problem is beyond doubt, but analytically it is essential to distinguish the "First United Nations" (the stage or arena for state decision making) from the "Second United Nations" (the secretariats whose staff work for the organization and have a certain margin for maneuver).[1] "There's a fundamental confusion between the UN as a stage and the UN as an actor," former assistant secretary-general Robert Orr summarizes. "As an actor, there's so little we can do, and often the people accusing us are the same ones who prevent us from being able to act."[2]

No one should be surprised about the realities of the First UN and the Second UN, which provide this book's focus. After all, member states establish priorities and pay the bills, more or less, thus determining the world body's agenda. To be sure, international civil servants would not exist without member states; but an institution of member states would not have a presence or impact without the administrative support of a secretariat. Success or failure in changing and implementing policy is not independent of states with their resources and vital interests. Yet there is more room for maneuver and autonomy on the part of international secretariats than is often supposed.

In addition, the "Third United Nations" appears in these pages as a component in some successes and failures, although it is not the focus and hence does not appear in later recommendations about future strategies. Its composition is simply too vast and amorphous to address here. For the sake of completeness, however, the reader should be aware that it consists of nongovernmental organizations (NGOs), independent experts, consultants, the media, for-profit corporations, and committed citizens who are integral to today's United Nations. They often combine forces around UN deliberations and operations. They include scholars, practitioners, and activists who maintain their independence but provide essential inputs into UN discussions, operations, advocacy, implementation, and monitoring. What once seemed marginal now is central to multilateralism. Numerous individuals and institutions that are neither states nor the creations of states (that is, intergovernmental bureaucracies) influence deliberations and decisions by member states and secretariats. The rebalancing of public and private, of states and markets, suggests the need to move beyond Inis Claude's 1956 textbook distinction.[3] Individuals matter – in governments, in the international civil service, and in global civil society.

A word is in order about "international community," a term that usually introduces confusion into analyses of multilateralism. International lawyers narrowly mean "peace-loving states" – euphemistically, the First UN. Other observers employ the term more expansively to connote not merely 193 member states – along with Palestine and the Vatican as non-member observer states – but also their creations in the form of intergovernmental bodies – that is, the Second UN. Still other commentators use "international community" to embrace not only states and international secretariats but also non-state actors operating internationally – that is, the Third UN.

What is the value of these distinctions? An adage comes to mind – success has numerous parents, but failure is an orphan. States are rarely willing to blame themselves for breakdowns in international society; and secretariats often indiscriminately blame governments for their lack of political will. The First UN of member states has a convenient scapegoat in the Second UN of international secretariats, and vice versa. To repeat, they are the preoccupation here.

Hence, blaming the world organization without distinguishing these separate actors obfuscates rather than clarifies analysis. The boundaries are porous, but properly apportioning the blame for failure or success – what Robert Cox and Harold Jacobson long ago called "the anatomy of influence"[4] – is a necessary and increasingly complex task that requires identifying the strengths and weaknesses of specific actors. An increasingly crowded international stage finds major roles and bit parts. States are still the marquee actors, and national interests have not receded as the basis for decision making; international secretariats serve these state masters but have more agency than many believe. These distinctions are important in exploring the implications of the counterfactual cases in Parts II and III because blanket statements about UN "success" or "failure" have little meaning without apportioning responsibility.

Member States and Secretariats, the First and the Second UNs

Unsurprisingly, the First UN has long been the focus of scholarship. After all, member states – fifty-one in June 1945 and almost four times that number today – determine what the world body does or does not do. Michael Barnett and Martha Finnemore distinguish five roles for the First UN: "as an agent of great powers doing their bidding; as a mechanism for interstate cooperation; as a governor of international society of states; as a constructor of the social world; and as a legitimation forum."[5] States pursue national interests from "high politics" in the Security Council to "low politics" in the boards and governing councils of UN funds and specialized agencies. States caucus in regional groups for the General Assembly and in smaller groups for numerous issues. Notions of the First UN find a home in virtually all theorizing about international relations: for a realist emphasizing self-interested states within an anarchical system; for a liberal institutionalist focusing on the costs and benefits of state cooperation; for a proponent of the English School analyzing the development of shared norms and values in international society; for a constructivist concerned with ideational change and identity shaping; and for a pragmatist seeking to legitimate specific values and actions.

The Second UN is also distinct, consisting of career and contractual staff who are paid through assessed and voluntary contributions. The international civil service is a legacy of the League of Nations, whose characteristics are enumerated in Article 101 of the UN Charter. A leading advocate for an autonomous Second UN was the second secretary-general, Dag Hammarskjöld. His May 1961 speech at Oxford does not ignore the reality that the international civil service exists to carry out decisions made by states; but it emphasizes that UN officials pledge allegiance to striving for a larger collective good rather than defending the interests of the countries that issue their passports. That senior UN posts are set aside for high-level officials approved by their home governments undermines the integrity of secretariats. Moreover, a shadow today hangs over the UN Secretariat as a result of events ranging from corruption in the Oil-for-Food Programme to sexual exploitation by peacekeepers.

Nonetheless, a basic idealism has animated the best of the Second UN. Autonomy and integrity are not unrealistic expectations for international civil servants. Today's professional and support staff number approximately 55,000 in the UN proper and another 25,000 in the specialized agencies. This number includes neither temporary staff in peace operations (about 125,000 military, police, and civilians in 2016) nor the staff of the International Monetary Fund (IMF) and the World Bank group (another 15,000). These figures represent substantial growth from the approximately 500 employees in the UN's first year at Lake Success or the 700 staff employed by the League of Nations.[6]

The Second UN typically receives little attention from analysts. But staff do more than carry out marching orders from governments. UN officials present ideas to tackle problems, debate them formally and informally with governments, take initiatives, advocate for change, and turn general decisions into specific programs of action and implement them. They monitor progress and report findings to national officials and politicians gathering at intergovernmental conferences and in countries with UN operations.

None of this should be a surprise. At the national level, it would be strange if civil service staff members took no initiatives or showed no leadership. UN officials are no different except that formal decision makers are government representatives in boards that meet quarterly, annually, or even once every two years. Decision making and responsibility for implementation in most parts of the UN system depend in large part on executive heads and senior staff.

The Third UN

From the outset, non-state actors have been in UN corridors and field projects. The Charter's 1945 Preamble opened with a clarion call from "We the Peoples of the United Nations," when one might have expected "We the Representatives of Sovereign Member States." Article 71 explicitly made room for NGOs. Nonetheless, the extent to which non-state actors have increasingly become a routine component of what passes for "international" relations by intergovernmental organizations is striking.

NGO involvement has been integral to UN-sponsored global

gatherings since the 1972 Stockholm Conference on the Human Environment, when the event's secretary-general, Maurice Strong, insisted on their presence. NGO parallel meetings, usually called "forums," have become a prominent fixture of deliberations and have been an important force in pressing for more forward-looking policies. For the Millennium (in 2000), 2005, and 2015 World Summits, special hearings involving NGOs were an expected part of deliberations.

Moreover, in terms of the delivery of development and humanitarian assistance, NGOs are crucial UN partners. Sometimes the funding goes directly to NGOs from private or government sources, and sometimes UN funds are subcontracted to nongovernmental partners that deliver goods and services.

Although the terminology may sound odd, such networks constitute the "Third United Nations." Many individuals who have played an essential role in the world organization's intellectual and norm-building activities as well as operations were neither government officials nor international civil servants. Moreover, many key contributors to ideas or operations as members of the First or the Second UN had significant prior or subsequent associations with a university, a think tank, a business, or an NGO. Many individuals have served as members or chairs of independent panels and commissions who examined emerging problems not yet on the international radar screen. The IPCC is a prominent recent example. Many also served as staff or board members of NGOs, and most have attended ad hoc global conferences that pull together a range of actors on the international stage.

The Third UN's influence on the world organization's thinking, policies, priorities, and actions is based on their independence from governments and secretariats. The members of the Third UN are "outsiders" – that is, persons who are not on the regular payroll of a government or a secretariat – who complement the "insiders" of the other two UNs in collective efforts to generate, debate, implement, and disseminate ideas and conduct operational programs. The "revolving doors" among the three UNs – including some individuals who may simultaneously be members of more than one – often blur distinctions between outsiders and insiders. A helpful distinction has been introduced by Roland Rich, who suggests that some members of the Third UN are more "formal" or "less informal," namely when a member state or a UN organization specifically requests an input from the Third UN – for example, Canada's convening the International Commission on Intervention and State Sovereignty (ICISS) or the special procedures of the UN Human Rights Council (HRC).[7] More recently, the Third UN has even been called upon to help define certain terms of interaction between the First and Second UNs, such as in the case of the use by the International Criminal Court (ICC) of an independent expert panel for defining and analyzing the practicability of court complementarity as it is described in the Rome Statute.

People who are neither government representatives nor international civil servants are often better placed to be more bold and critical, as well as to run operational risks. Anyone who has attended UN-sponsored global conferences is quite aware that secretariats who organize such meetings are joined not only by representatives of governments but also by a legion of NGOs, think tanks, and academics. The same is true of the board meetings of many UN funds, programs, and specialized agencies. And UN field projects are populated by many partners. Depending on the context and the time, the influence of Third UN, like that of the other two UNs, may be good, bad, or ambiguous.

Conclusion

A special section of the journal *Foreign Policy* in fall 2002 was titled "What Is the International Community?"[8] The article began with a soundbite: "Invoking the international community is a lot easier than defining it." It rarely makes sense to use the term in the restrictive international legal sense of "peace-loving states" because parsing the contemporary international community requires understanding the interactions among the three United Nations. Filling the glaring gaps in global governance leads us to urge that all parts of "the UN" – first, second, and third – continue to pool energies and make maximum use of respective comparative advantages. The notion of a three-faced UN is a contribution to the challenge of theorizing contemporary global governance. It builds on a growing body of work that calls for a conception of "multiple multilateralisms."[9]

This terminology resonates for students of international organization, even those who were raised on Claude's narrower framework. Scholars, especially those interested in global governance, increasingly examine the phenomenon of non-state actors, especially NGOs, as they intersect with the United Nations.[10] The number of non-official groups has expanded dramatically, while globalization has meant that communications and technological developments have increased the reach of their voices as well as their decibel levels along with operational contracts from UN organizations.

That said, the counterfactual reasoning in this book primarily emphasizes the arenas for decision making by the First UN of member states and the actions by individuals in international secretariats composing the Second UN. They are what most observers have in mind when analyzing the United Nations, and they can be directly affected by intergovernmental decisions and practices that can have an immediate and appreciable impact on making the world organization fitter for purpose.

2

FOUR UN AILMENTS

This chapter spells out four central problems facing the United Nations that should be kept in mind while examining the specific subsequent illustrations. The UN's main ailments are: unreconstructed state sovereignty; North–South theatrics; atomization; and lackluster leadership.[1]

Sacrosanct State Sovereignty

Many of the most intractable challenges (ranging from pandemics to the proliferation of WMD) are transnational, and addressing them successfully requires policies and actions that are not only multilateral (involving more than two states) but also global. The policy authority and resources necessary to tackle such problems, however, remain vested in individual states rather than in the collective United Nations. Established in 1945 by sovereign states seeking to protect themselves against external aggression, the UN was not built to confront many of today's numerous threats. The disjuncture between the nature of a growing number of problems and available solutions within the UN goes a long way toward explaining the world organization's recurrent difficulties on many fronts and the often fitful nature of what essentially are tactical and short-term responses to dangers that require strategic transnational thinking and sustained global attention.

The logic of the international system continues to reflect the basic principle of sovereign jurisdiction, which has its roots in the 1648 Peace of Westphalia. Only rules that states approve consensually, and only those intergovernmental organizations that they establish voluntarily, see the light of day. Because it was constructed to produce order and to buttress central authority within states, sovereignty also necessarily means that central authority in international society and relations remains anemic at best, non-existent at worst. All territorial states came to be seen as equal in the sense of having ultimate authority to prescribe what "should be" in their jurisdictions; and sovereign equality is the most essential building block of the United Nations as spelled out in Article 2 of its Charter.

The study of international relations reflects what political scientists label "anarchy" – no overarching authority exists beyond individual states. Despite the notion of the sovereign equality, all sorts of unequal relations have existed and have even been formally approved. That there are five permanent members (China, France, Russia, the United Kingdom, and the United States) of the Security Council (P-5) with a veto is one of many manifestations of inequality.[2]

Indeed, the widespread exceptions and routine violations led Stephen Krasner to characterize sovereignty as "organized hypocrisy."[3] Contemporary interpretations of sovereignty vary. At one end of the spectrum are diplomats who tightly embrace it for flexibility – this group includes not only those from many developing countries but also "new sovereigntists" in the United States and elsewhere in the West. At the same time, there are those who are passionate about the construction of human rights norms as a step toward breaking down the national barriers supposedly protecting war criminals or murderous dictators. In between are more ambivalent observers, among them those who see globalization's erosion of sovereignty as having pluses and minuses.

Not surprisingly, proponents of the main theories of international relations – realism, institutionalism, and constructivism – also vary in their appreciation for sovereignty's inherent value and relevance for global problem-solving. For realists, sovereignty is the only way to think about world politics and foreign policy. For liberal institutionalists, it can be accommodated by pursuing enlightened policies within intergovernmental organizations to foster cooperation and reduce transaction costs. For constructivists (or ideationalists), sovereignty is contingent, and so its meaning can be altered over time by individuals and states as their thinking and norms evolve.

National interests are the overwhelmingly acceptable basis for governments to make decisions, which explains the narrow national rather than global calculations by major, middle, and minor powers alike. Going it alone is easier for such hegemons as the United States and China, but the United Kingdom, Brazil, and even Palau or the

Maldives follow the same logic. Sovereignty thus explains the current multilateral system and its dire straits.

Most states value sovereignty more than supranational or even international cooperation. In countries that won independence after protracted nationalist armed struggles, anticolonial impulses survive in the collective memory, although their justifications sometimes get short shrift in the West. Algerian president Abdelazia Bouteflika's remarks during the 1999 General Assembly capture this reality: "We do not deny that the United Nations has the right and the duty to help suffering humanity, but we remain extremely sensitive to any undermining of our sovereignty, not only because sovereignty is our last defence against the rules of an unequal world, but because we are not taking part in the decision-making process of the Security Council."[4] In an understatement by the Council on Foreign Relations president Richard Haass, "Americans have traditionally guarded their sovereignty with more than a little ferocity."[5]

In short, every state argues that only its government and not outsiders can determine what is best for its citizens. The perpetuation of state sovereignty – the idea that each state should be free from outside interference as it exercises absolute authority over a given population and territory – as the essential organizing principle of world politics affords newer, smaller, and less powerful states an equal legal footing and a seat at many international high tables alongside older or more powerful states. It also guarantees some order and predictability within what Hedley Bull long ago called "international society"[6] because of the shared interests and identities that emphasize the creation and maintenance of norms, rules, and institutions. Indeed, state sovereignty is not only a functional but also a political value that allows national societies to make choices and hold international organizations accountable.[7]

International cooperation reflects agreements among sovereign states – letters are delivered, flights take off and land, and trade grows steadily. However, such accords fall far short of giving international organizations the wherewithal to extract compliance from states that fail to abide by the terms of their agreements or that simply opt out. The UN Charter's ban on the use of military force except with the Security Council's authorization or in self-defense, for example, is regularly ignored but rarely with consequences for those who flout it.

As the peoples and states of the world become more interconnected, the need for more effective international management increases. Terrorism, HIV/AIDS, economic crises, refugee movements, nuclear proliferation, and climate change cannot be adequately addressed by states acting individually to protect only their own citizens or territory. For instance, with widespread global travel, to halt the spread of an infectious disease within its own territory a state must also expend energy and resources to prevent the spread of disease elsewhere. Even then, absent a high degree of international cooperation, health crises can linger or spread widely at an alarming rate. Some may view actions such as the containment and eradication of infectious diseases as a moral imperative, but it is equally a practical necessity. Recent demonstrations were the Ebola outbreaks in Africa in 2014–15 and when tourists contracted the Zika virus in Latin America in 2016 and took it elsewhere, leading some Olympic athletes to avoid the Rio competition. "On a small, densely populated, highly connected planet," David Hulme reminds us, "a problem in a faraway place can soon become a problem anywhere."[8]

As peoples and states realize that their own welfare can be substantially affected by decisions taken elsewhere, demands can increase for more robust international management, which causes narrow notions of sovereignty to be questioned and sometimes modified. Americans are interconnected with Hondurans for trade in bananas; but they can do without the fruit or find alternate sources of supply. By contrast, in 1990 Americans were interdependent with the Organization of the Petroleum Exporting Countries (OPEC) for trade in oil. As such, energy was a necessity for which rapidly rising costs from Kuwait's takeover by Iraq caused major disruptions in the US and world economies. Thus, interdependence requires redefining some issues that were formerly considered domestic and inconsequential to be international and significant because of their material or moral pertinence.

Still, most states refuse to cede authority to international organizations. The George W. Bush administration's 2001 ceremonial gesture to revoke (by "unsigning") the earlier Clinton administration's signature of the Rome Statute establishing the ICC is a case in point. Although the court in many ways reflected American inputs and values, the United States refused to become a party – lest the court infringe on sovereign prerogatives.

Indeed, political efforts to go beyond or substantially alter the state-centric order seem to be moving backwards despite the growing number of problems recognized as global. The disarray in Europe as a result of the common currency crisis was already evident before populist votes in favor of Brexit and an inward-looking US president in 2016. "Many efforts for international cooperation, institutions and organizations are declining and weakening," summarizes Daniel Deudney. The paradox is clear: "There is a widespread sense that problems are growing faster than solutions."[9]

25

In brief, state sovereignty is the fundamental organizing principle for international relations generally and for the United Nations particularly. Lasting and meaningful solutions to such transboundary problems as pandemics and terrorism, to failing states and to climate change are impossible when sovereigns reach decisions based on narrowly defined interests and can opt out of agreements that prove inconvenient or costly. Westphalian sovereignty is a chronic ailment for the United Nations that could be lethal for the planet.

North–South Theatrics

Beginning in the late 1940s and gaining speed during the 1950s and 1960s, former colonies created two key coalitions through which they articulated their security and economic interests vis-à-vis the major powers – the Non-Aligned Movement (NAM) and the Group of 77 (G-77). In addition to the East–West rivalry that maintained the frigid temperatures of the Cold War, another rigid dichotomy was mapped onto the globe – the North–South divide. While the East–West split disappeared with the implosion of the Soviet Union, the division of the world into camps representing the North (developed countries) and the South (developing countries) has survived despite its irrelevance in a globalizing world. Many parts of the UN system, even the more "technical" of organizations such as the WHO or the UPU, are still likely to organize conversations around the simplistic and anachronistic division between the supposedly uniformly affluent North and the poor "Global South" – the current preferred label. Seemingly the only way to structure international debates is to organize a joust between the wealthy industrialized West and the proverbial "Rest."

Conor Cruise O'Brien described the United Nations as "sacred drama,"[10] which is certainly an apt characterization of the strange (and inaccurate) geographical terms describing the two major but ageing troupes of actors and their various roles in global theaters. Amateur or even professional geographers may have trouble without a special compass. During the Cold War, the "West" or "First World" consisted of industrialized countries (North America, Western Europe, Japan, Australia, and New Zealand), while the "East" or "Second World" consisted of the Soviet Union and its allies in Eastern Europe. They contrasted with what at the outset of the 1950s Alfred Sauvy first called the *tiers monde* (Third World) – that is, everyone else.[11] Whatever their actual hemispheric locations – Taiwan is nowhere (i.e., is not a UN member), and Israel is part of the "Western and

26

other" group – the "developed" countries of the former East and West today constitute the "North" and the "developing" countries the "South." In more recent years, the adjective "global" has been inserted in front of the Global South.[12]

The first visible manifestation was at the Asian-African Conference – the momentous political gathering in Bandung, Indonesia, in April 1955. African-American novelist Richard Wright wrote that it cut "through the outer layers of disparate social and political and cultural facts down to the bare brute residues of human existence: races and religions and continents."[13] The key figures were the "giants" of the first generation of Third World leaders: Indonesian president and host of the conference, Sukarno; Indian prime minister Jawaharlal Nehru; and Egyptian president Gamal Abdel Nasser. Also present were Ho Chi Minh, leader of the Democratic Republic of Vietnam; Kwame Nkrumah, the future prime minister of Ghana; and Zhou Enlai, foreign minister and later prime minister of the People's Republic of China.

The original motivation for Bandung was to find a path between the Soviet Union and the United States within the confines of the United Nations. Specifically, many newly independent countries were irritated by their inability to secure UN membership because of superpower jousting. No new members had been admitted since Indonesia in January 1950 because neither Moscow nor Washington would agree to have an additional member from the other's camp.

Eventually Bandung led to the formation of the NAM – representing those countries claiming to be aligned with neither Moscow nor Washington. Following the 1955 conference, the Afro-Asian Peoples' Solidarity Organization was founded at a meeting in Cairo, and then a more moderate group gathered in Belgrade in September 1961, at the First Conference of the Heads of State or Government of Non-Aligned Countries. However, despite rhetoric, "most nationalist movements and Third World regimes had diplomatic, economic, and military relations with one or both of the superpowers."[14] Indeed, amateur lexicographers might have problems in drafting a common-sensical dictionary entry for "non-aligned" because over time the NAM included such Soviet lackeys as Fidel Castro's Cuba and such American ones as Mobutu Sese Seko's Zaïre. But at the least the logjam in admitting new UN members disappeared.

Working in parallel with the NAM but concentrating on economic issues, another amalgam was the "Group of 77"; and here amateur mathematicians require a special calculator. Established in June 1964, the G-77 was named after two new members joined the original seventy-five (which included New Zealand) in a working caucus that

27

gathered to prepare for the first United Nations Conference on Trade and Development (UNCTAD). The numbers continued to grow, and New Zealand departed. Currently with over 130 members, the original label remains.

The crystallization of developing countries into a single bloc for the purposes of international economic negotiations was a direct challenge to Western industrialized countries.[15] The Third World's "solidarity" resulted in cohesion for the purposes of early international debates. It meant that developing countries were in a better position collectively to champion policies that aimed to change the distribution of benefits from growth and trade,[16] just as they sought some middle ground on security issues through the NAM.

The Cold War's chasm between East and West has disappeared, but the UN still struggles with the anachronistic North–South axis. The predictable antics between the industrialized North and the Global South impede any sensible regrouping of voices. Dramatic and largely symbolic or theatrical confrontations, rather than a search for meaningful partners, remains. With consensus as the preferred route for discussions, lowest common denominators enable 193 states (the current UN membership) to adopt resolutions, work programs, and budgets. Countries interpret them in the way that they deem fit or simply ignore what they dislike.

It remains politically correct to speak of the Global South as if it were homogeneous, with little hesitation in grouping the economies of Singapore and Chad or the approaches to military affairs of Costa Rica and North Korea. If one probes deeper and adds a dash of cynicism, it appears that powerful governments in both the North and the Global South are comfortable maintaining this fiction because it permits them to avoid any substantial democratization of international relations. They embrace fixed roles and oppose any worldwide democratic means for dealing with globalization – the North because global democracy would challenge privilege, and the South because global democracy would require local democracy or could, as Martha Finnemore and Kathryn Sikkink suggest, strengthen the domestic audience demanding political reforms.[17]

On some issues – such as emphasizing the importance of the General Assembly, where each state has one vote – developing countries maintain consistently common positions. In such instances, the North–South divide continues to be somewhat salient. Frequently, developing countries subdivide into political subgroupings according to an issue: that is, countries that are radical or moderate, Islamic or non-Islamic, mutually intra-regional or interregional, maritime or

28

landlocked, and experiencing economic growth or stagnation. Even within the Western group, there have always been differences, more easily aired after the disappearance of the East–West divide.

So, where are we after so many performances? The artificial division of the world into the North and the Global South is a crass oversimplification that overlooks substantial parts of reality. This frequent default option continues because no other template is readily available. Such rigid categories are more helpful for diplomats hoping to write simple scripts for drama in various UN diplomatic amphitheaters rather than for either serious negotiators or analysts attempting to move beyond the paralysis and sterile confrontation that characterizes most UN deliberations.

Atomization

As we learned earlier, the generic label attached to the organizational chart of the entire United Nations is "system," even if the term implies a coherence and cohesion that is uncharacteristic of its actual structure or behavior. Nonetheless, using its non-imperialist credentials to midwife the birth of many developing countries and help establish political, administrative, and economic institutions in them, the UN took on the task of "development." The decentralized, functionalist roots of the system were present from the outset, but a prolific and haphazard growth in the UN system has exacerbated centrifugal forces.

Mobilizing consensus about alternative structures and priorities is difficult, to say the least. With close to 200 member states and the use of the UN as a platform to discuss anything to which the words "international" or "global" can be attached, there is virtually nothing that is not on the agenda. Institutional relationships also reflect overlapping missions, competition for limited resources, and the desire to keep abreast of what is "popular" with donors (i.e., considered worthy of financial support). UN organizations are not unlike other institutions that seek to exclude rivals or to cooperate, depending on incentives.[18] The competition within and among secretariats – sometimes helpful, sometimes hurtful – influences the production and application of ideas and the conduct of operations.

In speaking about the relationship between UN headquarters and specialized agencies, readers should recall the horizontal nature of authority in the system. "The orchestra pays minimum heed to its conductor,"[19] wrote Brian Urquhart and Erskine Childers about a

UN PRINCIPAL ORGANS

GENERAL ASSEMBLY

SECURITY COUNCIL

ECONOMIC AND SOCIAL COUNCIL

SECRETARIAT

INTERNATIONAL COURT OF JUSTICE

TRUSTEESHIP COUNCIL[6]

Subsidiary Organs

- Main Committees
- Disarmament Commission
- Human Rights Council
- International Law Commission
- Joint Inspection Unit (JIU)
- Standing committees and ad hoc bodies

Funds and Programmes[1]

UNDP United Nations Development Programme
  - **UNCDF** United Nations Capital Development Fund
  - **UNV** United Nations Volunteers

UNEP[8] United Nations Environment Programme

UNFPA United Nations Population Fund

UN-Habitat[8] United Nations Human Settlements Programme

UNICEF United Nations Children's Fund

WFP World Food Programme (UN/FAO)

Subsidiary Organs

- Counter-Terrorism Committee
- International Tribunal for the former Yugoslavia (ICTY)
- International Residual Mechanism for Criminal Tribunals
- Military Staff Committee

Functional Commissions

- Crime Prevention and Criminal Justice
- Narcotic Drugs
- Population and Development
- Science and Technology for Development
- Social Development
- Statistics
- Status of Women
- United Nations Forum on Forests

Regional Commissions[8]

ECA Economic Commission for Africa

ECE Economic Commission for Europe

ECLAC Economic Commission for Latin America and the Caribbean

ESCAP Economic and Social Commission for Asia and the Pacific

ESCWA Economic and Social Commission for Western Asia

Departments and Offices[9]

EOSG Executive Office of the Secretary-General

DESA Department of Economic and Social Affairs

DFS Department of Field Support

DGACM Department for General Assembly and Conference Management

DM Department of Management

DPA Department of Political Affairs

DPI Department of Public Information

DPKO Department of Peacekeeping Operations

DSS Department of Safety and Security

OCHA Office for the Coordination of Humanitarian Affairs

ODA Office for Disarmament Affairs

OHCHR Office of the United Nations High Commissioner for Human Rights

OIOS Office of Internal Oversight Services

OLA Office of Legal Affairs

OSAA Office of the Special Adviser on Africa

PBSO Peacebuilding Support Office

SRSG/CAAC Office of the Special Representative of the Secretary-General for Children and Armed Conflict

SRSG/SVC Office of the Special Representative of the Secretary-General on Sexual Violence in Conflict

SRSG/VAC Office of the Special Representative of the Secretary-General on Violence Against Children

Figure 2.1 The UN System at a Glance

Source: www.un.org/en/aboutun/structure/pdfs/UN%20System%20Chart_ENG_FINAL_MARCH13_2017.pdf.

The United Nations System

Research and Training

UNIDIR United Nations Institute for Disarmament Research

UNITAR United Nations Institute for Training and Research

UNSSC United Nations System Staff College

UNU United Nations University

Other Entities

ITC International Trade Centre (UN/WTO)

UNCTAD[1,6] United Nations Conference on Trade and Development

UNHCR[1] Office of the United Nations High Commissioner for Refugees

UNOPS[1] United Nations Office for Project Services

UNRWA[1] United Nations Relief and Works Agency for Palestine Refugees in the Near East

UN-Women[1] United Nations Entity for Gender Equality and the Empowerment of Women

Related Organizations

CTBTO Preparatory Commission Preparatory Commission for the Comprehensive Nuclear-Test-Ban Treaty Organization

IAEA[1,3] International Atomic Energy Agency

ICC International Criminal Court

IOM[1] International Organization for Migration

ISA International Seabed Authority

ITLOS International Tribunal for the Law of the Sea

OPCW[3] Organization for the Prohibition of Chemical Weapons

WTO[1,4] World Trade Organization

- Peacekeeping operations and political missions
- Sanctions committees (ad hoc)
- Standing committees and ad hoc bodies

Peacebuilding Commission

HLPF High-level political forum on sustainable development

Other Bodies

- Committee for Development Policy
- Committee of Experts on Public Administration
- Committee on Non-Governmental Organizations
- Permanent Forum on Indigenous Issues

UNAIDS Joint United Nations Programme on HIV/AIDS

UNGEGN United Nations Group of Experts on Geographical Names

Research and Training

UNICRI United Nations Interregional Crime and Justice Research Institute

UNRISD United Nations Research Institute for Social Development

UNISDR United Nations Office for Disaster Risk Reduction

UNODC[1] United Nations Office on Drugs and Crime

UNOG United Nations Office at Geneva

UN-OHRLLS Office of the High Representative for the Least Developed Countries, Landlocked Developing Countries and Small Island Developing States

UNON United Nations Office at Nairobi

UNOP[2] United Nations Office for Partnerships

UNOV United Nations Office at Vienna

Specialized Agencies[1,5]

FAO Food and Agriculture Organization of the United Nations

ICAO International Civil Aviation Organization

IFAD International Fund for Agricultural Development

ILO International Labour Organization

IMF International Monetary Fund

IMO International Maritime Organization

ITU International Telecommunication Union

UNESCO United Nations Educational, Scientific and Cultural Organization

UNIDO United Nations Industrial Development Organization

UNWTO World Tourism Organization

UPU Universal Postal Union

WHO World Health Organization

WIPO World Intellectual Property Organization

WMO World Meteorological Organization

WORLD BANK GROUP[7]

- **IBRD** International Bank for Reconstruction and Development
- **IDA** International Development Association
- **IFC** International Finance Corporation

Notes:

1 Members of the United Nations System Chief Executives Board for Coordination (CEB).

2 UN Office for Partnerships (UNOP) is the UN's focal point vis-a-vis the United Nations Foundation, Inc.

3 IAEA and OPCW report to the Security Council and the General Assembly (GA).

4 WTO has no reporting obligation to the GA, but contributes on an ad hoc basis to GA and Economic and Social Council (ECOSOC) work on, inter alia, finance and development issues.

5 Specialized agencies are autonomous organizations whose work is coordinated through ECOSOC (inter-governmental level) and CEB (inter-secretariat level).

6 The Trusteeship Council suspended operation on 1 November 1994, as on 1 October 1994 Palau, the last United Nations Trust Territory, became independent.

7 International Centre for Settlement of Investment Disputes (ICSID) and Multilateral Investment Guarantee Agency (MIGA) are not specialized agencies in accordance with Articles 57 and 63 of the Charter, but are part of the World Bank Group.

8 The secretariats of these organs are part of the UN Secretariat.

9 The Secretariat also includes the following offices: The Ethics Office, United Nations Ombudsman and Mediation Services, Office of Administration of Justice and the Office on Sport for Development and Peace

This Chart is a reflection of the functional organization of the United Nations System and for informational purposes only. It does not include all offices or entities of the United Nations System.

Published by the United Nations Department of Public Information   DPI/2470 rev.5 —17-00023—March 2017 quarter-century ago. These battle-scarred bureaucratic veterans point out that the UN is not comparable to the hierarchical structures of most governments. The heads of agencies are appointed by different bodies with different priorities and budgets; their headquarters are located around the world, and their leaders may even choose to skip "cabinet" meetings held a few times a year.

The result is feudal kingdoms (the individual organizations) and feudal barons (their executive heads). The coalition of state interests and international civil servants who oppose an integrated UN system has helped cripple it by maintaining this structure. Organizations may be effective in working on aspects of a given problem, but we can certainly do better than to justify the continuation of the so-called system with that vacuous rationalization. As longtime UN hand Andrew Mack aptly summarized, "The UN system can be appropriately described as an 'organized anarchy' – which is not, or not necessarily, an oxymoron."[20] The system has an organogram but lacks a centralized authority structure. To adapt Gertrude Stein, "There's no there, there." Such generalizations have always rung true, but in the twenty-first century particularly so. Meanwhile, the mixture of security, humanitarian action, peacebuilding, and development has heightened the imperative for change.

Intersecting and overlapping responsibilities are obvious from a quick glance at the UN's organizational chart (see figure 2.1); but less obvious is the absence of any meaningful hierarchy. The tidy organogram is misleading because the secretary-general is only *primus inter pares* (first among equals). Furthermore, the chart does not contain the geographical locations (fourteen countries, fifteen cities) for even the headquarters of the various parts of the world organization itself and of the UN system. The problems from such dispersion are exacerbated by funding patterns (short-term and increasingly voluntary rather than longer-term and assessed or obligatory).[21]

The world body's extreme decentralization means that efforts to identify coherence inevitably are frustrated. The UN system's "operational activities" accounted for about $48 billion in 2015, the latest year for which reliable data are available (see table 2.1).[22] These figures do not include the World Bank and the IMF, which are *de jure* but not *de facto* part of the system. The UN development system alone includes more than thirty major organizations (variously called funds, programs, offices, and agencies); there are also an equivalent number of supportive functional commissions and research and training organizations that double that figure.

The solutions to the dispersal of UN efforts and resources –

consolidation and centralization – seem as obvious today as they were in 1969. At that time, Robert Jackson was given a task that resembled that of the 2006 High-Level Panel on System-Wide Coherence. The stated objective of both was to alleviate the chronic disease of feudalism, but then as now it is seemingly impossible to transform the UN system. In *The Capacity Study*, Jackson decried the absence of an institutional "brain," a lament echoed by the development economist Ignacy Sachs, who was also categorical about the UN's failure to establish a powerful central development agency: "It is perhaps the most important failure at the institutional level for the United Nations that, on the pretext that everyone is concerned with development, the UN never even bothered to create a strong center capable of articulating and stimulating thinking about development."[23]

If we fast forward to 2006, then secretary-general Kofi Annan asked a blue-ribbon panel to propose how to make the UN system act as a unit instead of a series of disjointed parts. It proposed that *Delivering as One* (DaO)[24] would require consolidating the activities of all organizations into three pillars for development, human rights, and the environment. Like Jackson's study thirty-seven years earlier, the recommendations fell on deaf ears. As former under secretary-general Margaret Joan Anstee summarized, "*The Capacity Study* has sometimes been dubbed the 'Bible' of UN reform because its precepts are lauded by everyone but put into effect by no one."[25]

Efforts since that time revolve around creating "One UN" at the country level in order to reduce transaction costs by host governments, donors, and UN organizations. However, the collective memory is short. In the early 1990s, fifteen unified offices were created in the former Soviet Union but were rapidly undermined by institutional rivalries. This effort is a microcosm of failed efforts at restructuring elsewhere. Proposals to create a single governing board for the UN's own myriad special funds and programs, for instance, are regularly met with guffaws.

The desperate need for centralization and consolidation is apparent, but equally obvious is that leaving the system alone is the only real option because inertia is so overwhelming, which leaves hoping for the best from ad hocery and luck. If donor countries would back their rhetoric with resources, however, perhaps consolidation and centralization could result. The mobilization of "coherence funds" for UNDP resident coordinators in the eight country experiments with DaO were carrots to foster more centralization, as was the MDG Achievement Fund sponsored by the Spanish government from 2007 to 2013. Despite some encouraging signs, the jury is still out

Table 2.1 Total Expenses by UN Organizations, by Expense Category, 2015

Organization	Development Assistance	Humanitarian Assistance	Peacekeeping Operations	Technical Cooperation	Normative, Treaty-related and Knowledge creation activities	Total
UN Secretariat	582,924,374	1,660,844,517	31,885,124	206,135,486	3,131,350,404	5,613,139,905
DPKO	–	–	8,759,159,000	–	–	8,759,159,000
FAO	453,401,243	351,253,953	–	–	414,580,192	1,219,235,388
IAEA	–	–	–	85,078,775	485,464,989	570,543,764
ICAO	–	–	–	93,062,362	101,741,485	194,803,847
IFAD	168,226,000	–	–	–	–	168,226,000
ILO	–	–	–	235,448,643	424,298,000	659,746,643
IMO	–	–	–	12,456,876	55,597,927	68,054,803
IOM	276,484,052	802,435,134	–	510,778,263	4,424,219	1,594,121,668
ITC	102,654,000	–	–	–	–	102,654,000
ITU	–	–	–	10,575,729	181,257,316	191,833,045
PAHO	–	–	–	1,379,321,927	–	1,379,321,927
UN-HABITAT	26,940,529	16,941,918	–	53,513,506	69,666,063	167,062,016
UNAIDS	–	–	–	293,936,807	–	293,936,807
UNDP	5,057,413,898	–	–	–	–	5,057,413,898
UNEP	–	–	–	–	559,703,000	559,703,000
UNESCO	457,494,625	–	–	152,498,208	152,498,208	762,491,041
UNFPA	924,276,000	53,099,687	–	–	–	977,375,687
UNHCR	–	3,278,871,762	–	–	–	3,278,871,762
UNICEF	2,782,751,274	2,294,850,382	–	–	–	5,077,601,656
UNIDO	244,140,762	–	–	–	–	244,140,762
UNITAR	–	–	–	–	23,473,000	23,473,000
UNODC	–	–	–	278,919,255	–	278,919,255

						Total
UNOPS	75,788,000	46,808,000	228,053,000	320,877,000	–	671,526,000
UNRWA	–	1,333,774,841	–	–	–	1,333,774,841
UNU	–	–	–	–	74,632,000	74,632,000
UNWOMEN	314,974,000	–	–	–	–	314,974,000
UNWTO	–	–	–	3,367,651	23,646,012	27,013,663
UPU	–	–	–	2,572,012	76,693,746	79,265,758
WFP	334,399,615	4,559,072,778	–	–	–	4,893,472,393
WHO	152,507,344	480,376,391	–	253,135,298	1,852,641,282	2,738,660,315
WIPO	74,981,000	–	–	–	276,858,000	351,839,000
WMO	–	–	–	102,471,241	–	102,471,241
WTO	–	–	–	20,703,371	226,323,810	247,027,181
	12,029,356,716	14,878,329,363	9,019,097,124	4,014,852,410	8,134,849,653	48,076,485,266

Source: CEB, Budgetary and Financial Situation of the organizations of the United Nations System, Note by the Secretary-General, UN document A/71/583, 28 October 2016, Table 3.

as to whether financial incentives succeeded in changing the organizational culture for the better.[26] Donors are inconsistent; their contrariness in the various corridors of UN organizations is legendary. The very countries that bemoan incoherence also deploy delegations to different UN entities, which acquiesce in widening mandates and untrammeled decentralization.

In 2015, the seventieth anniversary of the signing and entry into force of the UN Charter could and should have drawn attention to the 1942–5 United Nations Alliance that gave rise to the world body and the fundamental underpinnings of contemporary global governance. While anniversaries are artificial "hooks," they nonetheless serve as reminders not to forget. The year 2014 marked the 100th anniversary of the outbreak of World War I and the 75th of World War II, and 2015 marked the 200th anniversary of the end of the Napoleonic Wars.[27]

Those armed conflicts led to experiments in international organization – the Congress of Vienna, the League of Nations, and the UN – after rampant nationalism and going it alone were exposed as empty vessels for postwar peace and propsperity. Instead the Cold War's end led to a huge collective sigh of relief. Meanwhile, more and more intractable threats to human survival with dignity – ranging from climate change to mass atrocities, from pandemics to terrorism – have become clearer and are obviously beyond the problem-solving capabilities of any of the UN's 193 member states, no matter how powerful. "Substantive changes in the past have required a cataclysm," writes Anne-Marie Slaughter, who continued with an obvious conclusion, "which the world cannot afford."[28]

Yet, among the trends moving in the wrong direction within the UN system are the approximately 80 percent of expenditures financed by voluntary and earmarked funds.[29] Donors, rather than beneficiary countries or UN organizations, dictate the use of "soft" or "non-core" resources – an increasing bilateralization of multilateralism. Between 1999 and 2014, total non-core resources increased by 182 percent in real terms, but core by only 14 percent. Moreover, significant core contributions subsidized earmarked ones. "As a result, funds and programs are left with very few resources to implement internationally agreed, strategic plans," concluded an ECOSOC team. "This also underscores a critical disconnection between the intergovernmentally agreed development priorities and strategies of UNDS entities and their actual activities on the ground."[30]

Lackluster Leadership

All bureaucracies share certain problems, but the United Nations has peculiar difficulties; and the deterioration over time of its independence, integrity, and competence is noteworthy. The UN's top official is commonly viewed as more "secretary" than "general,"[31] and other types of intellectual and operational leadership at all levels are more circumscribed and lackluster than they should be.

The Second UN consists of career and contractual officials who are paid through assessed and voluntary UN budgets. The possibility of constituting an independent group of internationally recruited people, who are paid as much as the world's best civil service but whose allegiance is to the welfare of the planet rather than to their home countries, remains a lofty objective. This idea was first spelled out in 1921 and known as the "Nobelmaire Principles," named after the chair of the League of Nations committee convened to codify the international character of secretariats.

During World War II, the Carnegie Endowment for International Peace sponsored a series of conferences to learn the lessons from the "great experiment" of the League of Nations with regard to creating an international civil service – or administration or bureaucracy – to attack international problems.[32] While the League as a political experiment failed, the international staffing was a successful legacy; and Charter Article 101(3) calls for the "paramount consideration in the employment of staff" to be "securing the highest standards of efficiency, competence, and integrity" while paying regard "to the importance of recruiting the staff on as wide a geographical basis as possible."

A leading advocate for the Second UN was Dag Hammarskjöld, whose speech at Oxford in May 1961 spelled out the importance of an autonomous and dedicated international civil service despite the fact that many thought this kind of "political celibacy" was "in international affairs a fiction."[33] His clarion call did not ignore the fact that the international civil service exists to carry out decisions made by states. But it emphasized that UN staff could and should pledge themselves to strive for a larger collective good.

Members of the Second UN are supposed to take orders only from the secretary-general or head of an organization. They are also supposed to be the most highly qualified persons for their work. However, from the beginning these principles have been systematically violated under pressure from greater and lesser member states.

Governments seek to safeguard their interests from the inside of secretariats, and many have relied on UN officials even for intelligence gathering. From the outset, for example, the permanent members of the Security Council made clear that their nationals were to be allotted positions in the second rank below the secretary-general. The P-5 also reserved the right to "nominate" (essentially to select) officials to fill the main posts in the secretary-general's cabinet. This procedure applies virtually everywhere to positions above the director level, and often far below (even entry level). The delegates of member states lobby for the appointments of their favorite candidates, while hiring the most qualified individual for the job often remains a secondary consideration.

Beginning in the 1950s and 1960s, the influx of new member states following decolonization led newly independent countries to clamor for "their" quota of posts, reflecting the bad example of the major powers. Such claims resulted in downplaying competence and exaggerating the importance of national origins as *the* criterion for recruitment and promotion. Geography trumps talent. Senior officials should not have on-the-job training; they should be superbly qualified *before* being recruited. Moreover, while politics and contacts are hardly unknown in recruiting personnel in many businesses and bureaucracies, the extent to which senior and even junior UN positions are assigned to curry political favor in national capitals is appalling.

Simultaneously, the world body suffers from weak retention of young qualified staff, as noted in a 2000 report published by the Joint Inspection Unit (JIU).[34] Recognizing that the UN must find a way to decrease the "steady outflow of young professionals through resignations," the report highlighted three problems: delays in recruiting candidates from the roster of those who successfully pass the National Competitive Recruitment Examination; job dissatisfaction among young professionals due to the failure to rapidly integrate them; and little support in aiding spouses to find employment in duty stations. Thus, while seemingly mundane, serious difficulties in recruiting and retaining qualified staff are worth emphasizing. People matter, for good and for ill.

Indeed, a small but intriguing and possibly precedent-setting first step in an unfinished journey was the effort to improve the process that resulted in the October 2016 selection of Secretary-General António Guterres. The 1-for-7-billion campaign began in earnest in 2015 to increase the transparency of the process. This civil society effort opened up deliberations so that candidates were subject to public hearings and obliged to produce vision statements; and some participated in open debates. At the very least, the effort altered previous procedures in which the P-5 behaved much like a papal conclave, working in secrecy to make their recommendation while other member states awaited the white smoke to emerge from the Security Council chamber so that they could rubber stamp the appointment in the General Assembly, as called for in UN Charter Article 97.

Hopefully, there will be knock-on effects at every level and for every part of the UN system. In May 2017, for instance, Tedros Adhanom Ghebreyesus was voted WHO director-general, the first election conducted under more open and democratic procedures – including almost two years of active campaigning by six candidates and a secret ballot by ministers of health from 186 countries.

Why are these fledgling steps consequential? The recruitment, composition, rewards, retention, and performance of international civil servants form a substantial part of what ails the world organization. International organizations are more than merely tools of states, and as bureaucracies they have authority and power; however, they also are dysfunctional like other bureaucracies.[35] The quality of the staff is a variable that can be altered more easily, swiftly, and cheaply than the other major maladies. Renewing and reinvigorating staff are critical tasks as we approach the third decade of the twenty-first century. If the members of secretariats do not, who will care for the world organization and the planet?

Conclusion

What ails the United Nations? Traditional state sovereignty; North–South theatrics; atomization; and lackluster leadership. Despite them, the world organization has made contributions to international peace and security, human rights and humanitarian action, and sustainable development. But it could and should have done more. Two "what ifs?" – the world without a UN or with a better one – are explored through counterfactuals. The storylines reflect mainly these four ailments and primarily the inputs from the First UN of member states and from the Second UN of staff members.

In 2008, shortly after leaving his post as deputy secretary-general and prior to becoming the UK's minister for Africa, Asia, and the United Nations, Mark Malloch Brown commented that no topic, not even sex, was more popular around UN water coolers than reform. Neither governments nor officials could, however, conceive "the scale of change required."[36] This book strives to indicate why significant reforms would make a difference.

The structure of UN organizations and the way that they are led are more liable to change than are state sovereignty and regional politics. Hence, the selection of Guterres as the ninth secretary-general was more crucial than many observers realize. There is considerably more room for altering the ways that secretariats do business and that leadership functions – from the lowest to highest rungs on the professional ladder – than many believe, and perhaps more than some governments wish.

Part II

The World without the UN and its Ideas and Operations?

The examples in the next three chapters recount dramatic instances for which UN ideas and operations have made a significant difference to our fledgling international society. The examples help to explore the repercussions of a world without the United Nations. To repeat, my overall objective is not to overstate the centrality of the world organization in international affairs but, rather, to explore the possible implications of the UN's absence in the areas of international peace and security, human rights, and development. After the next three chapters, it should be difficult even for a diehard skeptic to defend the proposition that the world would have been unaffected, or even better off, without the UN's ideas and operations over the last seven and a half decades.

The thought experiments in the next three chapters consist of highlighting what could have happened to both normative advances and concrete operations without an active United Nations. Drawing up a partial balance sheet of the historical record is a useful point of departure before dismissing cavalierly the role of multilateral cooperation in a world in disarray.

3

A MORE VIOLENT WORLD WITH DIMINISHED INTERNATIONAL PEACE AND SECURITY?

Part II begins the exploration of a world without the UN and its ideas and operations by using examples of timely contributions to international peace and security. While some are well known and others less so, chapter 3 suggests that the planet could have been plagued by even more violence and suffering without the UN's substantial contribution to ideas and operations since 1945.

Ideas

Many observers undoubtedly regard the United Nations as "brain-dead," but history suggests otherwise. Here we examine the fruitful inventions of peacekeeping and good offices as well as the meaning of the Charter's Chapter VIII.

"Chapter Six and a Half": Peacekeeping

The projection of military power under international control to enforce international decisions against aggressors was supposed to distinguish the United Nations from the toothless League of Nations. The veto for the five permanent members of the Security Council was supposed to provide an incentive to cooperate and keep the major powers invested in the organization. However, the Cold War immediately made such collaboration impossible – in fact, the first fifty *nyets* (vetoes) cast in the initial decade came from Moscow. Another way to keep the major powers in the same room was needed – one that would permit the world body to act within carefully circumscribed limits when the major powers agreed, or at least acquiesced, to a decision.

43

UN peacekeeping proved to be a useful vessel for navigating the turbulent waters of the Cold War. Its limited scope of activities, combined with UN neutrality, made it politically acceptable to the P-5. Although peacekeeping is not mentioned in the Charter, it became the organization's primary security function until the end of the Cold War, when more robust operations and even enforcement became possible.

The idea of using soldiers to keep the peace was first officially proposed during the 1956 Suez crisis. Contemporary accounts credit Lester B. Pearson, then Canada's secretary of state for external affairs and later prime minister, with proposing to the General Assembly that Secretary-General Hammarskjöld organize an "international police force that would step in until a political settlement could be reached."[1]

Some 500,000 military, police, and civilian personnel – wearing national uniforms but distinguished from their colleagues with their trademark powder-blue helmets and berets – served as UN peacekeepers during the Cold War, and some 700 lost their lives. Alfred Nobel hardly intended to honor soldiers when he created the peace prize that bears his name, and so unsurprisingly no military organization had received the prize between 1901 and December 1988, when that special breed of solidiers – UN peacekeepers – received the prestigious award.

The lack of any specific Charter reference to peacekeeping led Hammarskjöld to coin the poetic "Chapter six and a half," which indicated stretching the original meaning of Charter Chapter VI. As Secretary-General Boutros Boutros-Ghali wrote in *An Agenda for Peace*, peacekeeping "can rightly be called the invention of the United Nations."[2] The lack of a constitutional basis made an official definition of "peacekeeping" difficult, particularly because operations were improvised for specific wars. Former UN under-secretary-general Marrack Goulding nonetheless provided a sensible one: "United Nations field operations in which international personnel, civilian and/or military, are deployed with the consent of the parties and under United Nations command to help control and resolve actual or potential international conflicts or internal conflicts which have a clear international dimension."[3]

From 1948 to 1988, peacekeepers typically served two functions: observing the peace (monitoring and reporting on the maintenance of ceasefires) and keeping the peace (providing an inter-positional buffer between belligerents and establishing zones of disengagement). UN forces were normally composed of troops from small or non-aligned states, with permanent members of the Security Council and other major powers contributing only under exceptional circumstances. Lightly armed and neutral troops were deployed between opposing forces who agreed to stop fighting; peacekeepers rarely used force and then only in self-defense and as a last resort. Rather than military prowess, UN peacekeepers' influence resulted from the cooperation of belligerents mixed with the moral weight and diplomatic pressure of the international community of states, of which the presence of UN soldiers served as a reminder.[4]

Peacekeepers defend the status quo. With an armed conflict suspended, they create political space so that opposing sides can be brought closer to a negotiating table. The value behind this idea was dramatically illustrated during the 1973 Yom Kippur War, when the world came to the nuclear brink for the second time since 1945 – the first being the Cuban Missile Crisis. While Israel was reeling from the surprise attack on October 6th, which some compared to the shock after Pearl Harbor, the Egyptian Army had crossed the Suez Canal and columns of Syrian tanks had penetrated the Golan Heights. Having lost some 400 tanks and fifty aircraft, Israel considered using its undeclared nuclear arsenal, and the United States implicitly threatened the Soviet Union. Shuttle diplomacy and the Security Council's deliberations notwithstanding, the availability of a peacekeeping option was essential for the ceasefire between Egyptian and Israeli forces to halt the October War. It also made possible the agreements of January 1974 and September 1975 that authorized the supervision of Egyptian and Israeli troop redeployments, as well as established buffer zones.

Of course, peacekeeping operations do not guarantee the successful pursuit of negotiations; and they can be easier to institute than to dismantle, as this activity in Cyprus since 1964 demonstrates. Yet, during the Cold War, keeping the peace between two NATO allies (Greece and Turkey each supporting opposite sides) was essential to the stability of the Western Alliance. A different illustration of their utility comes from a negative impact: the termination of an operation can create a vacuum like the 1967 outbreak of the Arab–Israeli War following the withdrawal of UNEF I at Egypt's request.

The UN Disengagement Observer Force (UNDOF) was a classic example of international compromise during the Cold War, which suggests how the world could have been an even more violent place without peacekeepers. The first deployments reflected geopolitical balance in microcosm, with a NATO member and a neutral on the pro-Western Israeli side of the line of separation and a member of the

Warsaw Pact and a neutral on the pro-Soviet Syrian side. UNDOF was established on May 31, 1974, upon the conclusion of disengagement agreements between Israel and Syria that called for an Israeli withdrawal from all areas it occupied within Syria, the establishment of a buffer zone to separate the Syrian and Israeli armies, and the creation of areas of restricted armaments on either side of the buffer zone.

Despite the ongoing hostility between Israel and Syria, UNDOF has proven instrumental in maintaining peace on the Golan Heights. The size and weapons of the force are completely inadequate to halt any serious military incursions, but the two longtime foes want the force there. No major incidents between the two states occurred in UNDOF's jurisdictional areas between 1977 and the Syrian civil war, which has destabilized the Golan Heights[5] and increased rebel activity in the region. However, UNDOF's presence over almost four decades also demonstrated that, when the First UN is willing and the Second UN has resources for the task at hand, the world body can make a difference.

The man who helped give operational meaning to "peacekeeping," Brian Urquhart, summarized the necessary conditions for the successful implementation of traditional operations during the Cold War: consent of the parties; the continuing strong support of the Security Council; a clear and practicable mandate; non-use of force except as a last resort and in self-defense; and the willingness of member states to furnish military forces and adequate financing.[6]

From 1948 to 1978 the United Nations deployed thirteen peacekeeping operations. In the next ten years, no new operations materialized, even as a rash of regional conflicts involving the superpowers or their proxies sprang up.[7] The increased tensions between East and West spelled the temporary end of new UN deployments, especially after the Reagan administration's electoral platform of virulent anticommunism, rebuilding national defense, and fiscal conservatism. Determined to roll back Soviet gains, Washington scorned the UN as a pro-communist bastion and shunned peacekeeping operations. Central America, the Horn of Africa, southern Africa, and parts of Asia became battlegrounds for the superpowers and their proxies. This situation changed in Moscow with Mikhail Gorbachev and the advent of *glasnost* and *perestroika*, which led to a renaissance in UN conflict management in general and peacekeeping in particular.

The post-Cold War era also simultaneously led to a vast expansion of UN peace operations – an intriguing story later in this volume. However, it is worth noting that, in 2016, some 110,000 soldiers and police officers served in UN operations, 90 percent more than the number in the mid-1980s. Research calls into question the received wisdom that the world is more violent than it used to be.[8] The twenty-first century's first decade averaged 55,000 war-related deaths a year, whereas the Cold War between 1950 and 1989 averaged 180,000 a year. The subtitle for the *Human Security Report 2009–2010* is *The Causes of Peace and the Shrinking Costs of War*. The puzzling good news of only a modest uptick in total deaths from the early twentieth century results from a synergy of the demise of the Cold War, increasing economic interdependence and democratization, evolving norms, and, not incidentally, the UN's contribution to conflict management built upon the idea of peacekeeping.[9] Despite problems in execution and perennial funding shortages, the idea of utilizing lightly armed soldiers certainly bore fruit, not only because of their achievements but also insofar as their deployments laid the groundwork for more robust future peace operations.

Good Offices

Charter Chapter VI's rubric of the "peaceful settlement of disputes" contains the idea of behind-the-scene efforts by the UN secretary-general and other senior staff to explore openings for mediation and negotiations among belligerents. One of the lesser known results of this idea were UN secretary-general U Thant's efforts to help avoid a nuclear confrontation between Washington and Moscow. Few knowledgeable analysts would dispute that the Cuban Missile Crisis, which unfolded between October 16 and 28, 1962, was one of the most dangerous moments in recorded history, when during "thirteen days" the world came to the brink of annihilation.

The timeline of events, while well known, is worth restating. Missile bases, secretly under construction on the Caribbean island, were discovered by an American U2 reconnaissance aircraft on October 15, 1962. A week later, US president John F. Kennedy ordered a naval quarantine to prevent additional Soviet materiel from making its way to Cuba. American and Soviet naval vessels were in close proximity, with a Soviet submarine captain authorized to launch nuclear weapons. On October 27, an American plane was shot down over Cuba, bringing tensions between Washington and Moscow to a fever pitch.

U Thant's role as intermediary helped defuse the crisis. In his address to the Security Council on October 24, the acting secretary-general – the General Assembly had appointed him shortly after Hammarskjöld's death a year earlier – called for urgent negotiations. He informed the council that he had sent appeals to Soviet Premier Nikita Khrushchev and President Kennedy for a moratorium of two to three weeks – for the Soviet Union, the voluntary suspension of arms shipments to Cuba; and, for the United States, the voluntary suspension of the quarantine. U Thant also appealed to Cuba's president Fidel Castro to suspend the construction of military installations.

Khrushchev accepted the secretary-general's proposal on October 25. That same day Kennedy communicated his appreciation for U Thant's message, accompanied by his conviction that a solution required the removal of all nuclear weapons from Cuba. Soviet vessels continued toward the quarantined waters, while the secretary-general appealed to both leaders: Khrushchev to instruct Soviet ships to stay away from the interception area; and Kennedy to instruct US vessels to avoid direct confrontation. U Thant received assurances from each side and informed the other. On October 26 he sent a message to Castro about encouraging responses and requested a halt to military construction in Cuba. Castro complained bitterly about Washington but invited the secretary-general to Cuba.

Using the breathing space, Kennedy and Khrushchev agreed on the formula that eventually ended the crisis. U Thant traveled to Cuba on October 30–31 for conversations with Cuban leaders that permitted them to let off steam. Meanwhile Kennedy's October 28 letter to Khrushchev noted: "The distinguished efforts of Acting Secretary-General U Thant have greatly facilitated both our tasks." American and Soviet negotiators later sent a joint letter to U Thant: "On behalf of the Government of the United States of America and the Soviet Union, we desire to express to you our appreciation for your efforts in assisting our Governments to avert the serious threat to peace which arose in the Caribbean area."[10] In November, U Thant was unanimously appointed to a first five-year term as secretary-general.

Good offices have been a signature contribution by secretaries-general and other senior UN officials over the years, what Bertrand Ramcharan calls "preventive diplomacy."[11] It is unnecessary to argue that UN efforts in Cuba and elsewhere were a *sine qua non* to eventual agreements to appreciate the significance of additional room for maneuver.

Regional Arrangements

Regional organizations – when and where they exist, and when and where they are well endowed – can be an appropriate option.

Instability often poses a greater threat to actors close by than to those farther away, thus inclining the former to act more swiftly and vigorously. Even prior to widespread consciousness about them, Article 21 of the Covenant of the League of Nations noted the validity of regional understandings for maintaining peace.

One of the more controversial aspects in San Francisco was the balance between regionalism and universalism.[12] The creation of the Security Council, with its concomitant enforcement power, gave "the global" an edge over "the regional"; but Charter Chapter VIII, titled "Regional Arrangements," was a prescient and essential idea. "Subsidiarity" requires the organization closest to the conflict to act first, if possible, before calling upon the UN. That way, the Security Council maintains its distance and neutrality; and it remains an option if regional efforts fall short.

Article 52 of Chapter VIII declares, "Nothing in the present Charter precludes the existence of regional arrangements or agencies dealing with matters relating to the maintenance of international peace and security" under the condition that "their activities are consistent with the Purposes and Principles of the United Nations." This article encourages states to consider regional organizations before the Security Council and also recommends that the council use regional arrangements. Articles 53 and 54 define relations between the UN and regional organizations by prohibiting the latter from taking peace and security measures without Security Council authorization and by insisting that regional organizations keep the council informed.

The active use of the veto throughout the Cold War not only prevented Security Council action but also meant that regional organizations provided Washington and Moscow with convenient pretexts for keeping disputes within organizations that were under superpower control. Crises in Guatemala, Cuba, Panama, and the Dominican Republic were relegated to the Organization of American States (OAS), dominated by the United States. Hungary and Czechoslovakia were in the jurisdiction of the "socialist community" of the Warsaw Pact, dominated by the Soviet Union. Thus, Article 52 permitted each superpower to legalize its attempts to keep order in its backyard without interference from the other.

Nonetheless, the UN's deficiencies and overstretch in the post-Cold War era, accompanied by the apparent strengths of regional organizations, unveiled the value in the vagueness of "region" as a concept and the purported better familiarity with local crises by the member states of regional organizations. The Charter's original framing proved prescient but ambiguous. Chapter VIII allowed governments

49

to fashion a variety of instruments. Although the commonsensical notion of "region" is geographic, the Charter's language meant that a region could be conceived geopolitically, culturally, ideologically, and economically. Such groups could include treaty-based organizations that predate or postdate the United Nations and ad hoc mechanisms. In addition to such geographic entities as the African Union (AU), the Organization for Security and Cooperation in Europe (OSCE), and the OAS, the Charter's definition also encompasses alliances such as NATO and broader cultural groupings such as the Organisation of Islamic Cooperation. Also significant are such "subregional" geographical units as the Gulf Cooperation Council (GCC) and the Southern African Development Coordination Conference.[13]

The end of East–West tensions diminished Western interests in many regional conflicts. Moreover, the so-called global war on terrorism (GWOT) introduced other priorities for the West, and increasingly for governments in other parts of the world as well. Regional approaches to crisis management remain an option. States near a country at war suffer most from the destabilizing consequences, and they thus have the greatest interest in finding a swift, lasting solution. They receive most of the refugees and bear the political, social, and economic consequences, willingly or unwillingly, of combatants from neighboring countries seeking sanctuary. They face the choice of pacifying and repatriating combatant and noncombatant aliens on their territory. Local conflicts and the consequent perceptions of regional instability dampen investment flows and retard growth, while at the same time diverting public resources away from social welfare and economic development into defense.

States from an area in flames seem to be well suited to mediating regional wars – they understand the dynamics of the strife and of the cultures involved more intimately than outsiders. Leaders are likely to have personal connections to the parties, which may be used to facilitate mediation. Regional powers or organizations may also be less likely to be perceived as illegitimate interlopers than extra-regional organizations. Finally, local armed conflicts are more likely to be given full and urgent consideration in regional gatherings than in global ones, as the latter have more extensive agendas and less direct interests in solutions to armed conflicts not in the backyards of their most powerful member states.

Such advantages of regional institutions in theory are not always matched in reality.[14] To begin, most such bodies are less capable than the United Nations. The comparative advantages of regional organizations may be offset by such practical disadvantages as partisanship, resource shortages, and intra-regional rivalries. Apart from unusual cases (especially NATO), and despite efforts to upgrade them, most regional organizations currently lack military capacity, diplomatic leverage, and economic resources. Furthermore, they are plagued by many of the same problems facing the world organization – lack of consensus, tepid commitments, and insufficient political will. Moreover, some of the factors favoring regional organizations are questionable. Actors within a particular area tend to suffer most from the destructive consequences of war among their neighbors, but they frequently have stakes in such armed conflicts, are committed to one side or another, and stand to benefit by influencing outcomes. And sometimes active participants seek to take advantage of the plight of rivals and can even fuel the continuation of war rather than its cessation.

Thus, interests are more complex than many of the proponents of regional organizations suggest. Shared interests in the public good of regional stability can be overshadowed by power struggles. In short, regional organizations, like their global counterparts, replicate power imbalances among members, and consequently decisions can reflect manipulation by the more powerful members at the expense of the weak. Finally, regional organizations have traditionally demonstrated structural weaknesses in confronting civil wars – today's growth industry for conflict managers.[15] This shortcoming flows in part from the doctrine of non-intervention in internal affairs, which is held sacrosanct by many leaders in the Global South recalcitrant to create precedents that might be used to justify intervention against them.

However, recent actions may necessitate a rethinking of these shortcomings because they reinforce the value of the ideas underpinning Charter Chapter VIII. The vocal and public endorsements of the Arab League, the GCC, and the Islamic League for establishing a no-fly zone in Libya were essential for Security Council resolution 1973, which facilitated NATO's air campaign. And later in Syria, the Arab League was clear in condemning Bashar al-Assad. Despite Security Council vetoes, threatened and real, from Russia and China, the Arab League put forward a peace plan and established the joint Arab League–UN mission led by a succession of special envoys – Kofi Annan, Lakhdar Brahimi, and Staffan de Mistura. The GCC approved a contested Saudi-led military intervention in Yemen in 2015, and the UN Security Council has followed up with an arms embargo against rebels. Regional organizations in the Middle East lack the military wherewithal to intervene, but their diplomatic contributions and initiatives can be essential for UN decisions and operations – for instance, in approving an arms embargo against rebels in Yemen or in the humanitarian intervention in Libya.

A different type of value for regional organizations is illustrated by the UN's creative use of them as subcontractors, especially in Europe, where such institutions are well funded; but those from developing countries could play a similar role if they were better equipped and trained. NATO's presence in Bosnia from 1995 until December 2004 and in Kosovo from 1999 to date are examples from the post-Cold War period. The operations in the Balkans were essential to make and keep the peace; the Security Council eventually blessed them all.

Regional organizations have also assumed specific mandates in support of UN objectives. In 1994, the then Conference (now Organization) for Security and Cooperation in Europe authorized troops from the Commonwealth of Independent States and other OSCE members to keep the peace in Nagorno-Karabakh, the Armenian-majority region within Azerbaijan. Similarly, in the same decade, ECOWAS authorized a contingent of largely Nigerian troops to stabilize both Liberia and Sierra Leone. Subsequently, these led to follow-on UN peace operations.

The record of non-UN peace operations – sometimes approved after the fact by the Security Council – have not always been superior to the UN's, with the exception of Europe's well-equipped ones. Yet the evident gap between the UN's capacities and persistent demands for military help can sometimes be filled by regional powers or coalitions of the willing, or even by hegemons.[16] The argument has become stronger in light of NATO's experience in the Balkans and the 2002 independence of Timor-Leste after the multinational Australian-led International Force for East Timor (INTERFET, 1999–2000) handed over operations in 2000 to the United Nations Transitional Administration in East Timor (UNTAET).

Events in Côte d'Ivoire further illustrated the possible impact of ad hoc regional arrangements and procedures in support of UN initiatives. Here the AU's unsuccessful diplomacy forced the Security Council to move, just as earlier ECOWAS had pressured the council to follow up militarily after an initial stabilization.[17] The absence of a meaningful threat to deploy military force in 2010–11 to oust incumbent Laurent Gbagbo and install Alassane Ouattara led to violent struggle. It was not until the 1,650-strong French Licorne force was unleashed as the vanguard of the UN peace operation, after a half-year of dawdling, that Gbagbo was ousted with relative ease. International inaction had abetted his intransigence as Côte d'Ivoire exploded; but eventually the reaction was forthcoming, and the regional ECOWAS was an essential element of the puzzle.

In short, their deficiencies notwithstanding, regional organizations have often been valuable diplomatic partners for the UN and sometimes have also been essential military ones. Weakness of regional organizations in the developing world could and should be upgraded. That said, without the military cooperation between the universal UN and regional organizations wisely spelled out in Charter Chapter VIII, the world would have been an even more dangerous place. And the potential for more UN military subcontracting and hybrid operations, involving better-endowed organizations in the Global South, is obvious.

Operations

This section fleshes out three underappreciated operational contributions to peace and security: monitoring WMD; disarming belligerents and eliminating WMD; and post-conflict peacebuilding.

WMD Monitoring in Iraq and Iran

The UN's efforts to grapple with threats to the peace from weapons of mass destruction began in the earliest days – the nuclear age dawned half-way between the Charter's signing in San Francisco in June and its entering into force in October 1945. Eliminating atomic arsenals and other weapons adaptable for mass destruction was the centerpiece of the General Assembly's first resolution in January 1946.[18] Although major powers have severely circumscribed the UN's efforts, the agenda item remained perennial and negotiation structures evolved. Without them, it is likely that progress to get nuclear arms under even modest control and surveillance would never have ensued. After all, the General Assembly was where countries debated many key issues that subsequently formed the basis for the 1968 Treaty on the Non-Proliferation of Nuclear Weapons (NPT), which in turn built on the key provision of General Assembly resolution 1665 (XVI) of December 1961. Moreover, it was US president Eisenhower's "Atoms for Peace" speech before the General Assembly in 1953 that laid the groundwork for the addition of the International Atomic Energy Agency (IAEA) to the UN family three years later. Some steps toward nuclear disarmament have resulted, and the Security Council has taken modest actions intended to avoid nuclear warfare. The UN also developed conventions, now ratified, to control landmines as well as chemical and biological weapons.

The long-standing efforts of the First and Second UNs to regulate WMD – nudged and pushed by vociferous NGOs from the Third UN – have met with varying degrees of success in two ways. First, the UN is a central forum for deliberations among states, most importantly through the General Assembly and its First Committee, as well as the Conference on Disarmament – which is not formally part of the UN but reports to the assembly and is staffed by UN officials.[19] The NPT is the most significant treaty concluded under UN auspices. The only countries outside the regime are India, Pakistan, and Israel; and in 2003 North Korea withdrew. The NPT rests on an asymmetric agreement between nuclear and non-nuclear states, committing the latter to forego acquiring weapons in exchange for nuclear technology for peaceful purposes, monitored by the IAEA. Another dimension is that nuclear-armed states are to reduce their stockpiles with the goal of total disarmament. September 11 increased the pressure to deter "rogue regimes" from acquiring nuclear and other WMD capabilities, which became more acute still with North Korea's acquisition of nuclear weapons and Iran's looming capacity.

In addition to the NPT, among other major treaties are the 1972 Biological Toxins and Weapons Convention, the 1993 Chemical Weapons Convention, and the Comprehensive Test Ban Treaty (which the General Assembly adopted in 1996 but has not entered into force). There have also been more moderate successes – in terms of the number of state parties and support of major military powers – including the adoption of the 2002 International Code of Conduct against Ballistic Missile Proliferation, known also as the "Hague Code of Conduct." The UN further plays a direct role in implementing arms control agreements – the IAEA conducts inspections to verify that nuclear materials and activities are not used for military purposes – and collaborates with the Preparatory Commission for the Comprehensive Nuclear-Test-Ban Treaty Organization and the Organisation for the Prohibition of Chemical Weapons (OPCW), discussed below.

Second, the UN has engaged in coercive disarmament and monitoring. Following the 1990–1 Gulf War, Security Council resolution 687 required Iraq to declare its WMD programs and facilities, imposed sanctions, and established intrusive inspection bodies, including the UN Special Commission (UNSCOM). Despite hurdles, it successfully determined the extent of the WMD program – uncovering nuclear, chemical, and biological aspirations – and oversaw the destruction of Iraq's chemical weapons and facilities as well as the country's biological weapons industry. UNSCOM's activities were impeded by Iraqi deception and compromised by its association with the US Central Intelligence Agency (CIA). Following a 1998 US cruise-missile attack on Iraq, revelations about the abuse by US intelligence agents led the regime to expel UNSCOM and ban IAEA inspections. Subsequently, the UN Monitoring, Verification and Inspection Commission (UNMOVIC) began with a clean slate and renewed inspections in 2002.

By the end of 2002, the George W. Bush administration was determined to overthrow Saddam Hussein's government, which purportedly had violated previous Security Council resolutions and again was developing WMD – threatening in itself and also because of its future availability for terrorist groups such as Al Qaeda. The United States and its coalition partners invaded in 2003 with Security Council approval and ousted Hussein, only to discover that there were no WMD in Iraq. Notwithstanding Washington's and London's military action in Iraq without UN authorization, US foreign policy often has been consistent with and supportive of international law and the UN. Despite the Trump administration's posturing and stumbling, such analysts as John Ruggie and John Ikenberry have aptly argued that the current generation of intergovernmental organizations reflects Western values and interests. [20] Moreover, the international legitimacy from a UN endorsement still matters even to an administration going it alone.[21] A fundamental point has not changed since 1945 – namely that the permanent members of the Security Council need to agree for it to be effective either diplomatically or militarily.[22]

Iraq has implications for our counterfactual ruminations about the UN's future role in disarmament. First, UNSCOM did a decent job. Despite Iraq's cat-and-mouse games, it found and destroyed much of the government's remaining WMD between 1991 and 1998, as confirmed by the 2004 report from the Iraq Survey Group (ISG).[23] Second, UN sanctions and national export controls may well have worked better than expected to prevent Iraq's purchase, acquisition, and development of WMD. Third, the painstaking analysis of UNSCOM data by UNMOVIC in 1999–2002 paid off. UNMOVIC documented WMD in a few months of in-country inspections with little additional intelligence gathering and limited cooperation from the Iraqi government. Indeed, the evidence was more persuasive than that from the American-led ISG after the 2003 war.

Whatever happens with the bellicose Trump administration, the UN's record is relevant when reviewing the original 2015 "Iran deal." After several years of negotiations, the P-5 plus Germany and the

EU arrived at an agreement to curb Iran's nuclear weapons capacity. Despite contestation about the agreement's desirability and chances for success, the follow-up monitoring relied on the IAEA. The history is worth a detour.

Unlike its non-declared but nuclear neighbor Israel, Iran has been a member of the NPT since 1968 and initially embarked on a comprehensive nuclear energy program with US blessings under IAEA auspices. After the 1979 Islamic Revolution, however, Washington suspended cooperation, which obliged Teheran to abandon its nuclear program. In 1989 Iran restarted the program by working with three sympathetic permanent members of the Security Council (France, China, and Russia) under IAEA supervision. In 2002, Teheran began construction of a nuclear reactor, a uranium enrichment program, and a heavy-water facility; and, although initially it did so without notifying the IAEA, Iran agreed to inspections in 2003.[24] It was found to be noncompliant with NPT obligations, especially enrichment, but Iran agreed to talks with France, Germany, and the United Kingdom.

The talks stalled in 2006, and the IAEA referred the case to the Security Council. While the NPT permits states to develop and use nuclear technology for peaceful purposes, those with such programs also potentially have the know-how and material capability to create weapons. In other words, they are nuclear weapon-capable, or "nuclear latent states"[25] – a categorization that includes Germany, Japan, the Netherlands, South Africa, Turkey, and Brazil. Iran claims the same capability to which all countries have a right under the NPT. Enriching uranium is necessary to produce nuclear energy, but further enrichment to weapons grade is a relatively modest additional step. Evidence that Iran was taking such steps prompted the IAEA to refer the issue to the Security Council in the first place.

A March 2006 presidential statement – often used when the council lacks the requisite consensus for a resolution – called on Iran to suspend enrichment and also to ratify and implement the Additional Protocol of the NPT that governs enriching technologies.[26] Iran refused, and the Security Council passed resolution 1696 under Chapter VII. Iran continued to defy the council, which imposed targeted sanctions in 2007 under resolutions 1737 and 1803. Russia also suspended building a nuclear power plant.

Iran successfully launched a ballistic missile in 2008 for its space program, but the possible dual use alarmed many, especially in Israel and the West. In March 2008, the Security Council tightened sanctions with resolution 1835, which banned trade of items with both military and civilian uses. Iran responded by testing intermediate and long-range missiles. US president Barack Obama promised dialogue, but optimism waned when Iranian president Mahmoud Ahmadinejad declared victory over the Green Movement in a disputed election in June. Iran also acknowledged a secret nuclear facility near Qom and test-fired more missiles. After Teheran rejected several IAEA plans in 2010, the three Western countries of the P-5 drafted resolution 1929, which expanded the arms embargo and tightened financial and shipping restrictions.

The Arab Spring's turmoil provided a temporary distraction. Russia and China refused to support stronger Security Council action, but by 2012 the EU and the United States imposed stronger sanctions of their own. Other countries to varying degrees reduced Iranian oil imports. Covert operations also exposed Iranian nuclear ambitions. The government, presumably, assassinated several Iranian nuclear scientists, and one defected to the United States.

Hassan Rouhani's election in 2013 renewed hope that diplomacy might work, this time with the so-called 6+1 talks (the P-5, Germany, and Iran). By summer 2015, Iran and its interlocutors agreed to a deal by which various sanctions would be progressively relaxed if international inspections confirmed that Iranian nuclear developments remained below a breakout level. In essence, Iran agreed not to seek to develop a weapon capacity for fifteen years in return for a progressive relaxation of broad and crippling UN sanctions. The Security Council endorsed the agreement in July 2015 with resolution 2231.

The 6+1's nuclear "deal," or the Joint Comprehensive Plan of Action (JCPOA), was adopted by the Iranian government on October 18, 2015; it immediately became the subject of much debate worldwide. Critics such as Israel contended that the terms did not solve the problem but "kicked the can" down the road. The Obama administration contended that continued sanctions and threats of force would not have the same leverage as the negotiated arrangement. Moreover, absent the agreement, Israel might strike Iran militarily, drawing the United States into yet another Middle East war and all but ensuring that Iran would "weaponize" its nuclear program.

It would be difficult to dismiss the UN's demonstrated WMD monitoring capacity, which was as essential to making possible the Iran deal as it was to ensuring WMD destruction in Iraq. The IAEA's finding of Iranian compliance with key JCPOA commitments led to the lifting of coercive sanctions by the United States and the EU.[27] Iran has, as required, removed and placed in IAEA-monitored storage about two-thirds of the 19,000 centrifuges at Natanz that had been devoted to uranium enrichment. Teheran has halted enrichment, a process essential for the production of bomb-grade fuel, and removed nuclear material from its once-secret facility at Fordow. It has reduced its stockpile of enriched uranium from 12,000 kilograms, with a purity as high as 5 percent, to 300 kilograms, with a purity of no more than 3.67 percent – thus, making it much less usable as the basis for weapons. The core of the Arak heavy-water reactor has been filled with concrete.

The bottom line, according to a 2016 *New York Times* editorial, is: "If Iranian officials decided to produce enough fissile material for a nuclear weapon, it would take at least one year; without the deal, it would have taken just two or three months."[28] Today, few experts dispute that it would take Teheran much longer. As the Israeli Defense Forces chief of staff stated, "The deal has actually removed the most serious danger to Israel's existence for the foreseeable future."[29] For all its detractors – following revelations about its collusion with the CIA in Iraq and in 2015 findings on Iranian JCOA compliance – the IAEA has nonetheless played an essential and beneficial role in making diplomatic solutions feasible and in forestalling intensified armed conflict. Having a respected international monitoring capability that is technically and politically legitimate has value for major and minor powers alike.

Disarmaming Belligerents and Disposing of Chemical Weapons

Nuclear weapons states have successfully sought to keep substantive negotiations among themselves, which has constrained UN disarmament and anti-proliferation efforts. Outside the field of nuclear arms, however, the UN has been able to exert more influence.

An essential component in most peace accords relates to disarming rebels and paramilitary groups, and one of the UN's singular contributions can be traced to the second generation of peacekeeping operations at the end of the Cold War. For instance, the UN demonstrated its disarmament capacity in conflict-ridden Central America, playing an essential role in establishing regional stability.

On March 27, 1990, Security Council resolution 650 established the UN Observer Group in Central America (ONUCA) to monitor and demobilize belligerents as a measure to implement the 1989 Esquipulas II Agreement (also known as the "Guatemala Procedure") at the request of Costa Rica, El Salvador, Guatemala, Honduras, and Nicaragua. ONUCA personnel facilitated the demobilization of the Nicaraguan Resistance and demobilized 260 resistance fighters in neighboring Honduras. Despite uncertainties, skepticism, and a threatened return to hostilities – including accusations by the Contras of ceasefire violations – late June saw the demobilization of armed and unarmed members of the resistance. ONUCA continued until January 1992 to monitor adherence to the Esquipulas II Agreement; during that time almost 20,000 Contras were demobilized in Nicaragua and 3,000 in Honduras, and over 15,000 small arms were destroyed.[30] This first UN peace operation in the Americas marked a crucial step toward national reconciliation in Nicaragua, a flash point for Cold War rivalries.

UN monitoring and disarmament capabilities have also been in evidence in the disposal of conventional weapons that caused unnecessary suffering to combatants as well as civilians. Global efforts to limit or eradicate them include the 1981 Convention on Certain Conventional Weapons and its additional Protocols (CCW) – which covers incendiary and blinding laser weapons, booby traps, landmines, and other unexploded ordinance, which its 2001 additions applies to both inter- and intra-national wars. Further, this 1981 text laid the foundations for the 1997 Anti-Personnel Mine Ban Convention (APMBC) and the 2008 Conventions on Cluster Munitions.

Very few people are aware of the work of the Organisation for the Prohibition of Chemical Weapons. Unlike the NPT, CCW, and the 1972 Biological Weapons Convention (BWC), the Chemical Weapons Convention (CWC) established an implementing secretariat, the OPCW, which oversees and verifies the destruction of declared chemical weapons; deactivates and destroys or converts for peaceful purposes chemical weapons production facilities; and inspects the production and, in some cases, the processing and consumption of dual-use chemicals.

The CWC contains other rigorous provisions. For example, its monitoring now routinely extends into the private sector – an unexpected extension. It provides technical assistance to a broad spectrum of countries. The OPCW has developed a peer-reviewed and certified analytical database with information on some 1,500 chemical weapons-related compounds. In addition, a network of protection experts consults regularly about how to improve responses to attacks and protect civilians.

By the end of 2016, 192 countries had ratified or acceded to the OPCW – Egypt, North Korea, Palestine, and South Sudan are non-signatories, and Israel has signed but not ratified. All declared their production capacities deactivated, with two-thirds of the declared facilities either verifiably destroyed or converted to peaceful uses. The inventory of all declared stockpiles is complete, but less than one-third of the declared 8.6 million chemical weapon munitions and 70,000 tons of declared chemical warfare agents have been verifiably destroyed. The OPCW has inspected about half of the possible 6,000 military and industrial sites in seventy-nine countries.

Just as the UN successfully disarmed belligerents in Central America, it also made substantial strides in 2014–15 to rid Syria of its chemical arsenal. The latter was noteworthy because it was widely viewed as "mission impossible."[31] The Security Council was completely useless in halting Syria's humanitarian disaster, but the conventional wisdom about a feckless Security Council must be tempered by its value in approving the joint undertaking by the UN and OPCW in the country. When chemical weapons were viewed as an unacceptable threat to international peace and security, the very same permanent and elected members of the very same principal organ agreed to eliminate Syria's chemical weapons. Within a matter of months, the UN/OPCW effort had eliminated virtually all the regime's lethal arsenal, which could have caused widespread slaughter and suffering.

Chemical weapons still menaced international peace and security, however, because the Assad regime deployed chemical weapons again in April 2017. Empowered by Moscow's tactical support and new-found willingness to shield the regime in the Security Council, Damascus released some of the small remaining stock that Assad had either withheld or illegally produced. The awful consequences of WMD – the images of suffocating children were even too much for the Trump administration, which responded in April 2017 with Tomahawk missiles against a government airbase – were a reminder nonetheless that these weapons are less threatening than they might otherwise have been because of a dedicated multilateral capacity. Would it have been better to have 1,300 tons more at Assad's disposal? When the First UN wants the Second UN's technical capabilities to be deployed, they work.

Post-Intervention Peacebuilding in Kosovo

Post-conflict peacebuilding has become a major multilateral undertaking, especially since the decision by the 2005 World Summit to create the Peacebuilding Commission (PBC) and its Peacebuilding Support Office (PBSO) and Peacebuilding Fund (PBF). Some argue that this endeavor is a UN comparative advantage and should become its principal operational focus.[32] Such potential is highlighted by post-1999 efforts in Kosovo.

Time and again Yugoslav president Slobodan Milošević blatantly disregarded negotiated agreements. The Serbian military launched an all-out campaign aimed at cleansing Kosovo's predominantly ethnic-Albanian population.[33] In March 1999 NATO began a bombing attack of Serbian targets that lasted two and a half months without Security Council approval because both Moscow and Beijing objected. Initially, the intervention accelerated suffering as 1.8 million Kosovar Albanians fled. It was difficult to sell aid agencies on the value of "humanitarian bombing";[34] but, as NATO's air strikes intensified, Milošević agreed to end the war and withdraw Serbian forces. Almost immediately refugees began returning home. The agreement included the deployment of an effective international civilian and security presence with substantial NATO participation, the establishment of an interim administration, the safe return of all refugees and displaced persons, the demilitarization of the Kosovo Liberation Army (KLA), and a self-governing Kosovo.

In a 14–0–1 vote (China abstained) on June 10, 1999, the Security Council adopted resolution 1244, authorizing an international civil and security presence in Kosovo under UN auspices. The post-intervention operation, unlike the original military intervention, had the council's imprimatur. The peace operation – the UN Interim Administration Mission in Kosovo (UNMIK) – was unprecedented in nature and scope. NATO authorized 49,000 troops (KFOR) to maintain order and security. Meanwhile UNMIK assumed judicial, legislative, and executive powers. Its terms of reference were to perform all normal civilian administrative functions, provide humanitarian relief (including the safe return of refugees and displaced persons), maintain law and order while re-establishing the rule of law, promote human rights, reconstruct basic social and economic infrastructure, and facilitate democracy.

The mission was path-breaking in making massive post-conflict peacebuilding a follow-on to humanitarian intervention. In addition to NATO's occupying force, UNMIK integrated several non-UN international organizations under a unified UN leadership: civil administration (UN Secretariat-led), humanitarian affairs (UNHCR-led), reconstruction (EU-led), and democratic institution-building (OSCE-led). The operation could hardly have been more ambitious or more successful. The undertaking of comprehensive civil administration included health, education, energy and public utilities, postal services and telecommunications, judicial and legal activities, public finance, trade, science, agriculture, environment, and democratization. Simultaneously, over 800,000 people had to be repatriated; 120,000 houses rebuilt; schools re-established; food, medicine, and other humanitarian assistance provided; electrical power, sanitation, and clean water restored; land mines cleared; and security ensured.

UNMIK's day-to-day functions are modest today. Military forces have been reduced, elections held, and rebuilding begun. Problems persist regarding continued ethnic violence, the status of the Serb minority, widespread unemployment, and a thriving sex trade. NATO and UNMIK have been criticized for not protecting Serb enclaves or confronting rioters,[35] which have plagued negotiations about the final status of the mostly Albanian province.

Serbia sought to retain sovereignty over the province and offered Kosovo the autonomous status that it had under the former Yugoslavia prior to the rise of Milošević. Yet Kosovo, backed by the United States and the EU, sought formal independence – indeed, in 2008, the Albanian majority had overwhelmingly approved it. That position was awkward because Security Council resolution 1244 reaffirms the sovereignty and territorial integrity of the Federal Republic of Yugoslavia, of which Kosovo was a part.

As of 2017, Kosovo is recognized as an independent state by 113 countries, including 109 UN member states. Kosovo is permitted to represent itself at international meetings, but only on the condition that the word "republic" does not appear in its title and that a footnote be included about Security Council resolution 1244 and the advisory opinion of the International Court of Justice (ICJ) in 2010 that Kosovo's unilateral declaration of independence did not violate international law.[36] This compromise represents a step toward EU membership for Serbia, which acknowledges Kosovo's existence but claims that it will never recognize Kosovo's independence.

While isolated violence continues in Serbian enclaves, postwar Kosovo has stabilized, and its status appears relatively peaceful – especially in comparison with the instability and violence so prevalent in other so-called post-conflict countries. Another exception would be East Timor, which also benefited from Western (in this case, mainly Australian) soldiers and investment. It would be difficult to believe that Kosovo and 90 percent of its population would be better off today without UN efforts, just as it would be for East Timorese. Rather than minimizing the relevance of these two small countries, the UN's potential for post-conflict peacebuilding should be better exploited in numerous war-torn societies.

Conclusion

This chapter has analyzed several timely and useful UN contributions to international peace and security. Ideas and operations since 1945 suggest how the planet could have been plagued by even more violence, war, and suffering without specific and successful efforts by the world organization. It is easy to dismiss theatrical efforts like the July 2017 General Assembly decision to adopt the Treaty on the Prohibition of Nuclear Weapons – without the participation of seventy member states, including all the P-5. It is harder to dismiss more pragmatic results, which is why we examined peacekeeping, good offices, and cooperation with regional organizations. We pointed to such specific inputs as monitoring WMD as well as conducting disarmament and post-conflict peacebuilding. In these arenas and others, the UN's contribution has been substantial.

4

A MORE REPRESSIVE AND UNKIND WORLD WITH DIMINISHED HUMAN RIGHTS AND HUMANITARIAN ACTION?

This second chapter in Part II continues to probe the implications of a world lacking the UN and its ideas and specific operational activities. The examination of human rights and humanitarian action illustrates how international society would have been even more repressive and unkind without substantial normative and operational inputs from the world organization.

Ideas

We begin our "what if?" exploration of human rights and humanitarian action with three extremely ambitious ideas: decolonization; the Universal Declaration of Human Rights (UDHR); and the responsibility to protect (R2P). In crucial ways, these normative advances are signature contributions by the United Nations to what Roger Norman and Sarah Zaidi have called "the unfinished revolution."[1]

Decolonization

A central idea circulating on the eve of the UN's creation was that peoples in all countries had the inherent right to determine their own political systems and be sovereign, to enter into whatever national and international agreements that their citizens and governments might choose. The collapse of the European imperial order and the achievement of national independence came within the UN's first quarter-century – although the Soviet "empire" resisted until 1989. Instead of the fifty-one original signatories of the Charter in 1945, there are flags from 193 countries currently flying in front of UN headquarters.

One of the six UN principal organs is the Trusteeship Council, which the Charter authorized to promote the advancement of the inhabitants of trust territories "towards self-government or independence." Initially there were eleven trust territories placed under its supervision. Soon a further seventy-two were identified as "non-self-governing." By 1959, eight of them had already become independent. Yet many countries argued that the Charter principles were being applied too slowly, and in 1960 the General Assembly passed the "Declaration on the Granting of Independence to Colonial Countries and Peoples." This called for immediate steps to transfer all powers to the peoples of non-self-governing territories, without conditions or reservations. In the next seven years, a further sixty former colonies, with a total population exceeding 800 million people, attained independence and joined the United Nations.[2]

The power of this notion is striking – it rapidly replaced the colonial paradigm that had been dominant state practice for centuries. In 1994, the Trusteeship Council effectively went out of business, although it remains a principal organ because the Charter has not been amended. A helpful historical perspective comes from Brian Urquhart concerning the pace of colonialization: "The avalanche started with the Indian subcontinent in 1947. And once that had happened, and with people like Ralph Bunche really pushing, by the mid-1950s it was clear that this was going to be a very rapid process." This was a change from what Urquhart and most of his contemporaries had imagined: "The original idea had been that all colonies would go through a period of trusteeship ... to prepare them so that they could manage their independence. But, of course, it never happened except with enemy colonies like Somalia."[3]

The appearance within a few decades of over one hundred newly independent countries changed the UN's character and dynamics. Thirty-two of the fifty countries present in San Francisco in 1945 were from what we now call the "Global South," but the vast majority were from Latin America, and only six were from Africa and Asia. However, within two decades more than half of the UN's member states were from the latter two continents. In fact, colonial rule had been delegitimized by the UN Charter, and no new colonies were formed in the last quarter of the twentieth century. And in the few instances when such attempts were made, there was immediate outrage (as in Indonesia's annexation of East Timor in 1975, which was reversed in 1999 under UN-supervised elections). Moreover, the few remaining colonies are mostly tiny islands.[4] Bolstered by the UN, the venerated first president of Tanzania, Julius Nyerere, summarized the impact: "colonialism in the traditional and political sense is now almost a thing of the past."[5]

Decolonization was not only a powerful idea in and of itself, but it also led to changes in the UN's programmatic focus. The Charter's daring main objective, "to save succeeding generations from the scourge of war," became less prominent as an organizational pursuit because the Cold War effectively paralyzed the Security Council. The Charter refers to development, which was viewed mainly as a means to attenuate armed conflict. For newly independent countries, however, economic and social development was the highest priority in its own right. Consequently, the agenda within the UN system was fundamentally reoriented; accelerated development became *the* principal work of the world organization.

Since 1945 the politics and policies of the First UN, and the composition of the Second UN, have changed beyond recognition. A fairer and more representative world body – albeit imperfect and chaotic – currently constitutes international society. While the relative merits of what Paul Kennedy has called the "Parliament of Man"[6] are disputed, and while the value of one-country one-voice is debated, decolonization was a necessary and essential contribution to contemporary world order. And the United Nations was the midwife.

Universal Declaration of Human Rights

Although the 1948 UDHR is the brightest jewel in the crown of UN contributions to human rights, it was neither the first nor the only precious stone in a gem-studded diadem. From his vantage point after over three decades in the Secretariat, Bertrand Ramcharan summarized that in San Francisco there was "a groundswell of sentiment that the 'new world order' should be built on a foundation of human rights."[7] Civil society organizations such as the World Jewish Congress, the Christian ecumenical movement, and the American Law Institute, as well as leading academics – the Third UN – were sketching blueprints for an international bill of human rights.

Governments, especially the leading powers of the time – the United States, the Soviet Union, and the United Kingdom – and Latin American countries, were supportive at Dumbarton Oaks. The Big Three in 1944 stated that the new organization should promote respect for human rights and fundamental freedoms. Such developments were in sharp contrast to the League of Nations, whose Covenant included no explicit references.

The First UN – with inputs from the Second and Third UNs – took two years to draft the UDHR. It would be shortsighted to ignore the conflicts underlying the declaration's language and the dissonance between it and the domestic practices of many signatories. Yet, without a negative vote, the General Assembly adopted it on December 10, 1948 – today celebrated as International Human Rights Day. The assembly's non-legally binding resolution listed thirty human rights principles that upheld perhaps sixty specific human rights.[8]

In *Human Rights at the UN: The Political History of Universal Justice*, Normand and Zaidi tell an extraordinary story: "The speed with which human rights has penetrated every corner of the globe is astounding. Compared to human rights, no other system of universal values has spread so far so fast." In his foreword to the volume, Richard Falk reinforces the point: "Among the most improbable developments of the previous hundred years or so is the spectacular rise of human rights to a position of prominence in world politics. This rise cuts across the grain of both the structure of world order and the 'realist' outlook of most political leaders acting on behalf of sovereign states."[9]

At the same time, Normand and Zaidi emphasize gaps between values espoused and rights implemented in every country. Although they have narrowed over the UN's lifetime, the absence of adequate implementation mechanisms for human rights remains a serious and debilitating shortcoming, contrasting sharply with the more powerful coercive tools to enforce international economic law, particularly since the 1995 emergence of the World Trade Organization (WTO). The paradox of the UDHR is that it serves "as both a source of universal values and an arena of ideological warfare."[10] Its rhetoric reaches the highest decibel levels, but enforcement machinery creaks weakly and is frequently contested. However, this arrangement was not by chance but by design. At the outset, Washington and London wished to avoid an activist system; and, when the United Kingdom decided to support limited actions, Moscow joined Washington in ensuring that implementation was secondary. Race relations, colonial possessions, and *gulags* were all factors.

While not discounting the lack of compliance with lofty norms, nonetheless the importance of human rights ideas shines through diplomacy and conversations at every level. Many observers argue that the boldest idea of all in the Charter is that all individuals have inalienable human rights.[11] In 1939, Churchill proclaimed that the war was being fought "to establish, on impregnable rocks, the rights of the individual." Roosevelt, in a speech to Congress in January 1941, announced his vision of security based on "freedom of speech and expression, freedom of worship, freedom from want and freedom from fear." Human rights appeared in background documents to the Atlantic Charter of 1941, as well as in the Preamble to the Declaration by United Nations in January 1942. The Allies employed human rights ideas to garner public support to defeat Germany and Japan.[12]

This type of initiative – naming and shaming is the main weapon of intergovernmental organizations – has since spread far and wide. It sprang from genuine US enthusiasm at that time for an international order based on rules and law. Such prompting led to a drafting commission in San Francisco tasked with defining universal rights. The result was the General Assembly's adoption of the UDHR. Together, the Charter and the Universal Declaration broke new ground and sowed the seeds for subsequent intrusions into what formerly had been considered the exclusive domestic jurisdiction of states.

In a speech at the United Nations upon the UDHR's adoption, Eleanor Roosevelt predicted that "a curious grapevine" would spread the ideas contained in the declaration far and wide, an exceptionally apt characterization for what has taken place.[13] The fruits of such efforts can be seen, for example, in the subsequent adoptions of the 1966 International Covenant on Civil and Political Rights (ICCPR), with its additional protocols, and that on Economic, Social and Cultural Rights (ICESCR). These documents, together with the Universal Declaration, collectively form what unofficially is known as the "International Bill of Rights."

International concern with human rights prior to World War II dwelled on the laws of war, slavery, and the protection of minorities. The UDHR is usually considered on a par with other great historical documents – for example, the French Declaration of the Rights of Man and of the Citizen and the American Declaration of Independence – and was the first truly *international* legal affirmation of the rights held by all.[14]

In retrospect, we can see how the Charter's language led to a different approach to the equilibrium between state sovereignty and human rights. The attempt to finesse the obvious tensions between them did not succeed completely, but the basis for sometimes weighing more heavily the rights of individuals than those of sovereigns was established and has made a difference. The East–West rivalry derailed efforts to convert the UDHR into a single covenant that all countries could ratify. Civil and political rights (rights emphasized by the West) were separated from economic, social, and cultural ones (emphasized by the East), which ultimately led to separate covenants agreed by the

General Assembly in 1966. As of 2017, about three-quarters of UN member states have ratified the ICCPR and the ICESCR.

An initial review of the UDHR took place in Teheran in 1968; but the 1993 Vienna one, forty-five years after the adoption of the original declaration, was more controversial. The main dispute centered on whether human rights were actually universal – as had been agreed in 1948 – or whether they were subject to local, religious, and cultural interpretations. Female genital mutilation in Sudan, the suppression of girls' education in Afghanistan, the repression of dissidents in Singapore, and the use of the death penalty in the United States are negative illustrations. In spite of the sparks over relativity, the 1993 World Conference on Human Rights reaffirmed their indivisibility and universality.[15] This occasion also led to the creation of the Office of the UN High Commissioner for Human Rights (OHCHR), something that had been on the drawing boards since 1947, when René Cassin proposed the establishment of the office of UN attorney-general. The 2006 creation of the Human Rights Council (HRC) is the most recent institutional advance.[16]

In short, since 1945, states have created international human rights obligations that restrict their operational sovereignty. International human rights law, nurtured on a global scale by the United Nations, regulates what policies states can adopt even within their respective territorial jurisdictions. International agreements have been followed occasionally by concrete, noteworthy developments showing the extent to which the global governance of human rights reaches deeply into matters that were once considered the core of domestic affairs. While the discrepancy between rhetoric and reality remains stark – as dissidents in Beijing or Harare or the denizens of Guantánamo could testify – human rights reality would be far worse without decades of UN efforts.

The Responsibility to Protect

One of the most dynamic of intrusions into sacrosanct state sovereignty began with the work of Francis M. Deng. As the representative of the secretary-general on internally displaced persons from 1992 to 2004, as well as the UN special adviser on the prevention of genocide from 2007 to 2012, he recast "sovereignty as responsibility." The notion was novel because "irresponsibility" – in the form of either state-sponsored repression or failure to curb abuses – was customarily viewed as acceptable as long as violations remained within national boundaries. Recent history is reminiscent of early social contract theorists' conceptualization of sovereignty as popular legitimacy – the consent of the governed. Deng emphasized states' responsibilities to their citizens. He argued that human rights reinforce rather than undermine authority: "Sovereignty is to me a positive concept, which stipulates state responsibility to provide protection and assistance for its people ... one can even add that the best way to protect sovereignty is to discharge the responsibilities of sovereignty."[17]

Some Security Council actions in the early 1990s helped to buttress a push for sovereignty as responsibility. For example, in 1991 it determined that human rights repression in Iraq threatened international peace and security. In 1992, it identified the lawlessness resulting from the breakdown of order within Somalia as a proper area for UN enforcement action. From 1992 to 1995, it argued that the dire situation in war-torn Bosnia was such that states and other actors should explore robust measures to ensure humanitarian access. Formerly, similar situations would have been considered the internal matters of states. But the grisly reality of twentieth-century Iraq, Somalia, and Bosnia, as well as during that period in Rwanda, Haiti, Kosovo, and East Timor – and of twenty-first-century Côte d'Ivoire, Libya, the Democratic Republic of the Congo (DRC), Sudan, Mali, the Central African Republic (CAR), and Syria – have come to be viewed as properly international concerns. The principle of absolute state sovereignty has yielded to a transnational demand for the effective protection of human rights.

The fate of civilians trapped in the cross-hairs of violence emerged as a mainstream concern,[18] accompanied by a more widespread demand for better management of pressing transnational problems – in this case, of human-made humanitarian disasters.[19] No idea has moved faster in the international normative arena than *The Responsibility to Protect*, the title of the 2001 report from the International Commission on Intervention and State Sovereignty (ICISS).[20] The basic idea of the R2P doctrine is that human beings sometimes count for more than the state sovereignty enshrined in UN Charter Article 2. As Kofi Annan told a 1998 conference, "state frontiers ... should no longer be seen as a watertight protection for war criminals or mass murderers."[21]

A blurring of domestic and international jurisdictions has taken place, which became more evident over the course of the 1990s with the willingness to override sovereignty by using military force to rescue menaced populations. The R2P rationale grew from Deng's "sovereignty as responsibility" to help internally displaced persons and Annan's "two sovereignties."[22] As a result, the four characteristics of a sovereign state (territory, authority, population, and independence) found in the 1934 Montevideo Convention on the Rights and Duties of States have been complemented by another: a modicum of respect for human rights. While that convention has not been amended, the discourse surrounding sovereignty nonetheless conveys its progressive *de facto* incorporation of rights.

The normative logic of R2P underscores a state's responsibilities and accountabilities to domestic *and* international constituencies for its human rights performance. Accordingly, a state would be unable to claim the prerogatives of a sovereign unless it lives up to internationally agreed upon responsibilities, which include respecting fundamental human rights and providing sustenance to its citizens. Failure to meet such obligations could legitimize the involvement of, or even military intervention by, the international society of responsible states.

Paragraphs 138–9 of the 2005 World Summit decision[23] show how policy and academic debates as well as actions are increasingly framed by *The Responsibility to Protect*.[24] The moral force behind the basic idea is that the welfare of humans sometimes trumps state sovereignty. Shortly after the publication of the report, former *New York Times* columnist Anthony Lewis described it as "the international state of mind."[25] Even one of its harshest opponents, Mohammed Ayoob, admitted its "considerable moral force."[26]

ICISS identified two threshold cases for the legitimate use of international force, namely large-scale loss of life and ethnic cleansing, whether under way or anticipated. It also stipulated that humanitarian intervention should be subject to four precautionary conditions: right intention, last resort, proportional means, and reasonable prospects of success. And, finally, the Security Council was the preferred authorizer of intervention.

ICISS pushed the normative envelope in three ways. One, it insisted that sovereignty also encompasses a state's responsibility to protect populations within its borders. Two, another conceptual contribution consisted of moving away from the rights of outsiders to intervene and toward an emphasis on the rights to protection of those who suffer from egregious violence. This perspective emphasizes the duty of states and international institutions to respond to grave violations of rights. Three, another contribution concerned not only the framing of responsibility to react in the face of mass atrocity crimes but also two other "responsibilities": to prevent reaching a stage when military force is required to stop carnage and to rebuild societies following an intervention. The spectrum of the responsibility to protect thus spells out a logic that attempts to placate those objecting to the use of outside military force because everything should be done to avoid it. However, in the face of mass murder and ethnic cleansing, military intervention is an acceptable last resort. In essence, R2P specifies that it is shameful to do nothing when conscience-shocking events cry out for action. It also is shameful to intervene to protect civilians – for example, in Libya – but then not to rebuild the authority that is destroyed in coming to the rescue.

Amidst modest achievements,[27] the First UN of member states at the 2005 World Summit nevertheless provided a resounding endorsement for this emerging norm more quickly than many had thought possible. As José Alvarez tells us, "traditional descriptions of the requisites of custom – the need for the passage of a considerable period of time and the accumulation of evidence of the diplomatic practices between sets of states reacting to one another's acts – appear increasingly passé."[28] The summit's final text reaffirms the primary roles of states in protecting their own citizens and encourages international assistance to weak states as a means of helping them to uphold that responsibility. The *sine qua non* of the Security Council's imprimatur – holding action in Syria hostage because of the double vetoes from Moscow and Beijing – has led some to call the summit's version "R2P lite."[29] Nonetheless, sovereignty's definition no longer includes a license for mass murder.

Some NAM members continue to chant ritualistic rejections – among staunch opponents are Cuba, Nicaragua, Sudan, and Venezuela. Most countries of the Global South, however, have remained in the R2P fold and voiced commitments during the annual interactive General Assembly dialogues that began in 2009.[30] Despite well-publicized grousing, research suggests support across the Global South.[31] "Sovereignty is like one of those lead-weighted dolls you can never get to lie down," writes Gareth Evans. "One might have thought that multiple changes in the global and regional landscape had worked in the modern age to limit the salience of the concept."[32]

New high-water marks in the acceptance of the R2P norm were its specific invocation in early 2011 by the Security Council to support military action for human protection purposes in both Côte d'Ivoire and, more controversially, Libya.[33] But with high tides come high risks. While few doubted that extreme measures were necessary to forestall likely massacres in Benghazi, criticism grew that NATO had unduly stretched its protective mandate to pursue regime change in Libya. The post-intervention criticism harkened back to earlier criticism of R2P as a Trojan horse for Western imperialism. Replacing a regime in the name of preventing human rights violations was a bridge too far for even some sympathetic supporters, let alone

Russia and China, whose abstentions had allowed resolution 1973 that authorized the Libya intervention.

The subsequent controversy, including a Brazilian initiative for "responsibility while protecting,"[34] coincided with the Security Council's paralysis over Syria, where the brutal suffering of civilians was far worse than in Libya. It will never be easy to reach agreement on how to handle the hardest cases. But there is little evidence that the gains of the last decade are in danger.

Political will remains problematic – as Darfur and Congo, let alone Syria, clearly demonstrate. The threshold for military intervention remains high, requiring not merely substantial human rights abuses but mass atrocities (genocide, war crimes, crimes against humanity, and ethnic cleansing). However, the new bottom line is clear: when a state is manifestly unable or unwilling to safeguard its own citizens – and when peaceful means fail – the resort to outside intervention, including military force (preferably with Security Council approval), remains a possibility. That this policy option exists at all represents a new middle ground in international relations: what constitutes state sovereignty has moved beyond the confines of the narrowest interpretation of the Westphalian order. That we can whisper "never again" and occasionally mean it reflects advocacy and action by all three United Nations.

Operations

Normative advances in human rights ideas have outpaced implementation. Nonetheless, UN operations have helped reduce the chasm between rhetoric and reality. Three are discussed: the Universal Periodic Review (UPR); international judicial pursuit; and succor and protection in war zones.

Universal Periodic Review

Another modestly encouraging result from the 2005 World Summit was the creation of the Human Rights Council. From the perspective of many capitals, the performance of the UN's Commission on Human Rights (CHR), which began operations in 1946, was nothing short of scandalous. In 2005, the fifty-three elected members of the CHR included Sudan, at the same time that its government was pursuing genocide in Darfur, and Zimbabwe, while it was rounding up critics as well as bulldozing the houses of 700,000 suspected opposition supporters. That China and Cuba played prominent roles and that Libya was a former chair added to the litany of embarrassments.

The summit replaced the CHR with a smaller HRC. The change in acronym was important, but the Human Rights Council was not transformed into a principal organ on a par with the Security Council. However, governments agreed to strengthen the Office of the High Commissioner for Human Rights, a 1993 addition to the UN's machinery, which was the secretariat for but still stood apart from the discredited commission and was staffed by professionals. The OHCHR both services the HRC and runs field missions, and its budget remains inadequate but has since doubled.

What is the HRC's balance sheet after over a decade? It certainly does not confirm that the council resembled more "a caterpillar with lipstick" than a "butterfly" – US ambassador John Bolton's dismissive imagery, which also ignored that UN larvae require nourishment by states to grow.[35] The Human Rights Council is required to meet only three times a year; but it has been in almost continual session from the outset, which has made human rights more of a full-time UN pre-occupation than an occasional pastime. The ability to call for special sessions has transformed the entity into a tool for crisis response as well.

Also on the positive side of the ledger would be the HRC's flagship procedure, the Universal Periodic Review, an innovative feature involving scrutiny by all HRC member states during their three-year terms. During the UPR Working Group's first session in April 2008, it was agreed that each country would be reviewed once every five years. The involvement of a review team of government-appointed experts – not the ideal way to ensure an independent evaluation – was a compromise. Although the first UPR of all UN member states was completed in 2011, robust follow-up mechanisms have yet to follow. Overall, the HRC seemed intent more on not offending the countries under review than on confronting abuses. Nonetheless, occasionally behavior was so egregious that it could not be ignored – for example, Libya was expelled and Syria condemned on numerous occasions, but Sri Lanka and Myanmar have so far escaped largely unscathed, certainly in relationship to the magnitude of their abuses of human rights.

In addition to a state's own report, there are ones from the secretariat (containing the findings of treaty bodies and special procedures) and from NGOs. This information is subject to debate by participating governments, although NGOs cannot take the floor during the final reviews and play less of a role than advocates would like. On human rights as on many other subjects, states try to limit non-state influence, but only with partial success.

The across-the-board approach emphasizes dialogue, and it privileges diplomacy over confrontation for government reports. As such, the UPR process permits countries to avoid addressing concrete instances of gross violations. Hence, the most concrete and consistent criticism of the UPR relates to stepping back from the harder-hitting procedures spelled out in human rights treaties. At the same time, the UPR's most significant benefit results from routinely subjecting countries to scrutiny about not having ratified treaties or respected commitments. There also is value in the reciprocity of states making specific recommendations to other states while also being obliged to accept them from peers.

Subsequent reviews are eventually supposed to focus on the implementation of recommendations from earlier ones. In the event of persistent non-cooperation, the HRC is mandated to urge the state under scrutiny to cooperate. And, after exhausting all such efforts, the Human Rights Council is supposed to address the persistent absence of implementation. It has yet to face this issue.

Many countries send high-level delegations when their UPR is under discussion, and so trenchant criticisms are at least heard by senior government officials. It has been proposed to be replicated for such other monitoring tasks as the SDGs. While a state is free to accept or reject recommendations, the open airing of problems constitutes a ritualized form of naming and shaming – the main item in the UN's toolkit. Countries have an interest in protecting allies with less than stellar human rights records – so, for example, the United States is unlikely to be harsh toward Saudi Arabia's policy toward women or Israel's toward Palestinians. Ramcharan sees an "Achilles heel" because "many member states with atrocious human rights records are treated by their peers with kid gloves."[36] Yet he estimates that acceptance rates on recommendations vary from 70 to 90 percent. Because human rights records are so sensitive, the UPR process has added value; it could add more still.

International Justice

The International Criminal Tribunal for the Former Yugoslavia (ICTY) and that for Rwanda (ICTR) called into question the automatic division between developed and developing countries in the pursuit of international criminal justice. The Security Council connected the dotted lines between armed conflict and accountability by expanding what constituted threats to international peace to include gross violations of international humanitarian law. In July 1992, resolution 764 reiterated that persons guilty of "grave breaches" of the Geneva Conventions in the former Yugoslavia were individually responsible. The resolution acknowledged the beneficial relationship between peace and justice. In October, resolution 780 requested the secretary-general to create a commission of experts to examine evidence about international humanitarian law. The commission's interim report recommended the creation of an ad hoc international tribunal and stated that customary law regarding war crimes established a legal basis for universal jurisdiction, and the Genocide Convention (Article VI) similarly had established a legal basis for an international tribunal.[37]

Security Council resolution 808 took the commission's advice and asked the secretary-general for proposals. He subsequently formulated a statute,[38] which the council approved unanimously in May 1993 by resolution 827. In December of that year, a significant indication of the broad support for this precedent came from General Assembly resolution 48/88, which welcomed the court's creation and encouraged states, intergovernmental organizations, and NGOs alike to make it function effectively.

In April 1994, the Security Council continued by condemning the violence and breaches of international humanitarian law in Rwanda. One measure of state reluctance was starting with a presidential statement, rather than a resolution, and avoiding use of the term "genocide";[39] but the council's president requested the secretary-general to draw up contingency plans.[40] A report issued in May by a special rapporteur appointed by the CHR to investigate allegations of genocide encouraged the Security Council, which acknowledged the gravity of the situation in June by using the "G" word in resolution 925.[41] The following month resolution 935 made another request of the secretary-general, to create a commission of experts to investigate breaches of international humanitarian law. Their interim report recommended the establishment of an international court,[42] leading the council to establish the Rwanda tribunal in November 1994 by resolution 955. The ICTR's statute was drafted by the United States and New Zealand with assistance from the new Rwandan post-genocide government. An elected member of the Security Council at the time, Rwanda had voted against the ICTR's creation because it lacked the death penalty and was in Arusha, Tanzania, rather than in Rwanda itself.

The legal basis for these tribunals was somewhat murky because the UN Charter does not explicitly authorize the Security Council to establish judicial bodies. That the council was acting *ultra vires* – beyond its legal authority – was raised during negotiations over both tribunals, especially by China and Brazil. However, Article 39 of the UN Charter gives the council the right to respond to threats to international peace and security, which is effectively the power to define both what counts as a threat and what counts as an acceptable response, including a judicial one.

The shortcomings of the ICTY and the ICTR (especially costs and the burden of evidence) provided the impetus to create a permanent court that could judge and perhaps deter future thugs, an idea that had been on the UN's agenda for decades. By the middle of the 1990s, governments across the North and the Global South, as well as NGOs, had formed coalitions to lobby for what soon would become the ICC.[43] A "like-minded group" assembled consensus at a preliminary diplomatic conference in Rome in July 1997. When the official UN Conference of Plenipotentiaries on the Establishment of an International Criminal Court – better known as the "Rome Conference" – convened a year later, a sixty-country coalition from the First UN joined forces with 700 members of the NGO Coalition for an International Criminal Court. The momentum was such that the Rome Conference itself – under UN auspices – moved toward a decision despite strong opposition from the P-5. Afterward, the signature and ratification processes proceeded on a fast track.

The need to set aside cookie-cutters for the First UN became clear. Progress on the rule of law instead of the jungle resulted specifically from ignoring the theatrical ideological divisions of North and Global South. While no two campaigns are identical, the push for an international criminal court mirrored efforts behind the Convention on Landmines insofar as both moved ahead with a broad-based coalition of NGOs and countries from the North and Global South.[44]

The ICC can prosecute offenses committed after July 1, 2002, but only when a domestic court is unable or unwilling to prosecute a crime that is either committed on the territory of a state party, by one of a state party's citizens, or is referred to the ICC by either the Security Council or through ad hoc self-referral by a non-signatory of the Rome Statute. This court of "last resort" has its headquarters in The Hague; since 2012 it has been led by Chief Prosecutor Fatou Bensouda.

In 2017, the ICC's 124 state parties – including many NATO partners but not the United States – were committed to prosecute individuals for mass atrocities. Another thirty countries have signed but not ratified, although a number of major powers (among them China and India) have done neither; and, symbolically, the United States and Israel took a previously unknown international legal step in 2002 when they revoked their signatures, and Russia followed suit in 2016.

Many found Washington's move away from its traditional role as the standard-bearer for human rights puzzling and a blow to the rule-based order that it had helped establish.[45] Indeed, the United States originally led the charge in the 1948 General Assembly to conduct trials in Nuremberg and Tokyo, as well as to establish such a permanent international criminal court following World War II's mass atrocities. In fact, the United States was also active in negotiations leading up to the 1998 draft of the Rome Statute.

That successive US administrations have remained outside the ICC fold demonstrates the degree to which even the world's most powerful states – whose sovereignty would be unchallenged – continue to resist meaningful international authority.[46] US objections reflect fear of an unrestrained prosecutor, contending that the court's procedures neither adhere to US Constitutional rights nor provide proper due process (primarily because of the lack of a trial by jury), and that the definitions of the crimes over which the ICC has jurisdiction are too vague. These objections underpin the argument that the court infringes upon US sovereignty and could limit the use of American military force.

Washington's opposition is more ideological than logical. The ICC's creation reflected "last resort" jurisprudence: the court is authorized to act only when there is no prospect of good-faith prosecution by the national court system in whose jurisdiction the Office of the Prosecutor identifies an alleged criminal whom it charges with specific acts within the ICC's jurisdiction. US fears about the crime of aggression – and possible limits on Washington's decision-making authority to use military force – were unfounded because that crime was only defined by the states parties in Uganda in June 2010; and that decision has yet to be ratified by two-thirds of them before the ICC can exercise jurisdiction over that crime. Likewise, Washington's concern for its military personnel and its argument that the ICC failed to provide due process (the lack of a jury) seemed hollow, because US military courts do not include juries and the United States routinely extradites individuals to countries that do not provide trials by jury.[47]

The lengths to which Washington has pursued its objections to the court were striking. By 2005, only three years after the ICC began work, no fewer than 100 countries had signed bilateral agreements with Washington not to extradite US soldiers or citizens.[48] In 2002, the US Congress passed the American Service-Members' Protection Act – dubbed "The Hague Invasion Act" to capture the irony of coupling military action against the city most identified with the rule of law – which authorizes the use of military force to liberate any American citizen detained by the ICC.

In 2005, the Security Council turned to the ICC to investigate genocide, war crimes, and crimes against humanity in Sudan. The United States could have vetoed the council resolution but abstained as the ICC's judgment was viewed as useful. Active opposition ended under the Obama administration, which included the ICC in its *National Security Strategy* of 2010[49] and in 2011 joined in the Security Council's unanimous resolution 1970, which referred Libya to the ICC. Nonetheless, Washington has maintained its opposition to the ICC's jurisdiction over US citizens, which certainly will not diminish under the Trump administration. The United States was the only non-party at the ICC's 2010 review conference to make pledges to help states build national capacity, while it continued to oppose the ICC's proposal to include aggression under its mandate.[50]

Lack of longitudinal data does not permit comparing the costs (high), criticism (widespread), and convictions (relatively few) of the permanent ICC in comparison with the ad hoc tribunals. The effectiveness of the former can be questioned[51] because, to date, it has cost over $1 billion but convicted only four of the thirty-nine indicted individuals. Rather than ceding to the temptation to dismiss the ICC's significance as more of a symbolic achievement than an effective means to identify and prosecute individuals who have committed mass atrocities, this section has suggested the possibility of finding different roles, different actors, different scripts, and different stages through which to move beyond the North–South theater and vacuous rhetoric that often paralyzes actions on human rights. The benefits of a more pragmatic and less ideological approach to international deliberations emerges.

The Geneva Conventions and the Genocide Convention require state prosecution under universal jurisdiction for mass atrocity crimes. Until recently, the historical record contained too many excuses and too little implementation. Over the last two decades, however, we have witnessed at least selective enforcement. As long as powerful and Lilliputian states privilege the politics of perceived vital interests over international criminal justice, accountability will remain inconsistent. Yet, the Security Council's creation of the ad hoc tribunals established a precedent for enforcement that has encouraged a nascent regime of international criminal justice underlying the ICC.

The need for turning a page on conflict is important – David Rieff, for example, has argued "in praise of forgetting"[52] – but confronting the truth and accounting for mass atrocity crimes is also necessary. The apparent difficulties faced in the pursuit of international justice notwithstanding, at least impunity is no longer guaranteed for some flagrant violators of international humanitarian law, a step in the right juridical direction.[53]

Succor and Protection in War Zones

The specter of rampant inhumanity throughout World War II led to hopes for the future – ironically, not the triumph of humanitarianism but, rather, a response to the utter desecration of humanity: the Holocaust, massive displacements, fire bombings, and the use of nuclear weapons. As we have seen, the search for human dignity led to the construction of such normative pillars as the 1945 UN Charter, the 1948 UDHR, the 1948 Convention on the Prevention and Punishment of the Crime of Genocide, and the 1949 Geneva Conventions (and eventually the 1977 Additional Protocols).

We have also witnessed burgeoning intergovernmental and nongovernmental machinery, which has provided life-saving assistance and protection for the 65 million people displaced by wars in 2016 – the latest record-breaking year. The United Nations Relief and Rehabilitation Administration (UNRRA), the first operational UN agency, which began in 1943, was revamped in 1946 as the International Rescue Organization before becoming the Office of the UN High Commissioner for Refugees in 1951. Although UNHCR was supposed to be temporary and limited to European refugees, it soon became permanent, with a global purview. The UN International Children's Emergency Fund – now better known by its acronym UNICEF – also was supposed to have disappeared – with the "E" indicating "emergency" – but it too became a permanent fixture and is one of the world's best-known humanitarian agencies. In 1942 a group of Quakers founded the Oxford Committee for Famine Relief (later shortened to "Oxfam") to respond to the famine in Greece during which an estimated 50 percent of children had died. Shortly after the end of World War II, Lutheran World Relief, Church World Service, and Caritas International came into being – founded by the Lutherans, the US National Council of Churches, and the Vatican, respectively. Many relief organizations that were established in response to the needs of European victims soon turned their attention to other countries and activities, including reconstruction, development, and poverty alleviation.

The end of the Cold War unleashed armed conflicts and resulted in the eruption of crises held in check by East–West tensions, which led to the proliferation of humanitarian agencies and the opening of resource floodgates. The budgets of humanitarian organizations registered a fivefold increase, from about $800 million in 1989 to some $4.4 billion in 1999, with an additional quadrupling to $16.7 billion in 2009. After peaking at just over $20 billion in 2010, the figures drifted downward, to $19.4 billion in 2011 and $17.9 billion in 2012, but then increased dramatically, to $22 billion in 2013 and $28 billion in 2015.[54] Even so, the January 2016 report of the High-Level Panel on Humanitarian Financing indicated that the new record for fund-raising still fell far short of the $40 billion needed.[55]

The tectonic political shifts with the thawing and end of the Cold War began the latest chapter in the international humanitarian system's history. One key characteristic is the dramatic expansion of "suppliers" – both the quantity and diversity of relief agencies. While the number of UN agencies has not really grown, the sheer expansion in NGO numbers is nothing short of remarkable. Setting aside for the moment what is and what is not a truly humanitarian organization, there are at least 2,500 international NGOs in the business, even if probably only 1 percent are truly significant.[56] One journalist cites UNDP estimates that there could be 37,000 international NGOs with some relevance for "the crisis caravan" and that, on average, 1,000 international and local NGOs show up for any contemporary emergency.[57] What two authors depict as a "swarm"[58] appearing for a new crisis can be explained by the proliferation of mom-and-pop aid deliverers and the reluctance to scale up because it requires loosing visibility and autonomy.

A detailed survey of US-based private voluntary agencies engaged in relief and development is undoubtedly indicative of more general patterns of considerable growth in today's marketplace that has taken place over the last three-quarters of a century. Shortly after the start of World War II, the number of US-based organizations rose to 387 (from 240), but the numbers dropped to 103 in 1946 and to 60 in 1948. However, they rose steadily thereafter, with especially dramatic growth from 1986 to 1994, when the number increased from 178 to 506 before reaching 543 in 2005.[59]

What about the number of aid workers worldwide? Abby Stoddard and her colleagues at the Overseas Development Institute hazard a guess of over 200,000.[60] But Peter Walker and Catherine Russ are undoubtedly closer to the mark in saying "We have no idea what size." Estimates include everyone from cleaning personnel and drivers in field offices to CEOs in headquarters. Walker and Russ prefer to extrapolate from Oxfam data to estimate probably 30,000 humanitarian professionals (both local and expatriate).[61]

In addition to the members of the UN system, among those that exert influence on the ground from outside a war zone are international NGOs; the ICRC; bilateral aid agencies; external military forces; for-profit firms; and the media. Diasporas – that is, scattered populations outside the affected country but still residing inside an "imagined community"[62] – can also be crucial. Operating alongside, and sometimes in opposition to, external agents in a war are local actors, which include NGOs and businesses as well as armed belligerents that can act as "suppliers" with access to suffering populations – at a price. In the face of soaring demands, the market has a remarkable capacity to expand the number and range of suppliers.[63]

Into this maelstrom, even in the worst of times as in Syria – after six years of civil war, with perhaps 500,000 dead and half of its pre-war population displaced inside or outside the country – the UN system is called upon to raise funds and orchestrate the outside humanitarian presence. While it is easier to emerge with less egg on one's face after a natural disaster – for example, in the heroic reaction to the 2004 tsunami – the UN's efforts to come to the rescue of war victims is a tougher last line of defense. The scramble for funds can be unseemly, but it would be hard to argue that war victims would be better off without the UN system delivering emergency supplies and protecting people during humanitarian catastrophes.

Conclusion

Slower decolonization? No universal rights standards? A license for state murder? The absence of international criminal justice? Fewer institutions and resources to react to mass atrocities?

Human rights and humanitarian action would hardly have been better without UN normative and operational advances over the last seven decades, as answers to these rhetorical questions make clear. It is helpful to keep in mind Martin Luther King's counsel in a 1965 speech in Montgomery, Alabama: "The arc of the moral universe is long, but it bends towards justice."[64] It is of course understandable that many – including victims, analysts, and advocates – are impatient about the pace and slope of the arc of change for human rights at the UN. Its institutional foundations are, however, firmly grounded; and they should be strengthened rather than undermined in the pursuit of a better world.

5

A MORE IMPOVERISHED AND POLLUTED WORLD WITH DIMINISHED DEVELOPMENT?

This final chapter in Part II explores additional illustrations – from the realms of development, poverty alleviation, and environmental protection – that probe the implications of "The World without the UN." It examines critical ideas and operations that have contributed to birthing and nurturing economic, social, and sustainable development. Chapter 5 explores how the planet could have been even poorer and more environmentally threatened without UN efforts since 1945.

Ideas

We begin by probing the UN's contribution to three crucial ideas with a direct impact on the prospects of many of the globe's most distressed citizens: the plight of the very poorest countries; the challenges of statistical measurement and standardization; and human development. Again, the argument emphasizes the value-added of the world organization without making the claim that it was the only or even the main variable to help explain steps in the right direction. While many factors and actors have contributed to improving the lives and opportunities of poor people and poor countries, the UN has played a notable role.

Least Developed Countries

By the late 1960s, the plight of the most disadvantaged countries became impossible to ignore, despite fear among the larger group of developing countries that any weakening of solidarity would open the way for the North to "divide and conquer" in economic negotiations with the Global South. In 1970, the UN's Committee for Development Planning established a working group to identify the neediest countries in order to make them eligible for special aid, trade, and investment measures. Three dimensions emerged as agreed criteria to be "least developed": low per capita income (less than $100 per year in 1968), low contribution of manufacturing to gross domestic product (GDP) (less than 10 percent), and low adult literacy (less than 20 percent).

In 1971 the UN so designated twenty-four such countries. Since that time, the UN has assembled more accurate statistics, and the number of countries that qualify has subsequently more than doubled, although a few of the original members have grown enough to graduate from the category. Highlighting their structural problems and agreeing about special measures on their behalf were made possible by the research and categorization. What started as a controversial notion has become an accepted part of international public policy.[1]

From the mid-1970s until 2001, UNCTAD was the secretariat for the UN system's work on least developed countries, after which it shifted to the UN Secretariat in New York. Jack Stone – UNCTAD's director of the Research Division and later of its Special Program for Least Developed Countries – recalled the struggle to launch this idea: "It was said that every agency in the UN system and every division in UNCTAD should emphasize work on the least developed countries ... yet without specifically or officially labeling a group of countries as 'least developed.'" Wealthier developing countries were afraid that a specific identification of "least developed" would mean less for them and drive a wedge in the Group of 77.

The creation of the category had results. Whatever the rhetoric, trade liberalization, foreign capital inflows, good behavior by multinationals, and a transfer of technology would not overcome the structural problems in the poorest countries, which required special measures, not just from the rich West but from better-off G-77 countries as well. Moreover, as a result of this category, other similar special measures (albeit slightly different depending on the statistical bases) were produced in the World Bank, the European Union, and Western donor governments. The outcomes were preferential trade, aid, and investment policies that favored those countries on the lowest rungs of the planet's development ladder.

Thus, the earlier undifferentiated endorsement within UN organizations of special efforts for all developing countries in the Global South was replaced by ones better tailored to individual circumstances. Given the accelerated development in many emerging economies and even middle-income countries, a basic sense of fairness and decency was generated from UN efforts on behalf of the least developed among developing countries. Despite concerns about the potential moral hazard of favoring the poorest – given that in many cases economic poverty was the consequence more of poor governance than of poor resource endowments or lack of comparative advantage – special aid, trade, and investment measures still helped the poorest of the poor. UN research and advocacy have meant that virtually all industrialized countries and the World Bank calibrate their activities and tailor delivery for levels of economic development. Moreover, it has become acceptable to channel other special attention and resources to such discrete categories among developing countries as the geographically disadvantaged (small island and landlocked) or those recovering from armed conflicts. Such ideas matter.

Quantifying the World

In one of the first comprehensive treatments of the UN's contributions to empirical analysis, Michael Ward noted that the availability of reliable worldwide data is an essential but relatively recent phenomenon. He distinguished three broad phases of UN statistical efforts that have helped to quantify the world and track the progress of, or in some cases the retreat from, agreed general objectives and specific economic and social targets. The first was an original and formative period, notably during the 1940s and 1950s, when basic data gathering and processing were required. The second phase consisted of a longer era of innovation and extraterritorial organizational activity to help spread common systems. The third and most recent phase, mostly since the 1990s, has been an era characterized by data systems maintenance and methodological consolidation. As Ward notes, "with the turn of the new millennium, the UN Statistical Office (UNSO) has moved back to center stage to begin forging new strategies."[2]

The UN has sometimes been an original source of new thinking but almost always an efficient promulgator of ideas wherever they sprouted. UNSO's role in the practical dissemination and transformation of statistical methods and standards has influenced the current shape of international statistical systems everywhere. The results are agreed measurements for launching and evaluating development and investment decisions.

In the post-Cold War era, UNSO has lost some of its intellectual authority as a result of budgetary and resource constraints, which have undermined its capacity to oversee the international statistical system. Indeed, UNSO ceded ground (and thus UN authority) to others, in particular the OECD. Having given up "the crown jewels of statistical measurement [it] conceded control of statistical authority to institutions committed to supporting the economic and financial agenda of Western orthodoxy."[3]

This story is worth telling because of the practical impact of this UN ideational undertaking. Formed in 1946, UNSO determined its main tasks to be the standardization of methods, development of common classifications, and coordination of data collection and sharing among countries and agencies. The early preoccupation was with gross national product (GNP), economic growth, and national accounts. While the issues of full employment and stable economic growth assumed prominence in postwar Europe, hunger and poverty were the overriding concerns in poor countries. National accounts won the day, and they determined macroeconomic responses in most developing countries. Bringing a Keynesian perspective to economic statistics contributed to growth but also placed the primary focus of data on national economic planning by governments to the detriment of the private sector.

The priority of establishing a system of national accounts (SNA) drove the early UN agenda. All countries were to implement this system in order to provide each government with standard tools for formulating macroeconomic policies. In 1952 Richard Stone and James Meade first proposed the SNA at the Organisation for European Economic Co-operation (OEEC, the predecessor of the OECD), which the UN took over, elaborated, and promulgated a year later.[4] This pioneering work created concepts and definitions that remain essentially unchanged to this day. GNP, GDP, gross national income (GNI), and their associated macroeconomic balances are universally recognized and understood.

Ideas that have worked and are now commonplace include SNA standardization, trade statistics, population, and demography. Another significant early UN initiative was including gender differences as essential data.[5] Other UNSO concepts, although scientifically sound and conceptually innovative, often fell on deaf ears. For example, although later they became widespread, at the time of their introduction the System of Social and Demographic Statistics (SSDS) and the early formulation of social indicators were judged conceptually inapplicable. Statistics on the distribution of income, consumption, and accumulation – for which there was a distinct lack of UN global leadership until the 1990s – were ignored by most governments until inequalities became overwhelmingly obvious to statisticians and the public in the twenty-first century. The work of the UN Research Institute on Social Development on measurement and social indicators during the 1960s and 1970s constituted an early critique of conventional data gathering by social scientists and the UN, a precursor to the Human Development Index of the 1990s discussed immediately below.[6]

There are other issues for which UNSO was less assertive and slower to take the lead: poverty measurement, the nature of deprivation, human rights, security, inequality, wealth, and the measurement of overall resource depletion. Rather than postwar European reconstruction, poverty and global inequality were the most important economic and social challenges facing the international system; and to its credit, UNSO confronted that statistical challenge.

Data to manage the global economy on a sustainable and equitable basis also were essential to hold governmental feet to the fire for a lack of fidelity to commitments and performance. That separate and doable task is discussed later in the chapter. UN ideas about quantifying the world helped make such monitoring possible and thus figure as an asset on the organization's ledger, and not one that can be discounted or ignored.

Human Development

Human development is an innovative UN idea, which moved people from the periphery squarely to the center of debate. The Preamble to the UN Charter referred to the dignity and worth of the human person, to equal rights for women and men, and to the need to promote social progress and better standards of living in the service of freedom. Human goals were embodied in the articles of association of several of the UN's specialized agencies. Already in 1944, what would become the FAO began the pursuit of ending hunger. UNESCO in 1948 recommended that primary education be free and compulsory worldwide. The WHO was established to address global health, which its charter defined as "a state of complete physical, mental and social well-being and not merely the absence of disease or infirmity." The primary focus of the ILO, established in 1919 as part of the League of Nations and continued in the UN system, was improving the conditions and social well-being of workers across the globe, and a 1944 wartime meeting in Philadelphia added the imperative of decolonization.

Bold intentions were always present but gained traction in fits and starts. For instance, in 1961, the First Development Decade's

Proposals for Action stated that "development concerns not only man's material needs but also the improvement of the social conditions of his life and his broad aspirations. Development is not just economic growth, it is growth plus change."[7] Notwithstanding these brave words, the UN was slow to develop an integrated framework for the system.

A vision of a people-focused development emerged in the 1970s when the ILO's World Employment Programme (WEP) launched an initiative to address people's basic needs. *Employment, Growth and Basic Needs: A One-World Problem* was the resulting synthesis and presented at the 1976 World Employment Conference.[8] Meeting basic human needs became dominant and captured the attention of donors and won the support of World Bank president Robert McNamara and others. The demise of this strategy in the early 1980s accompanied the rise of Thatcherism and Reaganism, the onset of world recession, and the priorities of banks to ensure that developing countries repaid debts. Structural adjustment dominated economic policymaking in Latin America and Africa beginning in the 1980s.

In 1990, the UNDP launched the *Human Development Report*, which explored and promoted an alternative to neoliberal analysis and policy. The annual reports brought the concept to worldwide awareness, gave it economic breadth and philosophical depth, and garnered media attention. In addition to reinforcing a new paradigm of human needs, successive reports expanded the approach to key sectors – inequality, public finance, participation, gender, economic growth, consumption, globalization, technology, culture, human rights, and international reform and cooperation.

Almost immediately, individual countries began producing their own human development reports to analyze their respective national problems and policies. In addition, the UNDP helped to sponsor regional versions, most notably the hard-hitting ones for the Arab and then South Asia regions. The intellectual foundation has since been strengthened since 2000 through books and articles and the quarterly *Journal of Human Development*.

The first *Human Development Report* reflected the philosophy of Mahbub ul Haq, its creator and first director. UNDP assembled a team of UN staff and outside experts, with subsequent Noble laureate Amartya Sen among them. Transcending conventional wisdom was made possible by replicating the principle pioneered by the UN's Economic Commission for Europe and the ILO's WEP: the report was issued under the authority of individual authors, seeking approval neither from the sponsoring UN organization nor from member states.

The first report defined human development as "a process of enlarging people's choices. The most critical of these wide-ranging choices are to live a long and healthy life, to be educated and to have access to resources needed for a decent standard of living. Additional choices include political freedom, guaranteed human rights and personal self-respect."[9] Later reports – and work outside the UN, especially in universities – progressively refined and elaborated the core concept. In particular, the framework now emphasizes broadening choices and strengthening capabilities, drawing especially on work by Sen and Martha Nussbaum.[10]

In explaining capabilities, Sen has consistently contrasted the great things that human beings can achieve with the limited possibilities enjoyed by most people. This tension "draws on the magnificence of human potentiality amidst the widespread experience of narrowly circumscribed lives. Lack of schooling, meager healthcare, inadequate economic opportunities, violation of political liberties, denial of civil rights, and other hostile winds can totally frustrate human beings despite their potential to ascend on the wings."[11]

Economic achievements measured by GNP per capita and human achievements measured by other indicators contrast sharply. Notwithstanding the correlation between them, evidence shows that many developing countries do poorly on social and human rights indicators in spite of growth – and vice versa. Yet the unabashed pursuit of growth is typically the central goal of economic policy-making. The *Human Development Report* uses four key indicators to determine how well or poorly countries are faring: HDI, the Human Development Index (a combination of life expectancy, literacy, and per capita GDP adjusted for purchasing power parity; GDI, the Gender-Related Development Index; GEM, the Gender Empowerment Measure; and HPI, the Human Poverty Index.

All such composite indicators can be criticized on technical grounds, but their mobilization value is clear. "We need a measure of the same level of vulgarity as GNP," Mahbub ul Haq said, "just one number – but a measure that is not as blind to the social aspects of human lives as GNP is."[12] Or, as Paul Streeten wrote, "There is considerable political appeal in a simple indicator that identifies important objectives and contrasts them with other indicators."[13] The UNDP's administrative and financial support proved critical for the promotion and spread of human development ideas. If they had been products only of scholars or researchers, the impact would undoubtedly have been weaker. The UN provided legitimacy and generated media attention. The HDI is now a widely quoted and influential indicator that provides a yardstick against which the impact of government policies and initiatives can be evaluated and compared.

"People are the real wealth of a nation," Haq wrote in the opening lines of the pioneering first report. "The basic objective of development is to create an enabling environment for people to enjoy long, healthy and creative lives. This may appear to be a simple truth. But it is often forgotten in the immediate concern with the accumulation of commodities and financial wealth."[14] The magnitude and value of this shift in thinking is hard to overstate.

Operations

The ideas just examined had observable operational implications for a wide variety of private sector, civil society, and intergovernmental actors – including the UN itself – and for a number of such policy areas as trade, aid, and investment. This section emphasizes operations – in particular, three whose impact was based less on intellectual breakthroughs than on the benefits resulting from universal buy-in and implementation: the elimination of the blight of smallpox; efforts to set and monitor goals; and exploring the natural environment by the Intergovernmental Panel on Climate Change.

Eradicating Smallpox and Confronting Health Threats

The elimination of smallpox provides a spectacular example of the value of a universal health organization in moving beyond vital interests artificially defined by national borders. A threatening problem was vanquished that otherwise would have remained costly. For more than 3,000 years, smallpox was a scourge of humankind – called "the red plague" or "speckled monster" – often accounting for 10 percent of annual deaths as late as the eighteenth century. Even after the discovery of vaccination in 1796 led to a marked decline of the disease in wealthier, Western countries, it continued almost unabated in Africa, Asia, and Latin America. Arguably the worst disease in history, it killed half a billion people in the twentieth century alone. In the 1960s, some 2 million people annually were still estimated to be dying of smallpox.[15]

In 1953, the WHO's first director-general, Brock Chisholm, made an unsuccessful attempt to persuade the World Health Assembly (WHA) to attack smallpox. Five years later, a Soviet delegate persuaded the WHO's governing body to launch a global program – but with only minimal funds. The organization itself was preoccupied with a major and eventually unsuccessful effort against malaria, and insiders were skeptical about the feasibility of smallpox eradication.

In 1966, the WHA agreed to intensify its efforts through the International Smallpox Eradication Program (ISEP), although doubts persisted. At that time, when the WHO's staff numbered some 3,300 persons, only about 150 professionals were overseeing smallpox programs in some fifty countries.

Once started, the effort advanced rapidly through mass vaccination campaigns, including freeze-dried vaccine delivery to tropical countries. A surveillance system was initiated to detect and investigate suspected smallpox cases to help contain outbreaks. The system was predicated on three givens: All countries should participate in conjunction with some form of regional and global coordination; flexible programs should be adapted to country-specific conditions; and ongoing laboratory and field research should evaluate progress and solve problems as they arose.

By the early 1970s, smallpox was in retreat. When a possible case appeared, flying squads made diagnoses, identified the infected, and vaccinated everyone exposed. By 1975, the number of countries with the disease had fallen from thirty to three – India, Bangladesh, and Ethiopia. By the end of the year, the last case of *Variola major*, the most serious form of the disease that killed one-third of infected individuals, was reported in a two-year-old Bangladeshi.

Attention then turned to Ethiopia, where the last case had been reported in August – but not before nomads had carried the disease across the border into Somalia, leading to an epidemic there in mid-1977. In October, the last case of *Variola minor* was reported there, and three years later – the time specified by medical protocols to be safe – the WHO declared victory. The total for the eleven-year effort was around $300 million, of which one-third was provided by international sources and two-thirds from affected countries. At the time, the total cost was the same as that for three US fighter-bombers. The world now saves $2–3 billion annually by avoiding the costs associated with the purchase of smallpox vaccine, administration (including applying international health regulations), and related expenses. This victory is one distinct economic, as well as human, measurement of the importance of redefining sovereignty to include fighting diseases far afield with as much vigor as those at home. Moreover, the eradication of smallpox is emblematic of the benefits from centrally coordinated efforts to promote international health and welfare by a universal organization.

A less heralded but nonetheless significant success story was the response to the first easily transmissible disease of the new millennium, SARS, the innocuous-sounding acronym for the deadly "severe acute respiratory syndrome." The WHO coordinated the international investigation with the assistance of the Global Outbreak Alert and Response Network and health authorities in affected countries, who helped provide epidemiological, clinical, and logistical support as required.

SARS is believed to have originated from somewhere in southern China around November 2002, to have crossed over to Hong Kong in February 2003, and then spread to Vietnam, Singapore, Mongolia, the Philippines, Canada, and Germany. Public health officials first recognized SARS at the end of February 2003. By the end of July 2003, more than 8,000 possible SARS cases and almost 800 deaths had been reported. Some borders were closed and economies were disrupted; for example, international travel and hotel occupancies fell sharply throughout Asia and the Pacific. Additionally, schools, hospitals, and the daily lives of millions of people were severely affected.

The WHO Secretariat in headquarters issued a "global alert" on March 2, 2003, about the outbreak of unexplained cases of atypical pneumonia. A few days later, it disseminated the symptoms to health authorities, airlines, and travelers and issued a travel advisory against people exhibiting the symptoms. The WHO activated its alert and response network, which brought together eleven laboratories in ten countries. Before long, it identified the cause of the disease as a new virus, the SARS Corona virus or SARS CoV, which had not previously been detected in humans or animals.

While twenty-six countries were affected, over 95 percent of those infected were in the western Pacific. Accordingly, in the Philippines, the WHO's Western Pacific Regional Office took the lead by supporting the healthcare infrastructure within affected countries, helping in particular to prepare for the virus leaping to their shores and collecting and providing the latest information to health officials in the region and worldwide.[16] In addition to its own staff, the WHO contacted professionals in epidemiology, infection control, laboratory diagnosis, and public relations. Infection-control equipment – the ubiquitous masks and gowns that quickly became the public face of the epidemic – were dispatched to vulnerable countries. A regional laboratory network was established under WHO auspices to carry out testing for countries with limited facilities. Local public health officials and WHO erected early-detection systems and procedures; they also established and maintained close liaison with the media in an attempt to raise public awareness without inciting panic.

For a new and rapidly communicable disease, the daily toll of SARS fell fast, and on July 5, 2003, Taiwan was the last area to be de-listed. In other words, as an integral part of the UN system, the WHO collected and collated data and acted as a clearing house for information. It promulgated the norms of safe international travel, and it informed and helped governments to institute preventive measures to contain and eliminate the threat. The UN system is a trusted agent because of its legitimacy, accumulated expertise, scientific objectivity, political neutrality, global footprint, and unmatched convening authority.

The international response to the avian flu pandemic (also known as H5N1, the disease's chief cause) was similar,[17] and the WHO acted as the coordinator of the emergency response system for the global health commons. Influenza "pandemics" can infect almost all countries – the Greek etymological origin of the word means "pertaining to all people." Under modern conditions of travel, transport, and communications, once an easily transmissible virus begins to spread internationally, it is virtually unstoppable, as cross-infection occurs with coughing and sneezing. Because infected people can spread the virus before they show symptomatic signs, the risk of spread is magnified by travelers; and epidemics become pandemics. The exceptionally severe 1918 pandemic killed more than 40 million people. The best and worst case estimates of an avian flu pandemic range from 2 million with a mild form of the disease to as much as 25 to 30 percent of the total population of the most severely affected countries. The surge in demand for emergency health and hospital treatment would overwhelm health services.

Just as SARS was being brought under control in Asia and the Pacific, the region was bashed by avian flu in mid-2003, resulting in the loss and culling of an estimated 250 million birds (mainly chickens) across several Southeast Asian countries. The countries affected, in chronological order from 2003 to the end of 2005, were South Korea, Vietnam, Japan, Thailand, Cambodia, Laos, Indonesia, China, Malaysia, Russia, Kazakhstan, Mongolia, Turkey, and Romania. It subsequently spread to South Asia, the Middle East, Europe, and Africa. In the four years after the disease was initially reported, 315 humans are known to have been infected, of whom 191 died.

At the same time, the politics of the WHO as part of the UN system also intruded in the form of the blanket refusal of the organization to permit Taiwan's involvement in activities because of China's objection to the breakaway city-state. This lapse in universalism was lamentable and predictable political correctness; and it was also dangerous because the "weakest links" work against the provision of a global

health public good, which "can only be provided with the active participation of *every* country."[18]

By way of further illustration, the eradication of polio, inspired in
part by the experience with smallpox, has also almost been achieved.
The vaccines invented by Jonas Salk (1955) and Albert Sabin (1962),
in combination with resources and cooperation that paid no attention to national boundaries, helped make the end of this disease
an imminent possibility. No cases of polio were reported after July
2014 until two were discovered in Nigeria in August 2016. However,
the ongoing efforts of the WHO and UNICEF, along with massive
support from the Gates Foundation and Rotary International, may
soon conquer polio.

The cure for many current health threats is a more inclusive redefi-
nition of vital interests and more operational reliance on universal
intergovernmental organizations to attack transboundary problems.
Among the important innovations have been the requirements for the
surveillance of infectious diseases, emergency medical controls over
outbreaks, rules that inhibit the spread of diseases across borders,
financial and material assistance to facilitate long-term health programs, and international legal reforms that promote access to health
programs.

As demonstrated in a spectacular fashion by efforts to eliminate
smallpox – and also by SARS, avian flu, and polio – the most critical
failures are not of science but, rather, of policy, politics, and governance. It is hard to imagine a better investment than smallpox's eradication, and harder still to imagine why similar calculations do not
apply to all global health threats – as a later discussion of HIV/AIDS
and Ebola demonstrates.

Goal-setting

International statistical standards were highlighted as an ideational
UN legacy that provided necessary metrics for the UN's operational efforts, especially in setting goals.[19] While less visible than
eradicating deadly diseases, such "operations" nonetheless have had
consequences.

Some of the earliest initiatives occurred in UNESCO regional conferences for the expansion of education from 1960 to 1980. Soon
after they began, US president John F. Kennedy proposed the First
Development Decade in a speech to the General Assembly, which led
to formulating UN development goals for the 1960s. Of particular
note were raising the annual economic growth rates of developing

94

countries to 5 percent and increasing annual foreign aid and investment of developed countries to 1 percent of gross national income.
Although originally dismissed as unrealistic, the goal for economic
growth was exceeded – developing-country growth rates *averaged*
5.5 percent in the 1960s, with fifty individual developing countries
exceeding the growth target. Moreover, total transfers reached 0.8
percent of GNI by 1970, about four-fifths of the target.

Over the years, the UN has set numerous goals for economic and
social development. *UN Contributions to Development Thinking and
Practice* reviewed some fifty individual goals, each with a quantified
target and a specific achievement date, a process that continues at
present with the SDGs.[20] The earlier goals covered faster economic
growth, higher life expectancy, lower child and maternal mortality, better health and reduced disease, increased access to education,
greater coverage of water and sanitation, reductions in hunger and
malnutrition, and moves to sustainable development – as well as
support for these efforts by the expansion of aid.

Performance of course varied by goal and period. While few goals
had been fully achieved, there were also few that could be considered
total failures. Progress on growth in developing countries continued
to improve in the 1970s – although after 1980 growth deteriorated
for most of the following two decades, with the notable exceptions of
China and select other countries in South and East Asia. Performance
on the social goals was generally better than on the economic goals,
and in some cases progress continued even during the 1980s (often
called the "lost decade"). For instance, the target of reducing infant
mortality rates to 120 per thousand in the poorest countries and to
50 per thousand in all others by 2000 was achieved in 138 countries.
Access to water and sanitation more than doubled over the 1980s.
Progress in reducing malnutrition, anemia, and iron and Vitamin A
deficiency was considerable over the 1990s.

Three conclusions emerge. First, although the record is mixed,
achievements have generally been more significant than commonly
thought. Second, the most serious failures were in sub-Saharan Africa
and other least developed countries. Third, except for the Scandinavian
countries, donor countries fell far short of the targets for aid, both in
terms of the 0.7 percent target for total aid as a percentage of GNI
and subsequent targets for aid to least developed countries.

The most recent UN initiatives for sustainable development have
come in two installments in the twenty-first century in the form of
the MDGs (2000–15) and the newer SDGs (2016–30). Here the discussion focuses on the former because it is premature to evaluate the

latter, which in many respects represent a missed operational opportunity, to which we return.

While South-versus-North confrontation continues as a fact of diplomatic life, some barriers came down during the Millennium Summit. Heads of state and government agreed to a declaration that was later translated into eight major goals (and eighteen targets): eradicate extreme poverty and hunger; achieve universal primary education; promote gender equality and empower women; reduce child mortality; improve maternal health; combat HIV/AIDS, malaria, and other diseases; ensure environmental sustainability; and formulate a global partnership for development.

The eighteen targets were specific and time-bound, which permitted quantifying what was to be achieved by 2015. However, the eighth goal, relating to a global partnership for development, had no target, which would have implied obligations for industrialized countries – clearly a sticking point with some governments, and especially Washington. The outset of the twenty-first century saw over 150 heads of state and government endorse the Millennium Declaration in General Assembly resolution 55/2 and later their incarnation as the MDGs.

The pursuit of MDGs signaled progress relative to the generally meager headway during the 1990s, especially in the poorest countries. Indeed, the 2015 final MDG report[21] showed that the proportion of people in dire poverty worldwide had been more than halved, an accomplishment achieved ahead of the target year; all developing regions achieved virtual gender parity in primary education; and the clean water access goal was reached, along with impressive results in fighting malaria and tuberculosis.

Of course, there were shortfalls, some substantial. Primary school enrollment still was not universal; chronic child malnutrition remained far too high; child and maternal mortality rates fell, but inadequately; and sanitation standards were short of their targets. While skeptics often indicated that the MDGs themselves deserve less credit for the plunge in poverty than growth in China and India, lifting more than 700 million people out of poverty by 2015 was the product of more than mere economic growth. The prospect of bad publicity for failing to meet international targets undoubtedly motivated at least some countries to adopt measures that they might not otherwise have done. While some pundits dismiss the impact of goal-setting, it is one of the ways to name and shame specific governments by holding their feet to the fire for poor results or lackadaisical efforts.

A few countries achieved all goals, but the majority fell short on several. Some, especially those prone to armed conflict, have not advanced in economic terms for more than a generation. For them, targets meant little. And those countries that were better off in 2015 than in 2000 may find it harder from their improved relative positions to attain the newer SDGs.

Developing countries found growing support for the previously agreed to goals among numerous donor countries, which provided a focus for official development assistance (ODA). Moreover, the World Bank and the IMF eventually joined in the consensus instead of remaining aloof from UN priority-setting, a departure from previous policy.[22] Increased attention also resulted. For example, the *Human Development Report* of 2002 and of 2003 emphasized strategies toward implementation; and reinforcing the MDGs was a major theme at the 2005 World Summit.[23]

The goals did not eliminate bureaucratic conflicts, but they focused policy on similar targets. It is difficult to judge the future relevance of the SDGs agreed in September 2015, but the tighter and more manageable MDG "model" may prove to be preferable to the successor SDGs, which have something for everyone. While they apply to all countries and involve multiple partners (welcome steps), they rely on self-monitoring by states, allowing governments to cherry-pick results to report or ignore, a topic to which we return.

In brief, a small group of UN staff compiled the MDGs into a single, succinct package that was measureable and time-bound. Although several UN organizations were slow to sign up, all eventually did, along with the World Bank and the IMF. The MDGs were the closest that the world and the world organization have ever come to a realistic and realizable development agenda. While it is impossible to draw unquestionable causal arrows, goal-setting was nonetheless a factor in improving country performance and many lives.

Changing the Bottom Line: the Intergovernmental Panel on Climate Change

Here a different twist is given to "operations," the work of a team of voluntary experts of the IPCC, and the UN staff servicing intergovernmental negotiations. The value-added of these UN-led efforts was evident in public policy debates and advances in public international law.

The 1988 establishment of the IPCC is a UN success story in filling an institutional void, which has made critical contributions to global environmental governance. A joint operational initiative by the

World Meteorological Organization (WMO) and the United Nations Environment Programme (UNEP), the IPCC is open to member states of both. It assesses the scientific, technical, and socioeconomic information relevant for the risks of human-induced climate change, its potential impacts, and options for adaptation and mitigation. The IPCC does so on a comprehensive, objective, open, and transparent basis but does not conduct research or monitor climate-related data. Its assessment reports, published every five to seven years, condense peer-reviewed and published scientific literature.[24]

The IPCC's mission is to analyze all aspects of climate change and formulate realistic strategies. The first assessment report served as the basis for negotiating the United Nations Framework Convention on Climate Change (UNFCCC). Even after entry into force of the convention, the IPCC remained the most important source for scientific and socioeconomic information and had a distinct impact on further work. The relationship between the UNFCCC and the IPCC has, in fact, become a model for interactions between scientists and decision makers. One essential principle is being policy relevant without being policy prescriptive. Other important factors are its scientific integrity, objectivity, openness, and transparency, which are achieved through the rigorous review process for its reports. The IPCC's adoption and approval process is open to all member states.

Between 1988 and 2016, the panel issued five assessment reports; a sixth is expected in 2022.[25] Each has presented a comprehensive overview of the existing stock of knowledge. The IPCC has also produced special reports on more specific issues. Its major achievement has been consensus among its more than 2,000 scientific members from over 150 countries about the unequivocal evidence of the human contribution to climate change. In the absence of drastic mitigation of emissions of greenhouse gases, the global temperature by the end of the twenty-first century is projected to increase by between 2 and 4 degrees. These numbers provided a base line for the Paris Agreement in December 2015.

A measure of recognition was that IPCC chair Rajendra Kumar Pachauri shared the Nobel Peace Prize in 2007 with former US vice-president Al Gore. The importance of epistemic communities is a key theoretical subject for contemporary international relations, but the IPCC is a powerful and pragmatic illustration of how an actual network of world-class volunteer scientists from several disciplines translated sometimes esoteric scientific findings into language understood by policymakers and politicians. This network put to rest the legitimacy of doubts – other than in the minds of ideologues –

regarding the human role in climate change. It has become harder to ignore record temperatures, storms, and other indicators. Agreement exists among virtually all knowledgeable experts that climate change is a looming threat requiring urgent action to reverse, or at least slow, human-induced damage.[26]

If we fast-forward to the twenty-first meeting of the Conference of Parties (COP21) at the UN Climate Change Conference in Paris in December 2015, we see a culmination of the UN's collective efforts that began with the Stockholm Conference on the Human Environment in 1972. The stage was set for talks in the French capital by the Obama administration's initiatives and high-level diplomacy with China.

One of the largest international conferences ever held, COP21 was attended by close to 50,000 participants, about half from governments and half from the non-state sector.[27] After two decades of negotiations, the conference sought a universal and binding agreement. On the eve of the opening, Bill Gates announced that he was no longer concentrating almost exclusively on health but was starting a multibillion-dollar clean energy fund for research and development. More countries, especially big polluters, signed up than expected. However, the bad news was that, even if states comply, temperatures at the end of the twenty-first century are expected to increase by 2.7 to 4.0 degrees Celsius, far above the 1.5 to 2 degrees agreed in Cancún in 2010. Many experts do not view the agreed targets as safe, but virtually all believe that going much beyond them would be catastrophic – all the more emphatic as 2015 registered record-breaking temperatures and volatile weather-related events that were broken again the following year.

At the end of the conference, many observers hoped that the glass was half-full because the text, which was unanimously agreed on December 12, asks every country to specify how it will cut carbon emissions through 2025 or 2030.[28] The countries that together produce over 90 percent of greenhouse gases (GHGs) created plans to curb emissions prior to the gathering. The UN secretariat's head, Christiana Figueres, recognized the voluntary nature of the plans by 195 countries and the European Union but noted: "Paris is not the final destination. It is, if anything, the departing station."[29] Moreover, while there is no legal requirement dictating how, or by how much, countries should reduce emissions, there are legally binding provisions to ratchet up the stringency of policies over time, to reconvene every five years beginning in 2020 to present tighter plans, and to meet every five years beginning in 2023 to report on progress using a common accounting system. The name-and-shame system also holds the potential that countries could enact necessary measures in order not to appear as laggards.

After treading water – including after the disastrous 2009 shipwreck at the COP in Copenhagen – governments began to respond in ways more commensurate with the nature of climate threats. The blueprint sets out what is required to get emissions to zero in the second half of the twentieth century. However, the necessary construction based on that blueprint will be impossible to execute faithfully without a change in approach toward traditional sovereignty, which emphasizes the logic of national rather than global interests and zero-sum rather than win–win calculations. As one demonstrator's sign in Paris put it, "There's no PLANet B."

In October 2016, negotiators reached a less publicized but perhaps more immediately important agreement in Kigali, Rwanda, to cut the use of CFCs (chlorofluorocabons) used in air-conditioners and refrigerators. While Paris pledges were just that – voluntary and vague and dependent on future political decisions – the Kigali agreement had the force of law, with specific targets, timetables, sanctions, and financing from rich countries to ease the transition in poor countries to more planet-friendly alternatives. The CFCs are only a small percentage of greenhouse gases, but they magnify warming with an estimated 1,000 times the impact of carbon dioxide.

The Trump presidency reflected, among other things, his baffling claim that climate change was a "hoax" and a "Chinese plot," as well as that environmental *de*regulation was desirable. His June 2017 withdrawal from the Paris Agreement was met with opprobrium worldwide – the former president of Ireland, Mary Robinson, went so far as to label the United States a "rogue state." Because four years are required before it goes into effect, however, the hope was that US voters would elect someone, almost anyone, else who would reverse Trump's myopic and immoral decision. Moreover, the economics of clean energy technologies – many US corporations lobbied unsuccessfully against the Trump decision – and the momentum of Paris undoubtedly will constrain damage by his administration. Indeed, the world's largest and third largest producers of GHGs, China and India, are scheduled to hit their 2030 targets for non-fossil fuel sources almost a decade ahead of the 2030 target date agreed in Paris.

The IPCC significantly contributed both to making climate change beyond serious scientific dispute and to making possible a series of diplomatic breakthroughs in Paris and beyond. Is it plausible that the planet would be closer to being on the path to a more sustainable future without efforts by the IPCC and various UN officials and secretariats?

Conclusion

A proper evaluation of the contribution of UN actors to sustainable development requires that we broaden perspectives to acknowledge cumulative impacts as well as come to grips with the difficulty of asking and answering questions about counterfactuals and of determining precisely why an international organization succeeds or fails.[30] What is important to our story is the positive collective impact of the UN system in promoting sustainable human development, especially since the 1970s. Such ideas as tailoring assistance to least developed countries, establishing global metrics, and placing human well-being at the center of development have been essential to human progress. And concrete international operations to eradicate infectious diseases, monitor agreed objectives, and establish the scientific bottom lines of climate change have demonstrated the utility of universal organizations of the UN system.

Self-satisfaction is hardly justified, however. There are growing inequalities within and between countries and three successive years of the warmest recorded annual temperatures and harsh climate catastrophes. Yet it is impossible to deny that the world would be a much poorer place and have an even more threatened environment without numerous UN ideas and operations. They have contributed to birthing and nurturing a more sustainable path to development than we would have had without them.

Part III

The World with a More Creative and Effective UN?

This part of the book probes the possibilities of the second counterfactual, namely of a fitter United Nations. Previous pages have documented primarily the foot-dragging and myopia of member states, an emphasis that continues here. In addition, as this book was being outlined, and the process to select Secretary-General António Guterres was taking place, several personnel issues arose that put forward the acute problems of the Second UN and, by implication, the potential pay-offs from improving its performance.

The issues on which the First UN of member states have fallen dramatically flat include several double vetoes in the Security Council to prevent action in Syria; short-sighted decisions in the Human Rights Council; and dramatic cuts in untied funding. The difficulties of calling upon states to redefine their own self-interests to include those of the collective fill volumes of international relations textbooks.

The next three chapters stress as well plausible improvements in the professional secretariat, which could and should be changed more readily than the myopic but tenacious calculations by states. While the iconic UN building in Manhattan has been renovated, the demeanor of the people working inside and elsewhere has not. Renewing and reinvigorating the staff is critical. If not the actual members of UN secretariats, who will care for the world organization and for the planet?

The first months of 2016 witnessed a distressing cascade of revelations about egregious ethical and management lapses by the Second UN. In March 2016, the UN's Office of Internal Oversight Services (OIOS) issued a confidential audit "of the management of the trust fund in support of the Office of the President of the General Assembly," which uncovered deficiencies and failures. The secretary-general

103

requested the audit *after* a former president of the General Assembly was indicted in New York for tax evasion involving $1.3 million in bribes. In an understatement, the report revealed multiple areas that need "strengthening for greater transparency, accountability and efficiency."[1] A *New York Times* op-ed by a long-serving official, Anthony Banbury, explained his early retirement because of "colossal mismanagement" and a "sclerotic personnel system."[2]

The next month witnessed an advisory panel of the United Nations Interim Administration Mission in Kosovo (UNMIK) issue an opinion that hundreds of internally displaced people were forced to live for years in "camps built on land known to be highly contaminated" and pointed to the obvious "failure to comply with applicable human rights standards."[3] In the same month, Transparency International published a study that graded the militaries that had provided troops to UN peace operations on a scale of A to F. In spite of rampant grade inflation, only one of the contributors of blue helmets scored better than D (high risk); six received an F (critical corruption risk); and the five largest contributors scored Ds and Es (very high risk).[4] The failing grades reflected "contributions" from UN peacekeepers to Haiti's 2010 cholera epidemic – the disease reappeared after nearly a century[5] and led to an apology in December 2016 from the outgoing secretary-general – and serial sexual misconduct by others. The latter first came to light in the 1990s in the former Yugoslavia and was later condemned by Kofi Annan on the basis of a comprehensive report by Zeid Ra'ad Zeid Al-Hussein, but it continued and became even more visible.

There is thus plenty of room to explore the second counterfactual: What might the last seven decades have been with a more creative and effective world organization?

6

A LESS VIOLENT WORLD WITH ENHANCED INTERNATIONAL PEACE AND SECURITY?

By scrutinizing ideas and operations that have failed or fallen short of achieving their intended outcomes for international peace and security, this first chapter explores the possibilities for a more effective UN in the arena that originally justified the organization's establishment. With different attitudes, perspectives, and commitments, chapter 6 points toward a more peaceful planet that could have resulted had both the First and the Second UNs more vigorously and rigorously pursued UN ideas and operations – not hypothetical or dreamy ones, but concrete ones on the agenda.

Ideas

The first section examines three notions whose impact could and should have been greater: disarmament and development; human security; and collective security. We need to pick up the pace to accelerate the implementation of ideas and initiatives that have more potential traction than is commonly thought.

Disarmament and Development

Ramesh Thakur and I have commented that, in the unfinished journey of global governance, major powers – and especially those with nuclear weapons and other types of WMD – prefer that serious discussions about controlling them be bilateral. The members in the club have expanded to include India, Pakistan, North Korea, and, undoubtedly, Israel; they join the P-5 in keeping multilateral deliberations at arm's length.

Linking disarmament with development, however, has long been on the UN's agenda. The results have been modest, but the topic has been one of the world organization's most sustained preoccupations. The link between disarmament and development is an adaptation of "guns and butter" – a trade-off of limited resources, with more for the military meaning less for social expenditures. However, as World Bank historians show, disarmament was neglected by the Bretton Woods institutions for four decades, after which it surreptitiously entered analyses of public spending. Even since the end of the Cold War, arms reduction has remained controversial.[1]

In contrast, all three UNs have actively advocated disarmament at various times. From the First UN, governments have introduced proposals linking disarmament with development. France began in 1955 by proposing that participating states agree to reduce military spending by a set percentage, which would increase each year. A common definition of military spending would be followed, and reductions monitored. The resources released would be paid into an international fund, 25 percent of which would be allocated to development.

In 1973, the General Assembly adopted a resolution calling for a one-time reduction of 10 percent in military budgets by the Security Council's P-5. Other states were encouraged to join, and 10 percent of the savings would be allocated to development. In 1978, several more proposals, including by Senegal and France, linked disarmament with development. The Cold War made such proposals dead on arrival.

Over the years, UN staff have explored related themes. For example, during the First Development Decade, governments discussed a proposal that as little as 10 percent of the savings from halved military spending could, if reallocated to development, accelerate economic growth in developing countries by an additional 1.5 percent per year (i.e., at the time, from around 3.5 percent to 5 percent annually).[2] To provide some contemporary perspective, total ODA in 2016 was about 1 percent of world military spending – which stood at $1.339 trillion.[3] The "what-if?" here relates to calculating the possible cumulative benefits of a half-century of not implementing that First Development Decade's recommendation.

The most creative and comprehensive of UN reports on the subject was the so-called Thorsson report of 1982 – which came from the Ad Hoc Committee of the Disarmament Commission named after its chair, Inga Thorsson, then Sweden's minister for disarmament. The 1973 Nobel Prize winner in economics, Wassily Leontief, made technical calculations and projections. The report brought together disarmament, development, and security. It analyzed the negative relationship between arms spending and economic growth in developing countries, and it criticized earlier studies by the Second UN for being too timid in the face of the First UN's obvious sensitivities. The report concluded that "the world can either continue to pursue the arms race with characteristic vigor or move consciously and with deliberate speed toward a more stable and balanced social and economic development. It cannot do both."[4] Yet the report was produced seven years before the fall of the Berlin Wall and thus without of the possibilities from the easing of East–West tensions.

The benefits of disarmament over the 1990s emerged in an unexpected way. The assumption over the decades had been that reductions in military spending would free up resources (mostly from developed states) that could be used for social spending, with a substantial proportion going to investments in the Global South. The reductions in arms spending by more than 25 percent from 1989 to 1996 in the United States and other Western countries, however, went elsewhere. Lawrence Klein and Joseph Stiglitz calculated how US decreases led to major reductions in the US deficit, which reduced interest rates and facilitated a long boom.[5] The knock-on effects throughout rest of the world spread the benefits and stimulated growth.

In other words, any peace dividend resulted primarily not from increased development expenditures but, rather, from decreased military spending that resulted in budgetary surpluses in many countries, most significantly the United States, which in turn allowed developed countries to spend more. Thus, the disarmament dividend envisioned by proponents of slashing military expenditures and plowing the cost-savings into development did not materialize; but the improved global economic and budgetary health resulting from military cuts permitted a positive outcome. The potential benefits to the lowest-income countries were often offset, however, by obligations under the structural adjustment policies championed by the Bretton Woods institutions and by the disruptive effects of local wars abetted by the small-arms trade.

Even before the beginning of the GWOT and the wars in Afghanistan and Iraq, military expenditures were on the rise. Early in the twenty-first century, world military expenditures were estimated to have reached about 2.5 percent of world GNP, an increase of 45 percent in real terms since 1998 – the low point in post-Cold War military expenditures. China and India have increased their military spending and arms exports, although Russia and Eastern Europe have recorded the highest growth in military spending. In 2007, the United States accounted for 45 percent of world military expenditures, though that figure dropped to 37 percent in 2015. More significantly, as of 2015, China accounted for 13 percent of world military expenditures, followed distantly by Saudi Arabia (5 percent), Russia (4 percent), and a collection of the United Kingdom, India, France, Japan, Germany, and South Korea, each spending about 2 to 3 percent of the world total. Although military spending in poorer developing countries forms only a small proportion of the world total, the drain of military expenditures in a number of these countries is substantial relative to their GNPs.[6]

What if secretariats had lobbied more effectively and if member states had implemented any of the forward-looking ideas about disarmament and development? Undoubtedly, we would have seen better international peace and security – and certainly not worse. More importantly, however, perhaps we would have witnessed improved economic and social prospects for many of the world's most impoverished citizens. Reallocation of even a sliver of the $1.4 trillion of annual world military expenditures could bring considerable benefits to individuals worldwide.

Human Security

An essential UN ideational contribution is "human security," arguably the most radical shift in thinking about conflict management since the UN's foundation. The notion first appeared in the UNDP's *Human Development Report 1994*: "The concept of security has for too long been interpreted narrowly: as security of territory from external aggression, or as protection of national interests in foreign policy or as global security from the threat of a nuclear holocaust. It has been related more to nation states than to people." At bottom, this report argued for the protection of people not just from military threats but also from a host of non-military ones to their lives and dignity. The expanded list included not only economic but also food, health, environment, and community insecurities. The report outlined key features: people-centered, universal, interdependent, and easier to ensure through early prevention than later intervention. According to the report, "Human security can be said to have two main aspects. It means, first, safety from such chronic threats as hunger, disease, and repression. And second, it means protection from sudden and hurtful disruptions in the pattern of daily life."[7]

The concept was in large measure the intellectual handiwork of Mahbub ul Haq and the UNDP's *Human Development Report* team, an instance of the Second UN operating with admirable intellectual independence. Oscar Arias, the Nobel Laureate and twice president of Costa Rica, also played a role. Credibility came because his country had abolished its army nearly fifty years earlier and proven the operational feasibility of non-military approaches to enhanced "security." Human security also reflected the continuation of skewed priorities after the Cold War.

Ironically, decreased East–West tensions were accompanied by the rapid proliferation of small arms and civil wars, which focused analytical attention on "new wars,"[8] and social insecurities encouraged thinking about people-focused security. From the seventeenth to the mid-twentieth century, conflict between states explained the vast majority of wars, which in turn contributed to crystallizing ideas about state security and vital national interests. But the late 1980s turned preoccupations away from the exclusive security of the state toward the security of individual human beings.

Human security was not without controversy, and there was no agreed definition. Nonetheless, within a decade the concept became central within the Second UN and several UN-related commissions. Moreover, several sympathetic members of the First UN (in particular, Canada, Japan, Norway, and Switzerland) publicly embraced the concept and pushed hard for it to guide UN activities. The relevance of ideas can be gleaned by seeing the extent to which subsequent government decisions about ODA and investment reflected a commitment to human security. However, many other states still do not heartily accept the concept. Still others resist replacing or supplementing state security because human security challenges sovereign prerogatives. The United States, Russia, and China appear to fall into this category, as do many countries in the Global South.

In moving away from the state and toward the individual, ambiguities still persist as to what exactly is being secured, a topic that is the subject of Neil MacFarlane and Yuen Foong Khong's *Human Security and the UN: A Critical History*.[9] One alternative conception is the protection of rights grounded in treaties and other international legal instruments. Another is "freedom from fear," the protection of people from threats of violence. A third engages the broader notion of sustainable human development, with human security encompassing economic, food, health, environmental, personal, community, and political dimensions. The first two echo, but go beyond, the laws of war.[10] Although MacFarlane and Khong applaud rebalancing state and individual security, they judge ill-advised stretching what counts as human security beyond protection from violence.

For example, while acknowledging the UNDP's seminal and

constructive role in focusing on "people," as well as highlighting "non-traditional threats," one official Canadian analysis suggested that the UN approach "made it unwieldy as a policy instrument." Moreover, it took issue with the original emphasis in the *Human Development Report 1994* on threats associated with underdevelopment, which led the UNDP to downplay "the continuing human insecurity resulting from violent conflict."[11] In order to emphasize the need for action in such instances, it argued for a narrower interpretation – one that focused on the protection of human beings from violence.

The UN initially followed this narrower approach. In September 1999, Secretary-General Kofi Annan delivered a report to the Security Council in which he outlined politically viable dimensions of human security by concentrating on armed attacks against civilians, forced displacement, the intermingling of combatants and civilians in refugee camps, the denial of humanitarian assistance and access, the targeting of humanitarian and peacekeeping personnel, the widespread availability of small arms and anti-personnel landmines, and the humanitarian impact of sanctions.[12] As he commented: "One has to be able to define it more narrowly than is being done presently for it to be meaningful and helpful to policy makers."[13] In short, if the meaning of human security included everything, the fear among many, even fervent, proponents was that it would catalyze not action but rhetoric.

In July 2000, the Security Council asked ECOSOC to address the structural causes of war and urged the more effective integration of efforts into ODA strategies. Annan reiterated his commitment to move the UN from a "culture of reaction to a culture of prevention";[14] and he underlined that structural conflict prevention consists mainly in encouraging sustainable development. He recommended addressing war's socioeconomic root causes, with a primary focus on decreasing such structural risks as inequity, inequality, and insecurity through UN development cooperation. In brief, the secretary-general pleaded for emphasizing "freedom from want" and "freedom from fear."

Yet, a dispute remained between the "development first" and the "security first" camps, although the two propositions are not mutually exclusive. The reports of the 2003 Commission on Human Security[15] and the 2004 Secretary-General's High-Level Panel on Threats, Challenges and Change (HLP)[16] emphasized that human well-being and the capacity of communities and individuals to protect their economic welfare are fundamentals of human security. This view built upon the *Human Development Report 1994* as well as a recognition that had been articulated earlier in the 1980 Brandt report by the Independent Commission on International Development Issues.[17]

A comprehensive approach to human security recognizes the inter-related actions required to deal with, prevent, and control the multiple causes of insecurity. It also emphasizes budgetary allocations and trade-offs: military expenditures should be compared with spending on non-military actions, such as for police to control urban crime or for public health to control disease. The case for taking account of the interactions and consequences seems clear. At the same time, sequencing and priority-setting are also essential, and so proponents of the broad notions have to go beyond recommendations to do everything at once and include every human malady in an undifferentiated and non-prioritized litany of security threats. Use of the term "security" is thought to indicate a seriousness that places an issue toward the top of the agenda. However, a "kitchen-sink" definition – that is, too much of a good thing – can render human security an analytically vacuous concept. Framing human security threats as organized violence prevents conceptual overstretch and circumscribes its scope to the meaning that the *Human Development Report 1994* and the secretary-general's HLP originally intended. While doing so fails to capture the full range of measures to counter all of the threats included by the most fervent human security proponents, adopting the narrow organized-violence criterion would be more manageable and build bridges to mainstream security thinking.

MacFarlane and Khong recommend restricting security threats to conscious ones against physical integrity, be they perpetrated by states, individuals, or groups. "Much of the literature on the broad concept of human security is simply an exercise in re-labeling phenomena that already have perfectly good names: hunger, disease, environmental degradation," Andrew Mack writes. "There has been little serious argument that seeks to demonstrate why 'broadening' the concept of security to embrace a large menu of mostly unrelated problems and social ills is either analytically or practically useful."[18]

In concluding this "what-if?" section, an important link to an earlier discussion is that the *Human Development Report 1994* regarded human security as a means to reduce military spending and shift resources to non-military investments. Oscar Arias set out details for a Global Demilitarization Fund[19] which could provide resources and incentives for disarming and demobilizing armed forces, reintegrating military personnel into society, reducing arms production, and encouraging civic participation in democratic political life. However, this fund has yet to see the light of day. The state remains the principal provider of security – which means military muscle in most countries – and thus arms expenditures and sales continue their upward trajectory, with no noticeable increase in the actual security of citizens.

Member states, secretariats, and NGOs have not done enough to advance a reasonable approach to human security; they have taken a solid idea and overstretched its meaning and thus prevented any significant operational application. It is hard to imagine that earlier concrete steps, however modest, to nurture and apply a narrower notion of human security would not have yielded a less violent world.

Collective Security Revisited: Korea and the Persian Gulf

The UN's primary purpose is, broadly, "collective security," a term that was applied to the League of Nations and thus fell into disrepute. The Charter's Preamble spells out the prime objective: "to save succeeding generations from the scourge of war." The primary mechanisms for collective security are the commitment to the peaceful settlement of disputes (Chapter VI), peace enforcement (Chapter VII), and respect for regional arrangements (Chapter VIII).[20]

This section explores UN theory and practice by examining the idea of collective security, which can be traced through a long history of proposals to restrict war and foster peace.[21] The central thread of the idea has remained constant over time: that all states would join forces to prevent one of their number from using coercion to gain advantage. Under such a system, no government could conquer another or otherwise disturb the peace for fear of retribution from all other governments. An attack on one would be treated as an attack on all. The notion of self-defense, universally agreed as a right of sovereign states, was expanded to include the right of the international community of states to prevent war.

The simplicity of the logic contrasts with the difficulties in the application of collective security. In theory, its success depends on three factors: consensus, commitment, and organization.[22] "Consensus" refers to the recognition by members of a threat to international peace and security. Members of a collective security arrangement, especially the most powerful, must agree that such a threat or breach of the peace has occurred, or they must at least stand aside when others wish to act. Since 1945, UN member states have inconsistently characterized uses of force, outside of self-defense, as a threat to or a breach of the peace.

If and when member states agree that some use of force is unacceptable, they must then agree on what to do. Should they impose economic sanctions, or use military force, or perhaps a combination of the two? Once a course has been charted, states must then be committed and have contingency plans in case it falters. They must be willing to bear the costs and sacrifice their national interests for the collective good – or define their vital interests as in some way coterminous with it.

Finally, if the first two conditions are met, then there must be organization. That is, agreed-upon mechanisms, rules, and procedures must exist to conduct an action for which there is consensus. If sanctions are imposed, how will member states enforce them, detect cheating, and evaluate impact? If military force is approved, which states will conduct operations, and how will they be monitored? The record of collective security is determined by its ability to meet the conditions of consensus, commitment, and organization.

The laudable idea has confronted the reality of world politics in four ways. One, some states have refused to join a collective-sanctioning effort because they have already defined their friends and enemies. During the Cold War, the United States would not have joined in a UN effort at collective security against one of its NATO allies, nor would the Soviet Union have done so against its Warsaw Pact allies. In an exceptional move, the United States opposed the British, French, and Israeli invasion of Egypt in 1956, and Washington eventually helped to roll it back diplomatically. But the United States never seriously considered UN sanctions against its allies at that time, precisely because it required their cooperation in the Cold War. Enemies and allies have shifted since the Cold War, but the desire to protect friends has not. Under collective security, all aggressors must be treated similarly.

Two, the fundamental problem of power makes it impossible to apply collective security against a nuclear state.[23] The Security Council is constrained by the veto; but, in any case, how could one justify the massive destruction that could result from trying to apply forcible measures against the P-5, or India, Israel, Pakistan, or North Korea, for that matter? And regulating powerful potential aggressors goes beyond nuclear-armed countries. Many states control sufficient conventional forces, biological and chemical weapons, or economic resources to render any potential exercise of collective security highly disruptive and costly to international society.

Three, collective security can be costly to supporters. That is, sanctions affect not only the aggressor but also the advocates. For example, states did not want to forego profits from the arms trade with South Africa during white-minority rule. It was one thing to accept that apartheid constituted a threat to the peace. It was another to bear the costs of coercive economic measures that cut both ways and negatively affected national economic interests. Similarly, UN sanctions against Iraq in the 1990s and against Sudan in 2005 were undermined by trading partners whose bottom lines would have suffered substantially from effective sanctions.

Four, collective security is based on the assumption that all victims are equally important, and that the international response should be the same for attacks on Bosnia or Armenia as for those on Kuwait or Germany.[24] Yet states differentiate between countries that are worth defending and those that are not – often, states judge that not all potential victims of aggression are worth expending blood and treasure. In the early 1990s, when Serbia sought to enlarge its territory at the expense of neighboring Bosnia, Washington declared that US national interests were not present and that Europeans should handle what was judged to be their problem. Later, when atrocities and regional instability led to increased demands for action, Washington and the rest of the Security Council finally reacted.

However, Chapter VII to reverse aggression by one state against another has been invoked successfully on two occasions. In June 1950, the temporary absence of Moscow from the Security Council (protesting Taiwan's occupation of the "Chinese seat" in spite of the 1949 military victory by the Chinese communists) permitted military action against North Korea and its allies for the invasion of the South. But once Moscow ended its boycott and entered the fray, the Security Council was paralyzed by the Soviet veto. The General Assembly's role in international peace and security increased with the passage in 1950 of the first "Uniting for Peace" resolution. It allowed the assembly to address North Korean aggression and continue the authorization. While North and South Korea are still technically at war, the UN authorization and action reversed the occupation and continues to make a difference along the demilitarized zone.

Iraqi aggression against neighboring Kuwait was rolled back in 1991 when the United States was willing to commit half-a-million military personnel (along with twenty-seven other states) to liberate Kuwait with the Security Council's unanimous support. UN actions in the Persian Gulf began in 1990 and set important precedents for collective security, humanitarian action, and sanctions, which were triggered on August 2, 1990, after Iraq's armed forces swept into neighboring Kuwait and quickly overran the tiny oil-rich country. The invasion encountered uniform UN condemnation, including the

114

Security Council's first unequivocal statement about a breach of the peace since Korea. From early August until the end of the year, the Security Council passed twelve resolutions, including comprehensive sanctions as a prelude to the first post-Cold War military enforcement action. Resolution 678 authorized "all necessary means," without restrictions on how much and how long force could be used. The United States had a blank check to pursue the expulsion of Iraq from Kuwait. The Persian Gulf War provided the first example of using the UN's security apparatus in an enforcement action in the post-Cold War era. Although successful in achieving its stated objective – expelling Iraq from Kuwait – diplomats, lawyers, and scholars continue to debate how this result was achieved. Yet there was no alternative to "subcontracting" to the twenty-eight members of the US-led coalition; in view of the UN's limited military capacities, such a procedure for enforcement seems inevitable for the foreseeable future.

The idea of collective security has shortcomings, to be sure, but it can make the state system more predictable and secure. We close by teasing out the counterfactual lessons from the first UN response to the attack on the Republic of Korea, which deserves more attention than is usual. Had the reaction been indifference, the population of one of Asia's most rapidly growing economies and democracies would now be enslaved by a dictatorial family pretending to apply communist doctrine. Judging by what the northern military did in occupied territory during the war, countless residents of South Korea would have been victimized for their political views. The productive South would not have been created but rather would have been held hostage as the larder for the North. Moreover, three of the P-5 (China, Russia, and the United States) would have felt a nuclear-armed presence on the beaches of Japan, including Okinawa, long before the rogue regime began successfully testing delivery vehicles in 2016–17. This reality would have increased the likelihood of World War III, which some in the US military, including Douglas MacArthur, unabashedly sought.

Without a robust reaction to the aggression in Korea, the United States – then and still the most influential UN member – would have been even more skeptical about UN cooperation than it would later become after the military deadlock in the peninsula and the later influx of independent countries – that is, long before the know-nothing Trump administration. Moreover, other valid lessons from the UN's Korean expedition would not have been learned: that a multilateral military force could be improvised; that the Security Council could legally act under Chapter VII even without the military force envisaged in the Charter; and that pouting and walkout tactics, on occasion, blow back.

Arguably, collective security has worked in the way that the Charter intended on only two occasions. Yet it is worth pointing out the obvious: when states decide to use the UN's decision-making machinery, it works. Moreover, collective security has worked, and it could be used more frequently.

Operations

The Charter of the United Nations was to be a giant step beyond the Covenant of the League of Nations because the Security Council would have teeth to enforce decisions. Although the Military Staff Committee and UN Standing Army envisaged in the founding document never materialized, we have already seen the value of the invention of peacekeeping. And numerous improvements to peace operations are feasible and would enhance international peace and security. Three are discussed here: a rapid-reaction capacity; better humanitarian intervention; and improved peacebuilding.

Rapid-Reaction Capability

Michael Smith, a seasoned UN veteran and scholarly commentator, notes that, despite successes, the UN's overall balance sheet contains serious debits; and it should and could have been more positive: "Too often the inappropriate behavior or ineffectiveness of peacekeepers has brought disgrace on the organization, while resistance to change from some member states as well as from within the various organs of the UN has hampered its agility and effectiveness."[25] It also is important to keep in mind that conflicting pressures within the various bureaucracies charged with peace operations can result in irreconcilable pressures that can help or hinder effective action and, in turn, lead to contradictory actions and statements.[26]

Countless reports have appeared with proposed reforms. The first in the post-Cold War era were Boutros Boutros-Ghali's *An Agenda for Peace* in 1992 and his 1995 *Supplement*.[27] Perhaps the most cited reform proposal was from a panel chaired by trouble-shooter Lakhdar Brahimi in 2000, which asserted that an overstretched UN also needed to learn to say "no."[28] The message was clear: UN civil servants should provide independent advice based on accurate assessments of options without considering what might be politically

116

popular or align with the positions of their political masters. In short, the Second UN was urged to tell the First UN in the Security Council what they *should* hear, not what they wanted to hear. Subsequent proposals came from the High-Level Panel on Threats, Challenges and Change in 2004;[29] the *New Partnership Agenda: Charting a New Horizon for UN Peacekeeping* in 2009;[30] and the High-Level Independent Panel on Peace Operations (HIPPO) in 2015.[31]

Although they have been inadequate, improvements have resulted, especially following the recognition of the overly ambitious agenda in the early post-Cold War era. While procurement, communications, and intelligence-sharing have improved, the central challenge remains: blue helmets and berets (the UN's distinctive military headgear) are lent by member states and remain under national command and control.[32] Most sweeping and sensible suggestions remain dead letters for numerous reasons, including member-state reluctance and internal bureaucratic resistance. Some 120,000 military and civilian personnel in fifteen missions with a budget of close to $8 billion in 2016 were accompanied by shortcomings that could be repaired.

One badly needed improvement jumps immediately to mind – a rapid-reaction capability. The Cold War made impossible the functioning of the Military Staff Committee by the P-5 called for in Charter Article 47; rather than attempting to re-create that missing capacity,[33] a more modest "what if?" concerns the plea from the first UN secretary-general, Trygve Lie, to establish a rapid-reaction force.[34] The UN's inability to halt genocide, particularly in Rwanda, brought renewed attention to the absence of this operational capability. In fact, over a dozen proposals emerged between 1948 and 1995 to fill the void,[35] including from such multilateral stalwarts as Canada and Norway. Concrete proposals have also come from US officials, for example in 2000 and 2001, when US congressman Jim McGovern proposed in bills 4453 and HR 938 to create a 6,000-person UN Rapid Deployment Police and Security Force. Such forces could have provided the secretary-general with a contingent able to deploy quickly in April 1994, for example, when General Roméo Dallaire, the Canadian commander of the UN Assistance Mission for Rwanda (UNAMIR), pleaded for additional troops; instead his requests met with a sharp reduction in his feeble forces.

In 2005, the emergency relief coordinator Jan Egeland put forward his proposal to establish a different type of rapid-reaction unit of 100 aid workers, which also went nowhere.[36] In 2006 a group of scholars and NGOs began championing the idea of a UN Emergency Peace Service (UNEPS) composed of 12,000–18,000 personnel of various backgrounds ready to be deployed in emergencies.[37] Such Third UN organizations as Global Action to Prevent War, the World Federalist Movement, and the Simons Foundation, the Ira and Miriam Wallach Foundation, and the Ford Foundation have repeatedly called for "a standing, individually recruited, service integrated, gender main-streamed service that can provide rapid response to outbreaks of gen-ocide, crimes against humanity, and other humanitarian disasters." The UNEPS is intended as a "first-in, first-out" force that can protect civilians more quickly and reduce the cost, number, and length of subsequent peace operations, which "often arrive on the scene too late and with a much too limited mandate to stop violence effec-tively."[38] The Canadian government argued more than two decades ago that "UN volunteers offer the best prospect of a completely reliable, well-trained rapid-reaction capability. Without the need to consult national authorities, the UN could cut response times signifi-cantly, and volunteers could be deployed within hours of a Security Council decision."[39]

Annie Herro, Wendy Lambourne, and David Penklis have applied counterfactual calculations to Rwanda (1993–4) and Darfur (2006–8), where military resources, political will, and mandates were far too little to protect civilians and deter atrocities. They conclude that "a UNEPS could respond to the domestic political backlash associated with 'body bags' when governments expose their nationals to security threats in countries which have little perceived economic, political or strategic significance." If a UNEPS had been deployed shortly after the killings began in Kigali, it could have slowed the slaughter and filled intelligence gaps that led to a flawed peace agreement, the abrogation of which led to the genocide. Similarly, in Darfur, a combat-ready UNEPS could have provided assurance to troop-contributing coun-tries that their personnel would be protected while simultaneously responding to local calls for "African solutions to African problems" with a regionally recruited UNEPS.[40]

No initiative has borne fruit thus far, and the financial and logis-tical constraints remain daunting – including a combination of widespread and general European unwillingness to increase defense spending along with a heightened global demand for peacekeepers. Yet the creation of standing rapid-reaction capability would undoubt-edly reinvigorate the UN and augment its legitimacy. At the outset of his first term, Ban Ki-moon indicated the need for a more inte-grated "emergency peace service" to combine military personnel with a range of civilian, police, judicial, governance, humanitarian, human rights, and development capabilities.[41] With the arrival of his successor António Guterres, circumstances may be opportune to revisit standing capacities. The 2015 HIPPO called it a "vanguard capability,"[42] but it would be a back-to-the-future idea from the first secretary-general that could bring significant benefits.

Better Humanitarian Intervention: Rwanda with Kosovo-Like Teeth and Côte d'Ivoire with Less Dawdling

What might have happened had the West in spring 1994 at least furnished the logistics to support an African intervention force for Rwanda that the Security Council agreed was necessary and that several African countries volunteered to staff? The lack of political will among the First UN in the Security Council is nothing new – although a more dramatic illustration than 800,000 deaths, or one-tenth of Rwanda's population, is hard to imagine – but here the analytical perspective is less geopolitical than administrative.

Unacceptable administrative reactions to courageous pleas from the field indicate the lack of appropriate reactions from the highest levels of the Second UN. Perhaps the most searing and well known was the cry in the wilderness of UNAMIR commander Dallaire for assistance and authorization to try – even symbolically – to halt the fast-paced genocide in Rwanda.[43] His *Shake Hands with the Devil* recounts how the Department of Peacekeeping Operations (DPKO) denied his calls for more combat troops and logistical support before the tragedy in April 1994.[44] Dallaire's repeated requests for reinforcements – at first a single and later four battalions – for his ill-equipped and under-trained force of about 2,600 (including 350 unarmed military observers) were denied by UN headquarters. Instead, Security Council resolution 912 *reduced* troop levels to 270 military personnel in line with the secretary-general's recommendation. This lamentable token presence reflected calculations about what major powers – particularly the United States, the United Kingdom, Belgium, and France – would approve.

While his argument that a force of 5,000 could have prevented the genocide is probably overly sanguine,[45] Dallaire's experience nonetheless illustrates how bureaucracy and lack of leadership thwarted decisive action. When he informed his superiors in New York of his intention to raid an arms cache, he was ordered not to take any action for fear of embroiling the UN more deeply. In the infamous exchange of cables in January 1994 (three months before the killing began), Dallaire informed DPKO headquarters that the *Interahamwe* – the Hutu paramilitary forces who subsequently inflicted the genocide –

119

were planning to exterminate Rwandan Tutsis and attack Belgian troops. Both predictions met indifference; both turned out to be true.

What if something like NATO's actions against Serbia in 1995 or in 1999 had been applied to Rwanda in April 1994? The counterfactual has additional bite because, following the murder of 800,000 Rwandans, France's Opération Turquoise actually deployed and successfully and quickly halted the fastest-moving genocide on record. While much criticism was later directed at France for having shielded *génocidaires*, the argument here stresses the tardiness of mobilizing political will to act in spite of universal condemnation. In fact, the Security Council lamented the tragedy but authorized nothing, despite pending African offers to intervene if logistic support were available.

Another illustration of foot-dragging involves France, and it arises from delays after post-election violence in Côte d'Ivoire. In many ways, this experience is even more intriguing for our counterfactual explorations, since half-hearted efforts were followed by meaningful military action – but this time by available troops already in the theater. The "what if?" thus requires asking about mobilizing political will not to authorize new troops but, rather, only to use those already deployed.[46]

The installation of Alassane Ouattarra and the surrender of former president Laurent Gbagbo followed a half-year of dawdling as Côte d'Ivoire's disaster unfolded. The turmoil accompanying the first electoral campaigns in ten years began before ballots were cast; and the election led to violence when Gbagbo refused to step down from his decade-long rule after losing to Ouattara, the universally recognized winner.

The UN Operation in Côte d'Ivoire (UNOCI) consisted of traditional peacekeepers whose presence had earlier been requested by Gbagbo's government. The UN refused subsequently to withdraw, despite Gbagbo's demands to do so, in the face of violence against peaceful protestors and the flight of tens of thousands. For three months, and in a typically desultory fashion, the Security Council dragged its collective feet and in real time observed refugees, massacres, full-scale civil war, and a ruined economy. On March 30, the council finally issued resolution 1975, which authorized UNOCI to "use all necessary means" – UN code for doing what is required to protect civilians.

That decision was the third in March 2011 that reflected the Security Council's reluctance to apply armed force and abetted Gbagbo's intransigence and facilitated the country's train wreck. That empty resolution-rattling ended early in April. Driven more by French domestic than UN politics, Paris authorized its 1,650-strong Licorne contingent, already in the theater of operations, to take robust military action as the UNOCI *avant-garde*. The violence ended quickly when Ouattara's troops, with French assistance, assaulted Gbagbo's residence and arrested him.

Posing counterfactual questions can be unsatisfying, but answers to the following two seem unequivocal: Was it necessary to observe war crimes and crimes against humanity as well as to foster the flight of a million refugees and a ravaged economy? The ICC subsequently indicted Gbagbo, who eventually was brought to The Hague in December 2011, but could he not have been inscribed on the docket and taken into custody earlier?

International action in Côte d'Ivoire was justifiable and doable, although it took longer than necessary. Even so, the benefits outweighed the costs for the intervening and neighboring countries. Washington had no dog in this fight, but its diplomatic engagement with regional and international partners unleashed French ground troops in combination with the modest UN contingent, which ended the violent electoral standoff, protected civilians, and permitted the country to resume its previous development path.

Libya with Robust Peace-Building

Ironically, the use of a Libyan operational counterfactual regrets the total lack of follow-up to an initial robust decision to intervene. Unlike Rwanda, Libya demonstrated the political will to deploy substantial military force in a timely fashion to prevent massacres in Benghazi in March 2011 – Security Council resolution 1973 authorized it to protect Libyans from the murderous harm that their president was inflicting. Colonel Muammar al-Gaddafi went beyond his usual verbal fireworks and threatened to crush the "cockroaches" and "rats" who opposed him. For those who recalled Rwanda's tragedy and similar ethnic epithets hurled by the murderous Hutu regime, Gaddafi's vile descriptions served as a wake-up call. However, whereas Rwanda benefited subsequently from a massive inflow of relief and, afterwards, peacebuilding assistance and investment, Libya received virtually nothing and could readily be classified as a "failed state." Peacebuilding is, of course, anything but simple. It is a complex constellation of efforts not only to reconstruct the physical destruction caused by war and intervention but also to address political, economic, and social institutions destroyed or undermined by armed conflict. Moreover, few tasks are as challenging as moving from the economics of war to the economics of peace.[47]

International military action began in March 2011 and marked a turning point in the post-9/11 intervention slump – other than modest efforts by the United Kingdom and France in West and Central Africa, there had been no serious military deployment for human protection purposes since NATO's 1999 Kosovo intervention. The Security Council's willingness to authorize "all necessary means" against Tripoli's rogue regime as it mowed down protestors momentarily seemed to signify a new dawn for R2P. The 22-member Arab League requested a no-fly zone; the overwhelming air power of France, the United Kingdom, and the United States gave meaning to Security Council resolution 1973 to protect civilians.

While President Obama asserted that he "refused to wait for the images of slaughter and mass graves before taking action"[48] against the Libyan dictator, he also was firm about limiting the US's role to "days not weeks."[49] With a public fatigued by Afghanistan and Iraq, boots on the ground in North Africa were out of the question. Less than two weeks after the March 19 enforcement of the no-fly zone (Operation Odyssey Dawn), the shared France–UK–US command was given to NATO (Operation Unified Protector) and supplemented with military support from the region (Qatar and the United Arab Emirates) and other Western air forces (Denmark and Norway). While Gaddafi's capture in October marked the end of an era, his brutal execution by rebels, the events of which were filmed on a mobile phone and seen by the world, tarnished the singular major human rights accomplishment of 2011.

It also complicated decision making for Syria after disgruntlement about regime change in Libya, although the feigned surprise among critics is hard to fathom. The purpose of international action in the face of abhorrent practices by a pariah regime like Gaddafi's should be to halt abuse and negotiate. However, if no such behavioral change occurs – and in Libya it did not, and there was never an indication of Gaddafi's willingness to stand down – a change in regime should not come as a surprise but as the logical outcome of deploying R2P military force.[50]

All decisions and actions, especially interventions, entail unintended and perverse consequences, and it is unreasonable to think that R2P undertakings will have fewer than other types. That said, the total absence of any military stabilization in Libya and of any effort to reconstitute the state is regrettable; it has transformed what may have been Africa's wealthiest country with the highest life expectancy into a completely collapsed state with an economy in shambles. The Islamic State has a growing presence and uses Libya as a transit and recruitment hub for foreign fighters and arms. With virtually no government control, militias run rampant and oil production has all but stopped. Local, tribal, regional, Islamist, and criminal groups have plagued Libya since the intervention; it has two governments, each with its own prime minister, parliament, and army. To the West, Islamist-allied militias control Tripoli and other cities; the so-called government expelled the parliament elected in 2014. To the East, the so-called legitimate government that is dominated by anti-Islamist politicians is exiled in Tobruk.

While the NATO intervention was justifiably motivated by humanitarianism – for the first time, R2P was used to justify military action against a functioning but aberrant government – the humanitarian situation has subsequently become dire.[51] Civilians in Libya suffer from civil war, general insecurity, political instability, and a collapsed economy. An estimated 1.3 million people (close to a quarter of the total population) require humanitarian assistance. Refugees, IDPs, and migrants have the most severe needs. Returnees and non-displaced Libyans in the most affected areas also require assistance. The healthcare system has virtually collapsed, so that hundreds of thousands lack access to life-saving healthcare and essential medicines. The most vulnerable individuals cannot be protected from the ongoing civil war and violence; the rule of law is a distant dream. Access to such essentials as food, shelter, water, and sanitation is problematic almost everywhere, driven by armed conflict, crime, violence, and the ongoing economic crisis.

In thinking about a more effective future UN, member states have to appreciate the extent to which investments in stabilization in post-conflict countries are cost-effective. Contrasting Rwanda and Kosovo with Libya, it is clear that the various UN organizations must pull together better after wars. In light of the growing demand and the recognized shortcomings,[52] it is worth delving more deeply into the decision to establish the PBC and its supporting office and fund, which resulted from the UN's incoherent presence in post-conflict activities.[53]

The PBC's creation in spring 2006 was a step toward improving UN efforts to prevent relapse by war-torn societies. Its mandate is to propose integrated strategies for post-conflict stability, ensure predictable financing for recovery, draw international attention to tasks, provide recommendations and information to improve coordination, and develop best practices. The PBC's Organizational Committee has thirty-one members: seven from the Security Council, seven from

ECOSOC, five of the main financial contributors, five of the top military contributors, and seven elected by the General Assembly to redress geographical imbalances that may result from the other criteria. The PBC also has country-specific committees with national representatives and relevant contributors.

The Organizational Committee is responsible for an expanding Second UN. The Peacebuilding Support Office (PBSO) oversees the Peacebuilding Fund (PBF), originally established with a target of $250 million. In 2015, deposits reached about $630 million, with a total portfolio of approximately $650 million.[54] The PBF aims to kick-start donor investments for longer-term recovery. The fund has the potential to reduce waste and duplication and to enhance coordination among financial sources.

During its first year, the PBC allocated some $35 million to Burundi and Sierra Leone. The PBSO approved emergency funding for Burundi, the CAR, Guinea, Côte d'Ivoire, Haiti, Liberia, and Kenya. In 2014, the PBC was one of the first to sound the alarm about the Ebola outbreak in West Africa, where yet another source of instability affected countries already on its agenda.

The PBC has recognized problems.[55] Reporting issues and miscommunications arise because it is a subsidiary of both the General Assembly and the Security Council. Moreover, as one analyst notes, "The advisory nature of the PBC – coupled with the stipulation that it 'shall act in all matters on the basis of consensus of its members' – seems at odds with the very concept of the body assuming the final responsibility for peacebuilding."[56] In addition, overlap and competition afflict the PBSO and the Department of Political Affairs and the DPKO. Nevertheless, the creation of the PBC, PBSO, and PBF was an essential collective step toward applying lessons from earlier UN post-conflict stability and reconciliation efforts to enhance coordination, efficiency, and effectiveness. Indeed, in operational terms, many donor countries are channeling more of their assistance to conflict-prone countries – about 40 percent of total ODA.[57] The PBC appears a comparative advantage for the United Nations, which is the only institution that combines military, humanitarian, human rights, and development services.[58]

The second salient issue returns to an earlier section because interveners abandoned Libya and were unwilling to provide time and space for post-conflict peacebuilding – "failing to plan for the day after" was, according to Barack Obama, probably the "worst mistake" of his presidency.[59] That Libya is becoming another Somalia leads to the overlooked third element of R2P – namely to rebuild – the impor-

tance of which was not only in the logic of ICISS's three-part responsibility but also General Colin Powell's so-called Pottery Barn rule:
"you break it, you own it." Calls for the institutionalization of a *jus
post bellum* as a kind of "Chapter VII½" reinforce this concept of
an obligation to rebuild in the aftermath of humanitarian crises and
certainly after an international intervention.[60] The counterfactual is
a straightforward one: What if the UN's post-intervention approach
in Libya had been characterized by a comparable political will to the
intervention? What if the post-intervention period had been characterized by a Kosovo-like presence? While its precise status as a sovereign
state is still subject to dispute, Kosovo has stabilized and appears close
to resolution, which contrasts starkly with the ongoing implosion of
Libya. What if Libyans had witnessed the kind of international and
domestic mobilization that has transformed post-genocide Rwanda
arguably into Africa's most stable and fastest-growing economy?

The rebuilding component of the R2P continuum – and the logic
that reaction by itself was bound to be ineffective – has been largely
ignored.[61] The wisdom of investing in peacebuilding in Kosovo (after
an intervention) and Rwanda (without the benefit of one) leads to
questioning international myopia in Libya and elsewhere. Doing
nothing has consequences.

Conclusion

This chapter has illustrated the proposition that the last seven decades
could have – not easily, but conceivably – been less violent and more
secure with more creative and effective First and Second UNs. The
modest contributions of disarmament and development, as well as
of human security, could have been greater had they been pursued
more vigorously by states and secretariats. There have been only
two instances of collective security, but there could have been more.
Similarly, the benefits should be compelling from the possible creation
and use in crises of a rapid-reaction capacity and better peacebuilding. And these eventualities should not be difficult to imagine in light
of successful examples.

In short, missed opportunities appear as debits in the UN's ledger,
but more could and should have appeared in the world organization's
asset column. Improving the UN's balance sheet should not require
pie-in-the-sky idealism; rather, it calls for the application of the kind
of support from governments and secretariats that occasionally have
been in evidence.

7

A LESS REPRESSIVE AND UNKIND WORLD WITH ENHANCED HUMAN RIGHTS AND HUMANITARIAN ACTION?

This second chapter of Part III explores additional cases that help illustrate the impact of a more creative and effective UN. It probes ideas and operations that could have made more significant contributions to improve human rights and humanitarian action over the last seven decades. Chapter 7 suggests how the planet could have been less repressive and kinder had UN ideas and operations actively under consideration been pursued more vigorously and effectively.

Ideas

Numerous illustrations in these pages have pointed to how UN ideas have changed the world and the world organization itself. In no arena is this reality more obvious than that of human rights and humanitarian action. The chapter details three partially missed opportunities: establishing a universal bill of rights; rewarding human rights whistle-blowers; and helping internally displaced persons (IDPs).

The Missing "Universal Bill of Rights"

The Covenant of the League of Nations largely failed to address human rights, although Article 23 indicated a concern with social justice. A substantial change was thus the desirability of including specific human rights in the UN Charter, whose preparations had begun before widespread knowledge about the Holocaust and other World War II atrocities, although subsequent revelations certainly accelerated the process of including rights in the UN's founding document.[1] Intellectual opinion, especially in the United States and the

United Kingdom, advocated human rights as a moral imperative for the war – a rationale echoed in the Atlantic Charter and Franklin D. Roosevelt's four freedoms. Latin American states joined in San Francisco to emphasize rights as a characteristic of civilized countries. Eleanor Roosevelt became an outspoken champion of human rights in general and women's rights in particular.

Unlike the Wilson administration in 1919, the Truman administration in 1945 pushed for specific human rights language and lobbied other great powers. This position was at odds, however, with not only gulags in the Soviet Union and British colonies but also the legal and widespread racial discrimination in the United States.[2] Perhaps Moscow viewed the language as a foil to deflect criticism from Soviet policies, especially since the Charter was vague and the Soviets likely foresaw no immediate application. Stalin viewed the general wording as instrumental to focus on communism's intended concentration on social and economic rights.[3] This was not the last time that Moscow underestimated the force of such international agreements – the 1975 provisions on human rights in the Helsinki Accords generated pressures that weakened European communism.[4] Meanwhile, Winston Churchill helped to author ringing pronouncements about human rights in order to highlight enemy atrocities, while perceiving no irony in Britain's continued unequal treatment of non-white peoples within its empire and with the understanding that UN norms would not apply to British colonies. In this way, he was not dissimilar from the American Founding Fathers two centuries earlier, whose proclamations about rights were not intended for women, slaves, or Native Americans. And certainly Roosevelt had no plan to end discrimination against African-Americans.

The 1945 language was vague but provided the legal cornerstone for later structures. The Charter's Preamble declares a principal purpose "to affirm faith in fundamental human rights." Article 1 specifies that one of the organization's central aims is to promote and encourage "respect for human rights and for fundamental freedoms for all without distinction as to race, sex, language, or religion." Article 55 imposes legal obligations on states to this end. The Charter essentially codified a commitment to upholding human rights before an agreed definition or list even existed, a task that was taken up with the drafting of the Universal Declaration of Human Rights.

After the General Assembly's passage of the UDHR in 1948, states turned to a more specific and thornier elaboration of the internationally recognized rights supposedly implied by it. By then, however, the Cold War had quashed the hopeful postwar vision of beginning

127

a journey toward an alternative world order with universal standards of protection. Rather than going further in 1948 to sketch a bill of rights, states decided to split the project into separate drafting exercises. As Christopher Roberts writes: "The international unity, success, and support for human rights that emerge in the standard story of the adoption of the UDHR are quickly overshadowed by the animosity and hostility that emerged during the key drafting period of the Covenant(s), from 1947 to 1954."[5]

The challenge was finding language that incorporated the East–West conflict and its divisions about how best to organize the postwar order. The rights in the ICCPR are well known in the West. They are "first generation," because they were first endorsed in national constitutions, and "negative," because civil rights block public authorities from interfering with the individual. Such rights include freedom of thought, speech, religion, privacy, and assembly. Some argue that they are the only true human rights or the most important, because they are necessary for an individual to obtain others.

Other commentators judge first-generation rights as less important because, without such material basics as food, shelter, healthcare, and education, these civil and political rights become relatively meaningless.[6] Hence, the other half of the drafting exercise focused on the ICESCR.[7] They are called "second generation" because they were associated with various twentieth-century revolutions emphasizing a redistribution of the material benefits of economic growth, and they are labeled "positive" because they obligate public authorities to take steps to ensure minimal levels of food, shelter, and healthcare. Such material rights are enshrined in welfare states throughout Europe, Japan, and Canada, and they receive at least rhetorical emphasis in many developing countries.

Proponents of the first generation offered numerous justifications for their privileged position. They were absolute and immediately achievable by legislative and judicial action; they required only the state to leave the individual alone. Such rights could serve as protection against governmental encroachment upon liberty and were viewed as low-cost investments in human well-being. In contrast, second-generation rights required costly state investments to provide education, healthcare, and housing – all of which later became aspects of "the right to development" – and could be achieved only gradually. Moreover, after being established, first-generation rights merely required vigilance to ensure their continuation; second-generation rights required governments to incur substantial, recurring material costs.

By 1956, the ICCPR and ICESCR were essentially complete. But another decade of contentious negotiations transpired before the General Assembly's formal approval in 1966. By 1976 both had entered into force. Few other states followed the example of the United States in accepting one (the ICCPR in 1992, with reservations) but rejecting the other (the ICESCR).

The 1948 UDHR and the 1966 covenants constitute what was missing from the Charter: an International Bill of Rights, or a core list that would have resembled the US Constitution's Bill of Rights. Most of the provisions in the covenants clarify and elaborate on thirty norms found in the Universal Declaration. Ironically, the two binding treaties – the ICCPR and the ICESCR – now buttress the non-binding UDHR. The Cold War delayed and politicized work to transform the latter into a single, binding treaty. Political and civil rights were decoupled from economic, social, and cultural rights. The West challenged the communist bloc for failures in civil and political rights, and the communist countries pointed fingers at the West's failures to address poverty amidst affluence.

The counterfactual of this long story concerns what could have been had the UDHR and the two covenants been integrated as originally planned. It is fatuous to speculate about having no Cold War for a half-century. However, it is not far-fetched to explore alternative pathways to a human rights consolidation because the decision to divide the bill of rights had consequences that are still imprinted on the First and Second UNs.[8]

The fragmentation of the universal project meant two separate sets of conversations, whose discourses were compartmentalized and insulated from each other, although the 1993 Vienna world conference reiterated the indivisibility of rights. The disconnect between the commonly accepted emphases in the West on individual and political rights, on the one hand, and the issues of development, trade, and finance reflected the absence – or at least the neglect – of economic and social factors within the mainstream, on the other. It is plausible that a more integrated approach could both have led to earlier discussions of gaps and inequalities and have mitigated the extremes of poverty and deprivation that have remained prevalent in spite of rhetoric about their reduction.

It was neither inevitable nor inescapable that economic and social rights were relegated to second-class status, and that civil and political rights were deemed largely irrelevant to global socioeconomic policymaking. Both member states and secretariats were at fault and could and should have integrated them. Efforts over the last two decades to "mainstream" rights in all UN activities were a belated conceptual and operational effort at integration across UN projects and programs. The fact that the crucial SDG #16 of "Peace, Justice and Strong Institutions" is the vaguest and most contested of the seventeen goals for the 2015–30 development agenda, and the one with the least specific objectives and indicators, is the most recent manifestation of the absence of integration of the two generations of rights.

Peacekeepers and Whistle-Blowers

International civil servants and peacekeepers should be held to the highest standards because international human rights have been ironed out and promulgated within the United Nations. The standard bearer ought to respect unequivocally the standards promulgated by it as the norm for the rest of the world. The performance of UN civil servants working on human rights often has disappointed, just as the behavior of blue helmets also has blemished the world organization's reputation.

Few cases have drawn as much and as damning attention as the sex scandal that arose in 2015 but had been ongoing for years. Nothing could be more important than accountability for those whose job description is to protect, not abuse, civilians. As Radhika Coomaraswamy, the former UN special representative for children in armed conflict, commented: "It is truly a frightening phenomenon when your protector becomes a predator."[9]

Perhaps most appalling in the latest scandal was the long history of inaction in the face of aberrant behavior. In response to allegations of sexual misconduct by peacekeepers in the DRC in 2004, the secretary-general asked Prince Zeid Ra'ad Zeid Al-Hussein – then Jordan's permanent representative and now UN high commissioner for human rights – to be his advisor on sexual exploitation and abuse by UN peacekeeping personnel. His 2005 *A Comprehensive Strategy to Eliminate Future Sexual Exploitation and Abuse in UN Peacekeeping Operations* recommended standard rules, a professional investigative process, and relevant "organizational, managerial and command measures."[10] Zeid argued that those guilty should be subject to disciplinary action and held financially and, where appropriate, criminally liable. The report failed miserably to staunch the culture of impunity.

Given the symbolic and actual impact of peace operations, it is impossible to deny that zero tolerance toward abuse is primordial. Echoing previously reported abuse in Haiti, Liberia, and the DRC, subsequent reports added troops from several African countries to the list of dishonor after finding that children had been molested and the UN had done nothing. Finally, in August 2015, the secretary-general asked the chief of the CAR mission – Babacar Gaye, a retired Senegalese general and veteran administrator – to resign after yet another Amnesty International report exposed the latest abuses. This virtually unprecedented action suggested that perhaps the UN was finally willing to act after almost 500 similar allegations had persistently surfaced between 2008 and 2013.

Cases of sexual trafficking and abuse by blue helmets suggest that the secretariat has cavalierly applied norms. Following widespread allegations of sexual abuse and misconduct – including trading money and food for sex with minors – by UN peacekeepers in the DRC in early 2005, the UN instituted a number of system-wide reforms but, at the same time, downplayed the extent of the scandal. When similar allegations surfaced later that same year in Burundi, Haiti, and Liberia, the UN was forced to acknowledge untrammeled abuses.

Secretary-General Annan promulgated a zero-tolerance policy toward offenders and convened in New York in December 2006 the High-Level Conference on Eliminating Sexual Exploitation and Abuse by UN and NGO Personnel, which agreed to a system-wide strategy to eradicate sexual abuse and exploitation. The resulting "Statement of Commitment on Eliminating Sexual Exploitation and Abuse" contains ten commitments to "facilitate rapid implementation of existing UN and non-UN standards relating to sexual exploitation and abuse."[11] Reports of sexual misconduct by UN peacekeepers have continued to surface, but statistics indicated a decline from 108 substantiated accusations in 2007 to eighty-five in 2008, sixty-three in 2009, thirty-three in 2010, and five by mid-2011. As the *New York Times* noted, "[M]ore than 200 such accusations remain unresolved, and the United Nations annual report on such crimes for 2010 noted that sexual activity with minors and non-consensual sex represented more than half of the reported accusations, little changed since 2008." In 2011, sixteen peacekeepers from Benin were repatriated from Côte d'Ivoire after Save the Children UK discovered that they had traded food for sex with underage girls.

Zeid commented at the time that the UN "doesn't know the evidence and has no way to follow up with the way the military decides to deal with this issue."[12] The result was evident in 2015 in the front-page headlines from a leaked document about French soldiers abusing children in the CAR; it was followed by reports about similar transgressions by troops from Equatorial Guinea and Chad and then, later, by peacekeepers from Burundi, Morocco, and the DRC.

Zero tolerance, the official UN policy since 2005, is a slogan and not a reality. After being debated in the General Assembly, the 2005 report led to DPKO's adoption of a "comprehensive strategy." Conduct and discipline units were established in nearly twenty peacekeeping operations to prevent, track, and punish gender-based crimes. The units "act as principal advisors to heads of mission on all conduct and discipline issues involving all categories of peacekeeping personnel in the missions." They are overseen by a conduct and discipline unit established in the DPKO, which in 2006 joined OCHA, UNICEF, and the UNDP to host the conference for UN and NGO personnel mentioned above.

Formal procedures to curb exploitation represent a first step in restoring the credibility of blue helmets. The military contingents, civilian police, military observers, civilian staff, volunteers, and subcontractors from each country have different procedures to handle allegations and complaints.[13] For military forces, it is up to the authorities of the various troop contributors to investigate and punish their own nationals – UN managers can only insist that they repatriate soldiers. In short, UN soldiers can only be punished by their home countries, which virtually never happens. Thus, formal procedures do not necessarily translate into either punishment or even attitudinal changes.

Over a decade ago, Refugees International suggested that procedures were ignored because UN culture bred tolerance for exploitation and abuse.[14] Anna Shotton, author of their 2005 report, nonetheless pointed to modest progress. Previously, the UN had occasionally repatriated uniformed personnel, but in the twenty months preceding her report it had completed 221 investigations, which resulted in firing ten civilian employees and repatriating eighty-eight military personnel, including six commanders.[15] Rapes often are dismissed as prostitution or "transactional sex" – a curious characterization when peacekeepers use food and other scarce items in countries rocked by war to entice and sexually exploit children whose families are starving. If we fast-forward to 2016, "There has been only one criminal charge filed in the 42 cases of sexual abuse or exploitation that have been officially registered in the Central African Republic, according to U.N. officials."[16]

Moving beyond the "boys-will-be-boys" attitude is an absolute necessity. The fact that no one replaced Zeid during the bulk of the Ban administration, in spite of continued abuses, was difficult to fathom. We have gone on at some length because it is impossible to imagine an issue that should mobilize consensus more easily than removing this most visible blight on the Second UN's field performance and reputation. Impunity for violating fundamental UN human rights clearly stands in the way of making peace operations as professional as they could and should be.

What could be done? Ironically, the 2015 human rights whistle-blower who leaked an internal report, Anders Kompass, was working for Zeid in the OHCHR; he was initially suspended for leaking a confidential and unredacted report. But the United Nations Appeals Tribunal issued an order to lift his suspension, which was "*prima facie* unlawful."[17] After having cleared his name, Kompass resigned in May 2016 and lamented the impunity for peacekeepers *and* the higher echelons of the UN civil service. Shortly before, the secretary-general had appointed a former peacekeeping assistant-secretary-general as a special coordinator. Paula Donovan of Code Blue, a campaign to end sexual exploitation by UN peacekeepers, commented scathingly that Ban Ki-moon had "appointed someone to *coordinate* what has been identified as just a failed, broken system."[18]

This is not the only such appalling example of the UN senior leadership's failing to respond appropriately. The courageous calls by UN special representative to Sudan, Jan Pronk, for help to halt genocide in Darfur met with similar silence from UN headquarters. Governments and the Security Council were collectively dragging their feet because robust action would have required financial resources and boots on the ground. What is harder to understand was the absence of outrage in UN headquarters when Khartoum expelled Pronk as *persona non grata* in late 2006. As an especially outspoken advocate, he had unflinchingly reported on violence against civilians perpetrated by government forces throughout his tenure as special representative. He was ordered to leave the country within seventy-two hours after posting information on his blog about two incidents of Sudanese government defeat by rebel forces. Accused of displaying "enmity to the Sudanese government and the armed forces," Pronk unceremoniously returned to New York after Annan recalled him for "consultations" ahead of the expulsion deadline.[19] The lack of support from the UN's top peacekeeping official at the time suggests an overly sensitive ear to the wishes of a sovereign state rather than solidarity with a forthright UN official who was trying to publicize Khartoum's reprehensible human rights violations.

All bureaucracies have their ups and downs, and the previous examples should not be taken to imply that there are not numerous instances of outstanding behavior by UN officials. But what is peculiar about the UN's human rights machinery is the visibility and extraordinary weight of the shackles of political palatability – measured by what major and even minor sovereign states consider acceptable. The lack of courage and independence by UN leadership is a critical weakness.

Moreover, to return to peacekeepers, zero tolerance for human rights abuses needs to become a fact rather than an aspiration. Such a change can only be accomplished when member states punish their own nationals to ensure that impunity disappears. Meanwhile, the Second UN of civil servants should also be held accountable, and courageous staff should be rewarded for exposing abuses. After leaving the world organization in disgust, Kompass summarized: "the benefit to the individual of not behaving ethically is perceived as greater than the cost of taking an ethical stance."[20] A potentially promising announcement came in March 2017, when António Guterres proposed stopping the reimbursement of countries that failed to investigate claims against their soldiers in UN peace operations and to place that money into a trust fund to assist victims. A related measure was to insist that all UN personnel acknowledge in writing that they understand the organization's policy against exploitation and abuse. He also called for a high-level meeting on sexual exploitation and abuses by the General Assembly.

Accountability and transparency are the main currency underpinning the UN's viability and reputation. They should never be compromised.

Internally Displaced Persons

The most reliable indicator of suffering in war zones is usually the number of "refugees" – that is, according to the 1951 UN Convention on Refugees, persons who because of a legitimate fear of persecution flee across the borders of their country of origin. Physical displacement is *prima facie* evidence of vulnerability, because people who are deprived of their homes, communities, and means of livelihood are unable to use traditional coping strategies for the hardships of war. Recent manifestations of such vulnerability include the grisly images of dead bodies floating in the Mediterranean and unseaworthy craft piloted by smugglers carrying tens of thousands of persons fleeing violence in Syria, Libya, Yemen, Afghanistan, and Iraq.

Yet, when victims are forced to migrate *within* their own countries, they often are even more vulnerable, largely because they lack the international protections afforded to refugees while continuing to be exposed to the dangers associated with remaining in war zones.[21] In 2017, for instance, Syria's 8 million IDPs were certainly not better off than its 4 million refugees. Whereas international law entitles refugees to assistance and human rights protection, no such guarantees exist for those who participate in an "exodus within borders."[22] Agencies seeking to help persons who have not crossed a border tyically require consent, in fact, from the very same political authorities responsible for displacement and suffering in the first place.

Over the past two decades, the ratio of refugees to IDPs – that is, between forced migrants who flee across national borders and those who flee violence but remain within their own countries – has seen a dramatic reversal. In 2016, the latest record-breaking year,[23] almost 65 million people (one in every 113) were displaced – about two-thirds of whom were IDPs; and these appalling figures do not even include the almost 20 million people who were displaced by natural disasters and development projects.[24] Furthermore, with violence escalating within and across states, and climate change and other environmental disasters impending, an increase in such victims is certain.

When IDP data were first gathered in 1982, there was one IDP for every ten refugees; at present, the ratio has flipped dramatically to 2:1 in "favor" of IDPs.[25] A normative journey began in 1992 when UN secretary-general Boutros Boutros-Ghali submitted the first analytical report on IDPs to the Commission on Human Rights (CHR). It approved controversial resolution 1992/73, which authorized the appointment of someone to explore "views and information from all Governments on the human rights issues related to internally displaced persons." Many states were uneasy with this intrusion into domestic jurisdiction, while many humanitarian agencies were leery about bureaucratic fallout and a negative impact on fundraising.

Shortly thereafter, Secretary-General Boutros-Ghali designated Francis Deng, a former Sudanese diplomat and a senior fellow at the Brookings Institution, to serve as his representative (RSG) on internally displaced persons but while maintaining his independent base at Brookings. Deng, together with US human rights advocate Roberta Cohen, his co-director at Brookings, directed a small secretariat at the Project on Internal Displacement. The CHR consistently extended the mandate for two- and three-year terms until July 2004, when Deng's extension encountered UN time limits. He was replaced by Walter Kälin (2004–10), a Swiss law professor at the University of Berne, whose title became RSG on the human rights of IDPs; Chaloka Beyani (2010–16), a Zambian national and law professor

THE WORLD WITH A MORE CREATIVE AND EFFECTIVE UN?

at the London School of Economics; and Cecilia Jimenez-Damary (2016–), a Phillipina NGO human rights lawyer specializing in migration and forced displacement.

What formerly was a blemish on the international humanitarian system has become an ugly structural scar. The fastest growing category of war-affected populations had, and still has, no institutional sponsor or formal international legal framework, leading Donald Steinberg – a former State Department official who now heads World Learning – to describe IDPs as "orphans of conflict."[26] Refugee populations continue to benefit from the UNHCR's institutional and legal efforts, but the anodyne "internal displacement" fails to convey immense human suffering and lacks policy punch. IDPs lack food, shelter, and physical and legal security and, according to a study by the Centers for Disease Control, could have death rates as much as sixty times higher than non-displaced populations in their home countries.[27]

In theory, the creation of a new agency specifically mandated to respond to internal displacement should have been straightforward, but there was neither political support nor resources. The next best thing would have been to endow an existing agency with the mandate for IDPs. And, finally, there was the possibility of enhanced coordination, the usual default setting within the decentralized UN system.

Given the similarity between the needs of refugees and IDPs, Deng and Cohen, as well as a number of other observers, considered the UNHCR to be the logical choice for the second option – "UNHCR plays the broadest role in addressing the problems of the internally displaced: it offers protection, assistance and initial support for reintegration."[28] The UNHCR was a good fit because of its human rights and humanitarian mandates. It also had a distinguished half-century of hands-on field experience in protecting and succoring uprooted people fleeing abuse by governments and insurgents.

The Second UN was divided. Some UNHCR staff favored adding the internally displaced to their agenda because they were in "refugee-like conditions" and mixed with refugees. Others objected, arguing that the responsibility for persons in their countries of origin would alter the UNHCR's character and undermine its primary mission. These "refugee fundamentalists" tried to keep the UNHCR's focus away from IDPs, warning that any shift in policy or practice would play into the hands of, and was perhaps even driven by, the interests of asylum countries seeking to limit flows of potential refugees.[29] They also feared that the UNHCR's involvement with IDPs would lead to conflicts with host countries and jeopardize its refugee protection mandate.[30] The result of keeping IDPs away from the UN agency best equipped to deal with them amounted to callously shunting aside the obvious needs of the internally displaced in exchange for the dubious advantage of respecting mandate purity.

The bureaucratic objections by other UN organizations and NGOs then officially killed the idea of putting responsibility for IDPs directly in the hands of the UNHCR. UNICEF and the WFP, along with NGOs through their consortium InterAction, sensed a threat to their territory and funding. They feared that the UNHCR would loom over them in size and authority. Consequently, Secretary-General Annan, who had supported the initiative, was forced to retreat when fierce aid-agency opposition was echoed by donors who preached coordination but had their own agendas, including protecting the territory and budget allocations of their favorite intergovernmental and nongovernmental organizations in quintessential patron–client relationships.

We have already seen why eyes glaze over at the mere mention of "coordination," wishful thinking without the requisite leverage to compel collaboration. Prospects for successful coordination continue to depend on getting the main UN operational agencies with a role for IDPs (UNHCR, UNICEF, UNDP, and WFP) and those outside the UN (ICRC, and the largest international NGOs) to pull together. Coordination depends on good faith and is entirely voluntary. Thus, no organization has a clearly mandated responsibility for IDPs, and no legal statute guides state or agency behavior.

The UN is the logical choice for orchestrating international humanitarian responses for IDPs, but their assistance and protection often involves usurping state sovereignty. IDPs are a domestic human rights issue, and repressive governments are unlikely to welcome international protection during a civil war. Over two decades later, serious gaps remain. Bureaucratic solutions over the years – task forces, meetings of leading agencies via the Inter-Agency Standing Committee (IASC), and "clusters" – have still not addressed the dire needs of these victims. On paper, an impressive organizational chart for coordinating assistance and protection for IDPs has at its apex the Emergency Relief Coordinator (ERC), who heads OCHA, with a line running down to the IASC and its working group. From there, lines run to the right and left to operational agencies and then down to the UN's resident coordinators in each country, who report back up to the ERC. However, the organization entrusted with overall responsibility for humanitarian affairs, OCHA, has neither the authority nor the resources to drive the system.

To say that no institutional progress has been made would be an exaggeration. A variety of intergovernmental, regional, and nongovernmental organizations now routinely include IDPs in their plans, projects, and programs – an improvement over the 1990s when even the categorization was disputed. Important donors over time have focused more attention and resources on the phenomenon. As a result, the ICRC and such major UN players as the UNHCR, UNICEF, and the WFP are obliged to publish reports to their governing bodies about how they have reoriented their IDP programming. The UNHCR's revised guidelines on the protection of refugee women, for instance, added IDPs, which has had a beneficial impact on delivery and protection.

Yet, to state the obvious, haphazard institutional progress falls painfully short of the size of the IDP problem, which remains an organizational orphan despite ideational and normative efforts. Even with the advent of such crises as Syria, IDPs were barely even mentioned as an aside in the Outcome Document for the September 2016 UN High-Level Meeting to Address Large Movements of Refugees and Migrants.[31] It is doubtful that the so-called Global Compact to be negotiated over the next few years will make meaningful headway.

The idea and norms for IDPs were an important point of departure at the outset of the 1990s, ahead of their time. What could and should have happened without resistance by the First and the Second UNs? Why do they continue to stand in the way of consolidated emergency delivery to and protection of IDPs? Sovereign sensibilities and turf-consciousness provide especially persuasive and prominent explanations. If an effective UN market were functioning, demand alone should have led to the creation of a separate entity for what is now the largest category of war victims. The hope that serendipity will lead to adequate coverage for IDPs calls to mind the characterization of second marriages by Oscar Wilde – the triumph of hope over experience.

Operations

At several junctures, including for IDPs, we have encountered the unhealthy rivalries within the United Nations, resulting in considerably less cohesion in field operations than one might expect from the so-called UN system. The first two illustrations of missed opportunities in this section concern concrete services for humanitarian emergencies and for women, while the third concerns the nascent

ICC. The reader can decide for herself about the relevance of the labe of "system."

1997's Humanitarian Almost-Reform

As a consequence of the phenomenal growth in resources available for the victims of war and for post-conflict peacebuilding, the main players in the UN's humanitarian system – the UNHCR, UNICEF, and the WFP – find themselves locked in competition with one another and other rivals in the system to garner the greatest possible share. Juxtaposing "humanitarian" and "business" is provocative yet accurate. The adjective customarily has uncontested positive connotations, while the noun is associated with wheeling and dealing. But money talks. Most UN organizations focused on development when that was necessary and fashionable with donors, but they increasingly are chasing more readily available humanitarian funding.[32] It is hard to improve upon a 2001 summary by the UK's Overseas Development Institute: "turf battles, empire-building, overlapping and conflicting mandates ... Tensions between staff in the field and headquarters, with each accusing the other of thwarting communication."[33]

The Cold War's end resulted in no transformation of international institutions but, rather, a huge sigh of relief. As we saw earlier, it permitted the explosion of crises frozen by East–West tensions; the proliferation of humanitarian organizations; and the mobilization of an ever-growing pool of funding. Total resources increased from about $800 million in 1989 to over $28 billion in 2015.[34] While the number of UN organizations has not grown, their budgets have (accounting for about two-thirds of total DAC humanitarian disbursements).

Over the past decade, governments have disbursed some $120 billion for humanitarian assistance. Whereas sixteen mainly Western states pledged their support to Bosnia in the mid-1990s, a diverse group of seventy-three donor countries attended the 2003 pledging conference in Madrid for Iraq, and ninety-two responded to the December 2004 tsunami. OECD governments almost doubled their assistance between 2000 and 2010, from $6.7 billion to $11.8 billion; in 2013 the figure stood at $14.1 billion. Meanwhile, the contributions from non-DAC donors between 2011 and 2013 increased from $.8 billion to $2.3 billion, representing about 15 percent of total official humanitarian aid, double the percentage from 2011.[35]

One need not agree with Naomi Klein's dismissal of emergency relief as "disaster capitalism"[36] to appreciate how the global bottom lines of some $18 to 25 billion in recent years, with personnel spread across the planet helping 75 to 100 million people, would strike most observers as a substantial business. James Ron and Alexander Cooley point to the impact of "the scramble" for resources and a "contract culture" that is "deeply corrosive" of the humanitarian soul.[37]

It thus is especially worth revisiting the dramatic mid-1997 "reform that almost was" in which newly elected Kofi Annan sought ways to consolidate the United Nations and ordered a system-wide review, with special attention to humanitarian and human rights operations. To spearhead the effort, he appointed Maurice Strong, the Canadian businessman and seasoned UN hand who had made his mark as head of two blockbuster UN conferences on the environment and as executive coordinator of the Office of Emergency Operations in Africa. His penultimate draft of reform proposals recommended centralizing responsibility for war victims in the UNHCR, and an appendix fleshed out the possibility of creating a consolidated UN humanitarian agency.

Resistance by the First and Second UNs, especially UNICEF and the WFP, resulted in the repackaging of the Department of Humanitarian Affairs (DHA) as the Office for the Coordination of Humanitarian Affairs (OCHA), quintessentially "old wine in a new bottle." The new acronym did not alter the prospects for pulling together the fragmented UN operational entities that help war victims. The final version of the 1997 reorganization consisted largely of "shell games," with loose coordination reaffirmed as the UN's mechanism of choice for dealing with urgent humanitarian crises, including internal displacement.[38]

The details of this failed consolidation are two decades old, but the tale remains disturbingly pertinent. Helping victims caught in the throes of war reflects the market, both for outsiders coming to the rescue and for the forcibly displaced.[39] While no one is in the "business" of being a humanitarian worker or contributing to an aid agency with the objective of making money, it is naïve to overlook the political economy of coming to the rescue. However, when UN mechanisms work – and we should not forget that many vulnerable victims are fed, housed, and protected – it is because of good faith and compatible personalities rather than through any coherent response structure that guarantees effectiveness.

Creative adhocracy has its limits, and any attempt to improve the performance of the international humanitarian system must involve consolidation and centralization (and a similar argument holds true for the UN development system, as we see in the next chapter). And when soldiers are involved, as they generally are in most war zones, even more planning and integration are required but typically are in short supply.[40]

As long as we are using market vocabulary, a new UN bottom line is: there must be fewer moving parts of the UN system, both in the humanitarian and in the development arenas. While many doubt my grasp of reality for uttering this proposal, it came close to implementation in 1997 until donor and bureaucratic politics reared their ugly heads. And, in another back-to-the-future moment, three respected humanitarian research institutions repeated the idea in preparation for the 2016 World Humanitarian Summit.[41] However, a modest but still precedent-setting consolidation of the kind needed across the system actually occurred in 2010, to which we now turn.

UN Women and the UNFPA: a Partial Consolidation

It is important to parse the 2010 establishment of UN Women, the only major recommendation implemented from the 2006 reform blueprint *Delivering as One* (DaO). Atomization often serves agencies and officials but not beneficiaries, and UN Women remains an anomaly that nevertheless suggests that consolidation is not impossible. It resulted from the fusion of four separate and often competitive programs in the system: the Division for the Advancement of Women, the International Research and Training Institute for the Advancement of Women (INSTRAW), the Office of the Special Advisor on Gender Issues and Advancement of Women, and the United Nations Development Fund for Women (UNIFEM).

The consolidation would have been even more encouraging had the UN Population Fund (UNFPA) – the organization's main operational entity for programming on behalf of women's reproductive health – been included. That consolidation proved unworkable because of the domestic politics in the United States that made progressive feminist politics, especially reproductive rights, of UN Women incompatible with Washington's conditioned support of the UNFPA. Even that reluctant and conditioned support turned into outright hostility in 2017, when the Trump administration cut completely the $70 million annual contribution to the UNFPA.

Nonetheless, prior to the 2010 fusion that resulted in boosting the position of women's human rights at the world organization, the UN system had never shuttered a major entity. A dominant theme in this volume is the seventy-year history of accretion and atomization. Hence, even the partial consolidation that resulted in UN Women is an encouraging example of what can be done when the politics are right.

In 2000, the Security Council passed resolution 1325 to ensure that peace operations and post-conflict reconstruction would be sensitive to gender and gendered inequalities.[42] To take stock after fifteen years and six additional resolutions, the Security Council approved a high-level review to assess national, regional, and global progress. Radhika Coomaraswamy, previously special representative of the secretary-general on children and armed conflict and special rapporteur on violence against women, led the group. Mainstreaming gender in peace operations still had not become standard practice, and the funding for programs supporting women in peace and security efforts remained "abysmally low."[43] The primary vehicle since July 2010 within the system has been UN Women. Evidence is unclear about donor priorities for gender equality, but UN Women has emerged as pivotal for international peace and security with obvious relevance elsewhere.[44] It has a seat at the high table for decisions about security and justice, gender- and sex-based violence, post-conflict humanitarian planning, and peacebuilding. This encouraging partial consolidation serves as a model for further centralization in other areas of the Byzantine UN system.

There obviously is considerable room to consolidate operational activities, for human rights and humanitarian action as for peace-keeping, peacebuilding, and sustainable development. In this regard, we would be remiss not to indicate partially successful efforts to create "One UN" in the development arena because it has direct application here as well. The term was coined to indicate efforts to take seriously the recommendations of *Delivering as One* – at the country level to reduce transaction costs by host governments, donors, and UN organizations. Modest efforts followed in 2006 after the report by the High-level Panel on System-Wide Coherence,[45] which proposed organizational changes to facilitate the implementation of the 2005 World Summit Outcome.[46] Calls for a more consolidated and better coordinated UN field presence have led to some convergence in about forty countries. While, except in a handful of cases, not achieving one leader, one program, one fund, and one office, UN organizations occasionally collaborate more closely. However, the collective memory is short. In the early 1990s, fifteen unified offices were created in the former Soviet Union but rapidly were undermined by rivalries. This microcosm of failed efforts at restructuring throughout the UN system underlines why, for instance, proposals to create a single governing board for special funds and programs are generally greeted with guffaws.

The UN system remains weaker and more wasteful than it should be. While current arrangements provide countries with choices for human rights and humanitarian assistance, the paucity of resources and surfeit of demand render "choice" a feeble defense for duplication, inefficiency, and counter-productive competition. In addition, the array of choices renders it impossible to maintain universal standards for rights or emergency delivery because countries can defect from one UN supplier to a competitor that ignores standards in order to get business.

In short, we need consolidation rather than hoping for the best from chance and fortuitous personal chemistry. If donor countries would back their rhetoric with cash, then perhaps meaningful consolidation along the lines of UN Women could result rather than endless chatter and business as usual. Donors are inconsistent; their contrariness in various UN corridors is legendary. The very countries that bemoan incoherence send different delegations with different instructions to different UN organizations, which result in widening mandates that facilitate untrammeled decentralization to a ferociously competitive network.

What is regrettable but can perhaps be tolerated as wasteful in more mundane development efforts becomes truly intolerable in the face of human rights abuses and acute humanitarian catastrophes where lives are at stake. There may be no miracle cure for the chronic feudal illness, but there certainly are palliatives. Ironically, 2017 was the first year in the first term of the ninth secretary-general. It would be shameful if the main result of his tenure is the further marginalization of the UN human rights and humanitarian system. Inertia is not a viable organizational strategy. Donors must cease talking out of both sides of their mouths and insist on consolidation and centralization rather than on the vacuous, half-hearted demands for increased coordination that ultimately serve only as a cover to leave bureaucratic things exactly as they are.

In this respect, UN Women could serve as a beacon – although not quite a "model" because, once established, it too energetically jumped into the competitive inter-agency fray by seeking its own separate country presence. Secretary-General Guterres simply must make streamlining the Second UN's machinery a priority, and he could and should begin with the entities of the UN proper working on human rights and humanitarianism, areas that he knows extremely well after a decade as high commissioner for refugees.

A More Muscular ICC

The experience of the United Nations War Crimes Commission (UNWCC) is an ignored international legal precedent from World War II. The seventeen-country commission approved 8,178 cases involving over 36,000 individuals in almost 2,000 war crimes trials for prosecution at a score of national civil and military tribunals across Allied states. Commission members submitted thousands of cases; when their charges were approved, they acted to pursue pros-ecutions in their own jurisdictions, leading to trials of Axis personnel from generals to low-ranking military and civilian perpetrators, from China to Norway. The Allies organized an extensive administration as part of the nascent United Nations to coordinate and support the prosecution of war crimes; this effort was not merely "victors' justice," because the UNWCC carefully ensured that cases were well founded and in line with domestic and international standards.[47] The breadth and depth of its work furnishes examples of political feasibility and law that can inform contemporary legal practice. It suggests that a more robust pursuit of war criminals at all levels was not merely a hope and a temporary reality at Nuremberg and Tokyo. Rather, it was an ambitious vision that could have been reinforced long before the 1998 Rome Statute created the ICC, which entered into force in 2002 after sixty ratifications.

Following the Cold War's end, massive atrocities demonstrated again the need for beefing up international justice. Moreover, short-comings in the ad hoc tribunals for the former Yugoslavia and Rwanda (including costs and the burden of evidence) exposed the desirability of a permanent court to prosecute individuals and act as a deterrent. By the middle of the 1990s, governments across the North and the Global South, as well as NGOs, had formed coalitions to lobby for what would become the ICC.[48] This "like-minded group" began with the modest hope of achieving consensus at a preliminary diplomatic conference in Rome in July 1997. When the official UN Conference of Plenipotentiaries on the Establishment of an International Criminal Court convened a year later, the sixty-country like-minded group rep-resented a formidable and persuasive coalition that joined forces with 700 members of the NGO Coalition for an International Criminal Court. The momentum was such that the formal Rome conference of 1998 moved toward a decision despite strong opposition from Washington, Moscow, and Beijing. Powerful and reluctant or hostile countries not only failed to ratify the Rome Statute but also at times actively sabotaged the ICC. Nonetheless, over much of the past two decades, a broad-gauged coalition of NGOs has worked in tandem with sympathetic governments from the North and the Global South. As a result, the ICC has proven resilient and implemented its mandate faster than many had initially predicted.

The ICC has opened investigations into Northern Uganda, the DRC, and the CAR upon requests by those governments, into Darfur and Libya with requests from the Security Council, and into Kenya *propio motu* by the prosecutor. The first chief prosecutor, Luís Moreno-Ocampo (2003–12), also submitted a request to investigate post-election crimes in Côte d'Ivoire in late 2010 and early 2011, which continue in the trial of Laurent Gbagbo, the first head of state to be taken into custody by the ICC (although in November 2011 he had already lost his re-election bid). The court has issued arrest warrants for three other heads of state, none of whom has success-fully been prosecuted: Sudanese president Omar al-Bashir (fugitive), Libya's Muammar el-Gaddafi (dead), and Kenya's president Uhuru Kenyatta (charges withdrawn).

Despite encouraging first steps, the ICC has retreated somewhat defensively in the face of a political firestorm among some African members. The growing continental disenchantment is troublesome because of the predominance of African cases on the ICC's docket. The regional breakdown of states parties is thirty-four in Africa; nineteen in Asia and the Pacific; eighteen in Eastern Europe; twenty-seven in Latin America and the Caribbean; and twenty-five in Western Europe and other states. At the outset, Africa had not only the most states parties but also the most enthusiasm for the ICC, spurred by Rwanda's 1994 horrors and South Africa's apartheid. Subsequently the continent has voiced the most unease because of the number of cases against African countries, and especially against sitting heads of state.

Although non-African investigations are under active considera-tion, the only individuals convicted to date have been Africans, among them the former DRC vice-president; and all others currently indicted are also African. Although the current chief prosecutor is herself from Gambia, and the African cases have mainly been requested by African countries, dissatisfaction seems to be growing. In October 2013, the AU's fifty-four members rejected a motion that African states with-draw from the ICC but nonetheless requested that cases against sitting heads of state be deferred until they left office. In January 2016, one of those scrutinized, Kenya's president Kenyatta, proposed that all AU members withdraw as a bloc; his proposal was popular, but no action followed. However, in October 2016 alone, three African states (Burundi, South Africa, and Gambia) voted to withdraw; a subsequent change in government caused Gambia to pull back from the announced plan, and a South African court declared its withdrawal "unconstitutional and invalid." But the damage was done, and, in November, Russia also decided to cut its ties – symbolically significant, as had been the George W. Bush administration's "unsigning" of the Rome Statute shortly before the treaty went into effect in 2002.

Moreover, having become a UN non-member observer state in 2012, the Palestinian Authority formally joined the ICC in April 2015 and has lodged two cases against Israel, regarding the construction of settlements and the conduct of the 2014 war in Gaza. This tactic is bound to raise predictable hackles in Washington and Tel Aviv. It is unclear what the future holds for this institution, as accusations of African bias continue to resonate in the battle to strip impunity from those who commit genocide, war crimes, and crimes against humanity.

The ICC's missed opportunities should be interpreted in light of what was in the policy mainstream during World War II. The UNWCC's earlier body of legal practice should alter the paradigm of international criminal justice, which has hitherto focused mainly on international tribunals rather than on the ICC.[49] The achievements of the twentieth and early twenty-first centuries come with a set of problems, particularly those surrounding speed, trial completion, multilateral participation, and costs. The breadth and depth of the UNWCC's work provides overlooked examples of political practice and law, which offer intriguing precedents and possible structures that could inform contemporary practice.

Here it is worth citing Andrew Hurrell's lament about the "relentless presentism" of social science[50] – narrowing one's intellectual and practical scope to take inspiration and lessons only from recent experiences. At best such myopia limits the range of innovation, policymaking, and breadth of understanding for contemporary issues, and at worst it leads to repeating mistakes. As Dan Plesch and I noted,[51] this oversight is a particular risk for the United Nations, whose roots have been remarkably under-researched. Its wartime origins and efforts to foster human rights and international criminal justice have a potential direct application today. The UNWCC's history has value not only in combating presentism but also in elucidating the origins and context for contemporary foot-dragging.

In attempting to contextualize the missed opportunities and potential for the ICC, we should recall, as has Carsten Stahn, that "international criminal justice is still in search of a 'UNWCC 2.0.'"

Ironically, modern academic debates and legal practice are going back to the future by revisiting the burst of innovation in the 1940s. Of particular note were complementarity, the prosecution of low- and high-level perpetrators, and the precedents of rape and sexual abuse as war crimes. However, contemporary ICC complementarity as embodied in the Rome Statute and subsequent academic literature barely scratches the surface of the UNWCC's efforts in terms of the scale of state obligations, participation, and the sheer number of trials.[52] In fact, modern complementarity seems as much a tool to preserve state sovereignty and protect national jurisdictions – as well as an acknowledgement of the ICC's inability to compel states to comply – as collaboration to prosecute mass atrocities and promote global justice. Yet the ICC's efforts, combined with increasing self-referrals on the part of member states as well as non-state parties (e.g., Palestine) and non-party states (e.g., Ukraine), suggest movement in the right direction, albeit unevenly and haltingly.

Thus, despite second thoughts by some African members and the long-standing reluctance of major powers, the setbacks for a more robust ICC in the twenty-first century appear modest in comparison with the precedents for the pursuit of international criminal justice. And the advances could and should be extended more energetically. Ramesh Thakur, in evaluating the pluses and minuses of the ICC and of R2P, summarized, "The world would be an even more cruel place for civilian victims without them."[53]

Conclusion

The missed opportunities resulting from inadequate pursuit and follow-up for a universal bill of rights, zero tolerance for abuse by peacekeepers, and IDPs suggest what could and should have been an even quicker bending of the long arc of historical progress for human rights and humanitarian action. Similarly, the enhanced operational effectiveness that would have resulted from a more centralized UN humanitarian system, an operationally fortified UN Women, and a less tentative ICC also suggest what could and should have been advances in the UN's human rights and humanitarian impact.

An example of the possible pay-off for improvements comes from considering the ongoing crisis of displacement in Europe. Media attention focuses on the populist political crisis from the blow-back of the influx of refugees. A picture is painted of refugees using various civil wars as pretense to seek a better life in Europe when they should have fled instead to areas more culturally, economically, or geographically "suitable." In fact, 86 percent of refugees fleeing civil wars fled to nearby middle-income countries outside of Europe (especially Jordan, Lebanon, Turkey, Ethiopia, and Pakistan). These data undermine the presumption by populist opponents of sheltering refugees in Europe because of what the UN's special representative on migration, Peter Sunderland, has called "responsibility by proximity." If "refugees are the responsibility of the world," then presumably "[p]roximity doesn't define responsibility."[54]

Such a holistic perspective on human rights and humanitarian response should be a quintessential UN one. Hyperbole about the scale of the current crisis should be put in perspective relative to previous postwar refugee flows – after World War I there were about 10 million displaced relative to a European population of 480 million; after World War II nearly 55 million relative to 540 million.[55] In the last two years, in contrast, perhaps as many as 1.8 million refugees arrived in Europe, which has a current population of 742 million, whereas Turkey, with a population of 74 million, received over 2.5 million.

UN contributions have been substantial, and this chapter suggests how the planet could have been less repressive and kinder had many human rights ideas and humanitarian operations been pursued more vigorously and in a more centralized fashion by both the First UN and the Second UN. This perspective should be a central component of the Global Compact that is supposed to emerge as a follow-up to the September 2016 UN Summit and the "New York Declaration for Refugees and Migrants."[56]

8

A LESS IMPOVERISHED AND POLLUTED WORLD WITH ENHANCED DEVELOPMENT?

By highlighting ideas and operations that could and should have made more significant contributions to sustainable development, this final substantive chapter continues to tease out the implications of "a more creative and effective UN." Chapter 8 explores how the planet could have been less impoverished and polluted with more equal development had many UN ideas and operations been pursued more energetically by states and international civil servants.

Ideas

Over many years, and in many contexts, I have argued that the UN's comparative advantage in sustainable development lies in its entrepreneurial, normative efforts – that is, in nurturing ideas and setting global standards and objectives. That said, the world body could have performed far better at numerous junctures. The prospects for a less impoverished and polluted planet are evident from three illustrations whose pursuit should have been more systematic and less ideological: the NIEO, the SDGs, and the right to development.

A New International Economic Order

While some might judge me daft for returning to the disparaged 1970s, an essential message was buried. Sustained attention could and should have been placed on measures to achieve a more egalitarian international system and to pursue national policies that combine redistribution with growth. It may sound hopelessly naïve even to utter the acronym "NIEO," but the sentiments motivating an economic order with a more just distribution of the benefits of growth can hardly be ignored in our world with its glaring and growing gaps of income and power.

The first decades of the twenty-first century displayed a growing awareness of and dissatisfaction with the kinds of unconscionable inequalities within and among countries that should have begun to be addressed in the 1970s but were not. Decades were lost until the various "Occupy" movements found echoes worldwide – including, ironically, the 2016 US presidential elections. They might well have begun earlier to push governments to address, or at least attenuate, the globe's now infamous inequality.

Concerns about the rich getting richer with their assets growing exponentially – while the middle and lower classes stagnate at best and become even poorer at worst – has resonance beyond academic debates. In the United States, no one disputed that disparities were at record-breaking numbers. US CEOs earned $373 for every $1 earned by the average worker (compared to *only* $42 in 1980).[1] The top 1 percent of Americans on average have over 38 times more income than the bottom 90 percent, and the top 0.1 percent more than 184 times their income share. Although global statistics pose significant difficulties in interpretation, they nonetheless are similarly depressing. The 1 percent of the world's wealthiest individuals control the same wealth as the world's poorest 95 percent.[2]

We return to controversial efforts to restructure relationships between the North and the Global South in the aftermath of the dramatic quadrupling in oil prices in 1973–4. A major shift in energy demand and supply resulted in a shift of global income to OPEC from both industrialized and developing countries without oil – sometimes nicknamed "NOPEC countries." Proposals for the NIEO consisted of an excessive shopping list of ideas to level the international economic playing field. Yet, the NIEO focused debate on a consolidated list of approaches that developing countries had put forward since the early 1960s, not all of which were unreasonable. However politically infeasible, they encapsulated the passionate call to alter relationships between the "haves" and "have-nots" – which still included oil-producers – to level the international playing field.

Yet "entrenched interest, national hubris, ideological divisions, and mindless militancy all played their part," as Mahfuzur Rahman has written about the NIEO's demise. "The idea of a new international economic order has long ceased to be a matter of serious discussion … [but] the story is worth recounting."[3] Stabilizing basic commodity prices had long been a fundamental demand of developing countries.

One of the key UN ideas was the Common Fund for Commodities. As many developing countries were dependent on raw materials for export earnings, wild fluctuations in commodity prices were a perpetual concern. The fund suddenly became a priority after OPEC overnight orchestrated a dramatic fourfold hike in the price of oil in October 1973. The first efforts to regulate price and supply had begun in 1949 among Venezuela, Iran, Iraq, Kuwait, and Saudia Arabia. Following a reduction in prices in 1960 by international companies, a conference was convened in Baghdad to set up a permanent organization, which was formed a year later in Caracas. Other countries joined over time. OPEC demonstrated the power of solidarity when it imposed an embargo on the United States and the Netherlands, which had supported Israel in the Yom Kippur War.

Bitter debates were mixed with the acute problems of non-oil-exporters, and the so-called North–South dialogue continued the confrontation. For instance, the Charter of Economic Rights and Duties of States was initiated by UNCTAD in 1972 and formalized in the 1974 General Assembly resolution 3281. The French government convened the Conference on International Economic Cooperation (CIEC) in 1975 to continue the "conversation" among fewer countries (twenty-five) rather than the entire UN membership. This "North–South dialogue" continued until 1981, and there were also the so-called global negotiations in a series of UN contexts. In actuality, a more accurate label was "dialogue of the deaf."

Ultimately, the Global South failed to change even the tone of discussions about prevailing inequities in the global political economy, although the NIEO's legacy reinforced for a time solidarity among developing countries. A former Dutch UN ambassador, Johan Kaufmann, attributed the NIEO's demise to the radical "confrontational style" of the Global South, deeming its semantics "too aggressive and abrasive."[4] The lack of constituency building among poor countries was one explanation, as was the unwillingness of wealthy states to consider redistribution.

While the NIEO litany is usually dismissed as wildly unrealistic, were the ideas really so outlandish? A heightened interest in reducing poverty and inequality has returned, but we have postponed a serious conversation for four decades. The individuals and countries that have paid the price of deprivation look upon the NIEO as a missed opportunity by the First UN. Sustained efforts should have begun earlier to improve the lot of nearly one-half of the world's population – more than 2.8 billion people – who live on less than $2.50 a day, including the 1.2 billion who survive in extreme poverty on less than half that amount. One-third of poverty-stricken individuals are children, of whom 22,000 die each day. At a minimum, we should have begun reducing these appalling numbers earlier.[5]

SDGs with Bite

Earlier we indicated the UN's value-added for goal-setting. Here, the "what if?" returns to that notion, but in order to criticize the lack of critical input for the visible recent version, the "Sustainable Development Goals." They represent a step forward by being universal, multi-sectorial, and multi-partner in aspiration. However, they also can be construed to have taken steps backward from the earlier (2000–15) "Millennium Development Goals," which had a sharper edge by being less numerous, more measurable, and time-bound; hence whether progress was achieved or not was visible instead of obfuscated.[6]

Starting in 2012, states and secretariats toiled on a new set of sustainable development goals to focus UN operations until 2030. In 2013, a high-level panel chaired by three serving heads of government proposed a new set of twelve goals and fifty measurable indicators, already a quantum leap in range and ambition from the earlier MDGs. The panel also laid down parameters, two of which were crucial. First, any new set of goals should build on the MDGs but should also have more breadth, including addressing concerns about economic growth and jobs, the promotion of peace and security, and inclusive governance. Second, they should be universal – that is, they should be directed at all 193 UN member states without distinguishing the "Global South" and the "North."

The panel's report was the starting point for work by an "open working group" (OWG), which began in 2013. Open consultations have the merit of being more inclusive through seeking wide consensus among states – a process that was not followed for the MDGs, which instead were drafted by a few UN officials. But this new agenda-setting was designed to fail. Without prioritization, countries will be able to say either "we have achieved what we said we would" (by cherry-picking), or "we have failed to achieve the SDGs" (because not even Switzerland could do them all).

As on other occasions, the hackneyed formula for UN consensus necessitates accommodating the aggregate of all state interests, as well as those of multiple lobbying groups and every UN organization. A year-and-a-half later, the OWG had a list of no fewer than seventeen development goals that threw up 169 explanatory paragraphs (with at least as many targets). The largest gathering ever of presidents and prime ministers – complete with a moral flogging from Pope Francis – at the September 2015 UN summit adopted "Transforming Our World by 2030: A New Agenda for Global Action."

Despite the length and grandiloquent packaging, several crucial and controversial issues were left on the cutting-room floor – forced displacement and massive voluntary migration, terrorism, armed conflict, religious fundamentalism, cyber-security, capital flight, corruption, post-conflict reconstruction, human rights in general, and LGBT rights in particular. The SDGs cater to lowest common denominators and do not even reflect significant institutional UN policies previously adopted at international conferences or introduced by the secretary-general. Moreover, in some cases they are also disingenuous – for instance, Washington and other wealthy capitals allowed the final document to contain the target of 0.7 percent of GNI as ODA. Only seven countries (Sweden, the United Arab Emirates, Norway, Luxembourg, Denmark, the Netherlands, and the United Kingdom) had reached the target by 2015, which others have rejected and have no intention of meeting (the United States, for instance, hovers around 0.17 percent).[7] Of what relevance is regurgitating previous broken promises? Such sleights of hand do not bode well for other targets. *The Economist* characterized the SDGs as "something for everyone [that] has produced too much for anyone."[8] Among them is a restatement and elaboration of most of the unrealized MDGs.

SDG 16 acknowledges that the main engine of development progress is national governance, which includes building strong and inclusive institutions, promulgating the rule of law, respecting rights, and reducing corruption and "all forms of violence." The final Goal 17 concerns the "means of implementation," which refers generally to substantial new resources. A central problem, especially pertinent for Goal 16, is that these last two umbrella goals shelter a large number of issues dear to the West and contested by many countries among the Rest. Goal 16 has no specific agreed targets, and, notwithstanding Goal 17's clarion call to financial or investment action, it leaves much to the imagination.

Although the United Nations has helped nurture some far-reaching ideas, the SDGs are hardly a shining accomplishment. The First and Second UNs have collectively patted themselves on the back for completing the job, with the result that colorful SDG banners are omnipresent in UN corridors, SDG pins are in many lapels, and even SDG footballs are being dribbled. However, the "achievement" amounted to staying in the same room long enough to agree upon a "laundry list" – a typical criterion of UN success. But precious little detail refers to the truly critical indicators of development progress. It is often said that UN processes are more important than products. The muddled process – to stay with the household imagery – produced the "kitchen sink" that is the SDGs.

Due to lack of strategic guidance from either the UN secretariat or knowledgeable advisers (who had been instrumental in devising the MDGs), the outcome is multilayered, duplicative, and incoherent. Within the verbal obfuscation and diplomatic jargon are some metrics by which progress could be measured. But many indicators are simply impossible to quantify. What would it mean, for example, to "build the resilience of the poor" (Goal 1), or "ensure sustainable food production systems" (Goal 2), or "increase substantially health financing" (Goal 3)? Every goal is peppered with worthy but vague exhortations.

The SDGs do not lack ambition, but any practical purchase will necessitate that critical choices be retrofitted onto this indigestible menu of aspirations. In some ways, the can has been kicked down the proverbial road as formulation of the actual contents of the agenda was initially postponed until March 2016, when the Inter-Agency and Expert Group – a subgroup of twenty-eight of the 193 national statistics offices that compose the UN's Statistical Commission – was to quantify targets. Choices are necessary because not all countries can meet all the targets. Perhaps more importantly, their sheer number means that reporting countries can obscure abysmal failures on some indicators with their more modest successes on others; the sheer number of indicators can enable countries to claim an inability to report, allowing them to emphasize those on which they have done well and ignore others. The MDGs, with a far smaller number of indicators, had the advantage of being used to name and shame governments.

Will all goals and targets be measured for all countries? Or a different set of goals tailored to each? Or a mixture? How will their detailed application be measured? While the SDGs refer to least developed, landlocked, and small island states, no mention is made of those prone to conflict, which face the greatest development challenges. While readily available metrics existed for virtually every country for every MDG, how will new SDG concepts such as security or governance be determined?

Even once the shaping and honing has been done, better capacities for gathering and interpreting statistics are required, but how can they be achieved? And, even if data are solid, who will monitor and interpret them? How can observers, as Nate Silver's best-seller asked, distinguish "the noise and the signal"?[9] Ominously, and as a concrete indicator of bad faith, some UN member states have asked that the word "accountability" be dropped from SDG documentation.[10]

Governments are the main obstacles to development yet are responsible for their own reviews. They must be held to account if this exercise is to have meaning, which will require hard-nosed tracking by local civil society organizations, international NGOs, and the UN itself. Indeed, the world body could emulate its own practice in the human rights domain with "universal periodic reviews" for every country's development performance.

What if the UN secretary-general and senior staff had exerted more intellectual leadership and pointed to how few (or perhaps many) clothes were on the SDG emperor? All is not lost, however, because the UN could reclaim the mantle of intellectual leadership by independently monitoring the SDGs and exposing good and bad performances.

The UN has managed to attract individuals who have demonstrated outstanding intellectual leadership. It has also played a pioneering role in the world of ideas, many of which have had remarkable impact. Even though many have been rejected, sidelined, or adopted only rhetorically at first, some UN ideas have emerged and become part of mainstream international discourse. These include everything from climate change to gender equality, from special measures for the least developed countries to putting people at the center of development, from human security to removing the license for mass murder from the attributes of sovereign states. It is no exaggeration to claim that such ideas have often been "ahead of the curve."[11]

The SDGs remain a missed opportunity to have identified priorities for investment, action, and sequencing. The First UN did what member states do in universal forums – pursue their interests and sidestep confrontation by adding more and more items. In this case, instead of resisting, the Second UN's interests were served by going along for the ride; staff were complicit instead of taking a stance.

The Right to Development

In contrast to the Convention on the Elimination of all Forms of Discrimination Against Women (CEDAW) and the Convention on the Rights of the Child, which have witnessed substantial progress since their ratification, the Right to Development was adopted by the UN General Assembly in 1986 but continues to be stalled. First conceived in the 1970s after years of debate, the Commission on Human Rights created a fifteen-member working group which met for five years of tortuous negotiations. In 1985, the working group presented its draft, which the General Assembly accepted by a vote of 146 to 1 (the United States) with eight abstentions (seven other Western countries and Israel).[12]

The Right to Development introduced two controversial notions. First, it established the idea of group rights – people or nation, ethnic, linguistic, or geographical – as long as it was possible to define obligations and for a duty holder to fulfil them. Second, advocates argued that it corrected the individualistic bias in the human rights tradition by introducing the collective rights of states to economic self-determination – known as "third-generation" rights to accompany the first (civil and political) and second (economic and social). The Universal Declaration had finessed this issue in Article 28: "Everyone is entitled to a social and international order in which the rights and freedoms set forth in this Declaration can be fully realized." In contrast, the Right to Development referred explicitly to such duties in Article 3:

> States have the duty to co-operate with each other in ensuring development and eliminating obstacles to development. States should realize their rights and fulfil their duties in such a manner as to promote a new international economic order based on sovereign equality, interdependence, mutual interest and co-operation among all States.

The controversies did not die after adoption. A number of developed countries expressed strong reservations, including Washington's ECOSOC representative, who declared bluntly: "the view that States had the right to development was unacceptable."[13] Although opponents saw the Right to Development as revolutionary and destructive, its defenders viewed it as having synthesized strands of human rights with development. Philip Alston, a distinguished human rights expert, described the controversy as "little more than an exercise in shadow boxing."[14]

The post-World War II political order – based on universal rules with an emphasis on human rights, self-determination, solidarity, and equality among countries – raised huge expectations of a brighter future for countries emerging from colonial rule.[15] Indeed, the UN's very creation unleashed expectations about the promotion and protection of human rights, including the enforceable one to development.

At present, however, a combination of globalization, unequal terms of trade, debt structures, and other economic and political constraints mean that many countries in the Global South are unable to pursue their chosen paths. The policies imposed by donor countries – including good governance and economic liberalization – may have obstructed as much as promoted development. Martin Khor has argued that "developing countries must have the ability, freedom, and flexibility to make strategic choices in financial, trade, and investment policies."[16] Without that ability, a country is not in a position to promote and protect the right to development of its citizens. "Self-determination" has been a buzzword since Woodrow Wilson; UN membership is one thing, but the right of a state to devise and pursue policies for itself that are suited to local political and economic conditions is another.

Despite well-known shortcomings, the UN remains the only global institution in which all governments can discuss and mobilize national and global resources to tackle the most intractable problems. Among other problems with the SDGs is their exclusion of the right to development. The mobilization of the private sector, civil society, foundations, and other stakeholders for the construction of a more just and peaceful world order as envisioned in the UN Charter and subsequent human rights conventions still is missing a foundation to foster their achievement. Moving "from broken promises to global partnership" is how David Hulme frames the need to revisit the missed opportunity of the right to development.[17]

Operations

This section evaluates additional UN shortcomings within operations dealing with infectious diseases and pandemics, on the one hand, and rejection of a central funding mechanism and avoidance of delivering as one, on the other. These indicate, again, that the Second UN – despite accomplishments – could and should perform better.

HIV/AIDS and Ebola without Political Appointments

We have encountered numerous threats – terrorism, economic crises, refugee movements, nuclear proliferation, and climate change – that are global in scope and which cannot be adequately overcome by states acting individually to protect their own citizens or territory. Health illustrates clearly this dynamic, which is why it was one of the first issues in the nineteenth century that facilitated international cooperation through the establishment of public unions.[18] Improving health, and particularly fighting infectious diseases, was an obvious transboundary menace to peoples and states even then.[19] That logic is more pertinent in today's world of near instantaneous global travel and interconnectedness. To halt the spread of an infectious disease within its own territory, a state must also expend energy and resources to prevent the spread of disease elsewhere, especially in countries that are less capable.

Tragically, initial efforts to tackle HIV/AIDS met with considerably less success than those for smallpox, SARS, and avian flu; they demonstrate how *not* to respond – namely, relying on narrower and backward-looking approaches to sovereignty and cooperation. Instead of seeing common threats and attacking them regardless of location, the approach to HIV/AIDS has been more piecemeal and oriented toward narrower conceptions of national interests.

While the virology and epidemiology of smallpox was a precondition for its eradication, the relatively early embrace of cooperation and transnational interests, rather than going it alone on a national basis, was even more essential to defeating the killer disease. The HIV/AIDS story is one of waking up after the disaster and proceeding with minimal international cooperation, including disputes over the patents governing life-saving palliative drugs (and the profits therefrom). Part of what the doctor should have ordered was a more inclusive definition of the vital interests of the sovereign members of the First UN along with more courageous action by the Second UN.

Already by 2007 at least 15 million Africans had died from AIDS since the start of the epidemic a decade-and-a-half earlier. In 2012 alone, 1.2 million people in sub-Saharan Africa succumbed to the disease.[20] However, by 2015, as a result of drug availability, the number of deaths worldwide had dropped to 1.1 million, although 2.1 million were still being newly affected. The HIV prevalence rate in southern Africa was breathtaking: in 2014, in Botswana, 25.2 percent of adults were infected; in Lesotho 23.4 percent; in South Africa 18.9 percent; and in Swaziland 27.7 percent.[21]

Prevention efforts are too late for the 36.7 million people now living with HIV and AIDS, and for many who still will follow. Indeed, the number of new infections daily is still around 5,700, with 2.1 million newly infected in 2015 (150,000 children). The UN originally set a goal to cut new infections by 25 percent by 2005, an objective that failed miserably as the toll doubled and doubled again. However, since 2010 the rate of new HIV infection has fallen by 6 percent, and by 50 percent among children.[22] In 2016, the UN reset the goal to halt the spread by 2030.

Among the more unsettling "what ifs?" relates to the WHO's early involvement with HIV/AIDS. Its initial efforts were ahead of the curve but then abandoned, leaving the world to pay the steep price in loss of life, economic performance, and insecurity. Early in 1986, the WHO still regarded AIDS as infecting the promiscuous few. It was Jonathan Mann, who died tragically in a plane accident in September 1998, who had convinced Halfdan Mahler, then WHO's director-general, that AIDS was not merely another infectious disease. It flourishes in, and reinforces conditions of, poverty, oppression, urban migration, and violence.

Mann persuaded Mahler that a pandemic was in the making and launched and took charge of a special program. The UN took the lead until Mahler's retirement in 1988, after which the WHO's AIDS program was slashed by the new director-general, Hiroshi Nakajima. Mann resigned in protest and pursued his crusade from Harvard University.[23] It is difficult to measure the role of homophobia in tardy responses and cutbacks, but it certainly was part of the explanation. So too was the stigma attached to a sexually transmitted disease, along with perceptions of culturally appropriate sexual practices.

By 1990, the sense of urgency about AIDS in industrialized countries had begun to wane. New drugs and other preventive measures available in the West meant that it was no longer viewed as quite the same threat to the developed world. At the same time, incompetent ministries of health in many developing countries denied the existence of the problem and refused to cooperate in data gathering. The WHO was laggard in building on its promising start, but it was not the only UN agency to cut AIDS programs. At UNICEF, the health division fought from 1992 to 1994 to avoid AIDS programming. Meanwhile, the UNDP attacked what remained of Mann's program at the WHO as too narrowly focused on bio-medical needs.

Finally, by the middle of the 1990s, donor governments began to push for the creation of a joint UNAIDS program, which was established in January 1996. UNAIDS attempts to pull together the efforts of eleven UN organizations; but the initial efforts were more politicized than they should have been, with disastrous results. The participating organizations cut back sharply on resources and personnel devoted to AIDS. World Bank loans dropped from $50 million to less than $10 million, while WHO spending dropped from $130 million to $20 million and UNICEF's from $45 million to $10 million.

In summer 1998, Gro Harlem Brundtland became the WHO's director-general. Her first two *World Health Reports*[24] emphasized tobacco and tuberculosis. While the latter kills one-third of those living with HIV/AIDS, nonetheless it was unacceptable that the 1999 report made no reference to the fact that HIV/AIDS surpassed all other causes of death in Africa. In a secretariat of more than 2,000 people, only nine WHO professionals worked on AIDS.

In January 2000, US vice-president and presidential contender Al Gore articulated Washington's new position before the UN Security Council, which was addressing Africa's social-cum-security ills: "Today, in sight of all the world, we are putting the AIDS crisis at the top of the world's agenda. We must face the threat as we are facing it right here, in one of the great forums of the earth – openly, boldly, with urgency and compassion."[25] Unfortunately, the HIV/AIDS story remains essentially different from that of smallpox because it is one in which the First and Second UNs awakened only after the disaster had struck. Needlessly, lives and retarded development and additional sources of insecurity were the price.

It would be a relief if governments had at least learned from the experience, but other infectious diseases continue to pose challenges for contemporary global health governance, and they too are approached with myopia. As the peoples and states of the world become more materially and morally interconnected, the need for more effective international management increases, but the sensitivities to the wishes of member states, large and small, can impede action by an overly cautious Second UN. The unnecessarily slow reaction to the 2014 deadly Ebola outbreak in West Africa startles but was bureaucratically predictable after a better appreciation of the HIV/AIDS experience. The WHO's politicized recruitment of key officials in Africa, which emphasized political connections over medical and management competence, was key to the tragically bungled 2014 response. A Geneva-based health institution and an independent panel sponsored by the London School of Hygiene & Tropical Medicine, along with the Harvard Global Health Institute, came to the same conclusion: the WHO's capacity for handling such pandemics needed to be protected from political and personnel meddling.[26]

The international response to the West African Ebola virus epidemic of 2013 to 2016 was a near miss. Earlier instances had fortunately been controlled, but the most recent was also the most widespread outbreak. Lost lives and widespread socioeconomic disruption in the region hit hardest Guinea, Liberia, and Sierra Leone. The fatality rate was about 70 percent, although among hospitalized patients it was less than 60 percent. Lesser outbreaks took place in Nigeria and Mali, and there were isolated cases in Senegal and the United Kingdom, along with the secondary infections of health personnel in the United States and Spain. The actual number of cases peaked in October 2014 and then, following the commitment of substantial international resources, began to decline.[27]

On March 29, 2016, the WHO terminated the Public Health Emergency of International Concern status of the outbreak and reported a total of 28,616 suspected cases and 11,310 deaths – although the organization believes that these numbers were substantial underestimations. It left about 17,000 survivors, many of whom report symptoms severe enough to require long-term care. In addition, there is an apparent ability of the virus to "hide" in a recovered survivor's body for an extended period of time and become active months or years later, either in the same individual or in a sexual partner.

The WHO was the logical leader, as it was earlier in smallpox and to a lesser extent in SARS and the avian flu; but clearly more vigilance is required to ensure the recruitment, promotion, and retention of competent technicians and to avoid political appointments "even at the risk of angering some of the 194 member states that govern it," as the *New York Times* reported. It must be able, the experts said, "to freely raise international alarms about an epidemic in a country without regard to that country's reputation."[28]

For students of international relations and international organizations, politics is, unsurprisingly, the essence; personnel appointments can hardly be expected to be "above politics." Yet, when purely political considerations so clearly trump competence and integrity regarding the appointment of personnel, both member states and "We the peoples" suffer from the ensuing public health hazards. The WHO's structure means that regional directors are supposed to take the lead in issuing quarantines and sanctions, but they are elected by member states. This process invariably means giving priority to governmental preferences rather than public health – illustrated by cover-ups and delays related to polio's comeback in Syria in 2013 as it initially was in Ebola's outbreak in Guinea in 2013.

A more recent illustration of the weight of politics versus public health arose in the midst of the high value of public investments in Rio for the 2016 Summer Olympics in comparison with overall concerns for containing disease. How seriously could the WHO weigh the views about Zika by some 150 health experts from two dozen countries who called for a delay in the games or a move to another site when such a powerful member state as Brazil wanted the danger to be minimal?[29] As it turned out, the games took place without any noticeable increase in Zika. Good luck prevailed, but the political and not technical health judgment predominated in the decision to keep the games in Rio.

Early in 2017 a new public–private partnership was formed, the Coalition for Epidemic Preparedness Innovations, to develop and stockpile vaccines against known viral threats such as Ebola and to push the development of research when new threats such as Zika emerge. Moral and practical concerns overlap. The combination of charities (e.g., the Gates Foundation), governments (e.g., Japan and Norway), vaccine producers (e.g., Merck and Pfizer), NGOs (e.g., Médecins Sans Frontières MSF), and the WHO is a powerful indication that a global pandemic could be a more likely way to kill millions than nuclear war or terrorism.

When the First UN wants international organizations to work and provides the requisite resources, the necessary technical and operational services can result. And when the international civil servants who are employed to attack a world problem are competent, motivated, and properly supported, they can help provide a global public good such as healthcare. As the case of HIV/AIDS and Ebola show, however, the planet's citizens cannot count on such results.

The UNDP as the UN's Central Fund and Coordinator

Funding to widen the avenues for development and the UN's comparative advantage in this arena came to the fore in the 1960s after debate had begun in the previous decade. With a half-century of hindsight, there is much to praise in what was pioneering: the range of issues; the vision, freshness, and subtlety of many policies; the clear focus on national action; and the first rush of goal-setting. There was also a more operational bent, the recognition of the crucial role that the UN's expertise and its country representatives – the on-the-ground agents – should and could play. In 1966, the United Nations Development Programme began operations, and over time its resident representatives became the coordinators for the UN system in each country.

In 1949 the UN began providing technical inputs through the Expanded Programme of Technical Assistance (EPTA), which pursued US president Harry Truman's Point Four proposal from his 1949 Inaugural Address. He believed that the United States should help less economically developed nations improve living conditions through sharing its more advanced scientific and technological "techniques." The UN Special Fund was established ten years later to finance such efforts. These two institutions together became the UNDP.

By that time, the World Bank had doubled its capital and shifted from post-World War II European reconstruction to development in newly independent countries. In 1960, it established the International Development Association (IDA), which provided low-interest loans on such soft terms as to amount to "grants" along the same lines originally proposed earlier for the United Nations. The World Bank, with strong US resistance, had opposed such a facility but shifted 180 degrees to support the proposal once it seemed that money would flow its way.[30] Its official history noted that the IDA "carried the genes of its third world and United Nations parentage."[31]

The row over whether the UN or the World Bank would get the cash explained the failure to launch the Special United Nations Fund for Economic Development (SUNFED): "That proposal stemmed from the need for developing countries, many of them recently independent, to have access to capital development finance at a cheaper rate than World Bank loans – especially the poorer countries," recalled the UN's first female under-secretary-general, Margaret Joan Anstee. "The 'S' [was] added when they discovered the acronym without it was 'UNFED!'"[32] The UN Special Fund was left to finance pre-investment studies, while the World Bank's concessional arm provided cheaper finance to poorer developing countries.

While investments in brick and mortar – factories, roads, ports, and communications – were necessary, they were insufficient, leading the UN to reorient toward investing in people. Technical "assistance" – which implied more of a one-way, top-down direction from the knowledgeable West to the ignorant Rest – gave way to a less paternalistic label of technical "cooperation." But the essential notion was a division of labor between the Washington-based international financial institutions with cash, and the UN system as the poor cousin's answer to the more costly investments that generally emanate from the World Bank, the IMF, other multilateral banks, and bilateral donors.

While the resources were modest, the main reason behind the creation of the UNDP was a hoped-for centralization of fundraising so that technical agencies could concentrate on specific inputs while the UNDP would raise the resources and help coordinate the potentially unwieldy members of the UN system. The first overview of the experiment was given to Robert Jackson, the Australian logistical genius who had saved Malta for the Allies during World War II and who had also worked miracles with the UN's first operational agency, UNRRA. His searing 1969 *A Study of the Capacity of the United Nations Development System* already lamented the fragmentation

163

and competition that has worsened considerably since.[33] Another giant of the early and mid-life United Nations, Brian Urquhart, remembered the almost uniform negative reactions from senior UN officials to Jackson's recommendations that threatened turf:

> He made a joke – well, he thought it was a joke – in the introduction ... that "there were a number of dinosaurs and cavemen in the system." And Paul Hoffmann, who was the head of the UN Development Programme among others, took violent umbrage ... It was ridiculous, because *The Capacity Study* was a perfectly sensible study, but, as so often happens, it was ruined by one sentence.[34]

What would have happened to the atomized UN system had the First UN, and especially the main Western donors, insisted upon Jackson-like centralization? Additionally, what if the leaders of the Second UN had wanted to provide coherent and cost-effective services rather than build feudal kingdoms? What if the UNDP had become a central source of funds and coordination rather than competing for soft monies and project execution with virtually every organization within the UN system?

While the need to confront global challenges has never been greater, the UN has never been more disjointed. The legendary waste and competition has ensured turf-conscious organizations that do not merit the label of "system." Every new problem or increased emphasis has led to new organizations or sub-units of established ones.

As noted earlier, the thirty (or seventy, depending on how one is counting) main entities of the UN humanitarian and development system function alongside an equivalent number of research and training organizations and functional commissions that do not figure in that total. The headquarters of the main organizations are in fourteen different countries (and fifteen cities). A group of independent ECOSOC advisers noted the tentacles of the UN development system (UNDS), for instance, in a 2016 overview:

> [T]he UNDS organizational arrangements at the country and regional levels are highly fragmented, which undermines the ability of these entities to deliver integrated support to the member states .... 24 UNDS entities, which represent approximately 95% of the UN Official Assistance for Development (OAD) expenditures (2014), maintained 1,432 UNDS offices in 180 countries across the globe .... These exclude multiple field offices of a UNDS entity within a given country. In 168 of these countries (93%), UNDS has five or more entities present and 65 countries (36%) have 10 or more entities present. A few funds and programmes (UNDP, UNICEF etc.) are physically present in over 120 countries.[35]

The UN's fragmentation, along with donor incentives, explains why individual organizations focus on their own substantive areas and eschew a tighter system. Backed by separate budgets, governing boards, and organizational cultures, as well as independent executive heads, an almost universal chorus sings the atonal tune praising decentralization. The UN's principal organ charged with oversight, ECOSOC, provides the main concert hall for this cacophony. What if the original design had been implemented and there were a central funding mechanism whose power of the purse could compel respect and cooperation? Would the UN system not have been less wasteful and have had greater impact?

Delivering as One

The latest major effort to overhaul operations was a follow-up to the 2005 World Summit, when Secretary-General Annan convened a High-Level Panel on UN System-Wide Coherence in the Fields of Development, Humanitarian Assistance and Environment.[36] Its recommendations figure in a report titled *Delivering as One*, but the chances for their successful implementation were close to nil. The high-level panel proposed consolidating the activities of the system's organizations into three pillars – development, human rights, and the environment – the latest installment in a long list of unsuccessful reforms.

In addition to the overarching recommendation in the title, the report argued for the creation of a UN Sustainable Development Board "to drive coordination and joint planning between all funds, programs and agencies to monitor overlaps and gaps."[37] The board was envisioned as an ECOSOC body, with heads of UN organizations serving ex officio. One of its functions would have been to oversee and approve DaO programs and funding. The panel also proposed the establishment of an MDG-funding mechanism to provide multi-year financing for one-country programs; the strengthening of international environmental governance; and the establishment of a UN entity focused on gender equality and women's empowerment (so far, the anomaly).

From earlier discussions, the reader undoubtedly will suspect DaO's current fate. There is still no effective center despite repeated pleas: in 1969, Robert Jackson lamented the lack of a "central brain"; there was a call in 1977 for a director-general of development (that is, a high-powered deputy secretary-general), and in 2006 for a development coordinator. There is no effective oversight body, which

ECOSOC was intended to become but never did. There is no single fund as EPTA was supposed to be in 1950, arguably the last year in which UN programmatic centralization prevailed.

The 2006 timetable has fallen far behind schedule, but some progress occurred in eight pilot countries (Pakistan, Vietnam, Tanzania, Rwanda, Mozambique, Cape Verde, Uruguay, and Albania). The mobilization of "coherence funds" to strengthen the hand of UNDP resident coordinators (RCs) in them provided carrots to foster more centralization, as was the MDG Achievement Fund sponsored by the Spanish government. Despite some encouraging signs, the jury is still out as to whether they succeeded in changing the organizational culture by altering financial incentives.[38] Some fifty countries subsequently have adopted DaO and been partially tempted by the possibilities for centralization,[39] and an independent evaluation commissioned by the General Assembly in 2012 found pluses.[40] As early as 2009, all the pilot and self-starter countries agreed at a meeting in Kigali that there is "no way back,"[41] which was echoed later in Hanoi, Montevideo, and Tirana.[42]

DaO benefits should be obvious: joint programming that is better aligned with national priorities and more demand- than supply-driven; more transparency for governments and other partners; clearer ideas about UN programming cycles; more predictability and clearer activities, results, and budgets; more joint monitoring and reporting with decreased burdens; and a better division of labor. In terms of efficiency, however, joint programming has thus far increased internal UN transaction costs, with more time and resources being spent on coordination; but some transaction costs with external partners, government, and donors seem to have decreased.

The 2012 evaluation also recorded debits. While joint programming has led to larger and more coherent efforts with stronger participation from non-resident agencies, it remains difficult to strike a balance between a few priority outcomes and inclusiveness. The single budgetary framework has enhanced transparency, but it has been applied in different ways in different countries, making the aggregation of data impossible. Perhaps most importantly, the function of UN RCs was strengthened – in particular, some 40 percent of such personnel are now from outside the UNDP, which had previously monopolized such positions. But the RC still lacks formal authority over teams within a country, with loyalties to parent agencies holding more sway than the horizontal accountability to the country-specific team members.

Consolidated funds to foster DaO have been held out as a lever for greater coherence. However, they vary significantly across countries –

for instance, they supply 33 percent of total requirements in Vietnam, but only 6 percent in Pakistan.[43] The size of these funds is small and dependent on a small group of donor countries – five contributed over 80 percent of total resources.

The greatest challenges remain for the single office. The 2012 General Assembly resolution 67/226 set up the quadrennial comprehensive policy review (QCPR, or a periodic overview of system-wide operations), which called for more "harmonization." The familiar plea is for UN organizations to reduce duplication as well as administrative and transaction costs through consolidating support services; to establish common services; to standardize procurement; and to emphasize the interoperability of planning.

While the principles of a common UN are gaining some traction, DaO's full benefits require substantially more robust efforts on many fronts, but two in particular stand out: an alignment of procedures and business practices across the headquarters of all UN organizations; and genuine integration rather than hoping that serendipity will produce results.[44] Without dramatic and substantial changes of the kind recommended by the 2006 panel, the cozy status quo will condemn UN development operations to irrelevance.[45] Nothing short of a strategic repositioning will help the UN rediscover its rightful place within the international system. Yet, so far, tinkering rather than structural change has resulted.

The consolidation into UN Women was the only substantial result from the 2006 recommendations. Generous funding was available for the first three years of DaO (2007–9), and $585 million was allocated to it from 2008 to 2011 through UN multi-donor trust funds that created incentives for governments and UN organizations. However, by 2011 the largest donors reduced funding after the financial crisis; so when new countries adopted the DaO approach it was without additional funding. The least progress was made in reducing transaction costs for national partners and UN entities because country-level UN staff had no mandate to change cumbersome procedures. There was almost no progress in tackling the bottlenecks caused by a lack of common IT and reporting systems, and no incentives for staff to reach out beyond their own organizations.

Although leaving the system alone typically is the only viable option because political and organizational inertia are overwhelming, support for more meaningful bureaucratic shake-ups may be increasing. Independent surveys conducted by the Future of the UN Development System (FUNDS) Project received almost 15,000 responses to four surveys from every part of the globe in 2010, 2012,

2014, and 2016, including from the private sector, NGOs, academia, and governments.[46] Respondents, 90 percent of whom were located in the Global South, agreed that the UN's neutrality and objectivity were strong suits, but decentralization was by far its glaring weakness. Over 70 percent also agreed that by 2025 there should be fewer UN agencies with dramatic changes in mandates and functions, including stronger NGO and private-sector participation. Nearly 70 percent of respondents supported the appointment of a single head of the UN development system, although views were split about a single headquarters. Almost 80 percent sought a single representative and country program in each developing country.

To be fair, fledgling efforts began under Secretary-General Ban Ki-moon. Some business practices were harmonized. More system-wide evaluations were attempted. A cautious plan to align seven research and training entities was proposed but scuttled by the host country. In an attempt to bring the different parts of the system together as well as involve more partners, the secretary-general launched several new ventures: Every Woman, Every Child; Sustainable Energy for All; the Global Education First Initiative; Zero Hunger Challenge; the Scaling-Up Nutrition Movement; and the Call to Action on Sanitation. These initiatives also demonstrated the proclivity for accretion, although they may encourage existing UN organizations to take charge and extend partnerships.

That even seemingly obvious steps remain under consideration and are viewed as stretches reflects the magnitude of the task faced by Secretary-General António Guterres. Since 1945, has the UN system witnessed evolution? Yes. Adaptation? Some. Transformation? None. Why consolidate and save money by reducing transaction costs in the Second UN when neither donor nor recipient countries of the First UN are the slightest bit interested in getting value for money? On the contrary, both sides enjoy the fruits of patronizing and being patronized. Moroever, hostility is evident in the General Assembly and other governing councils, for instance, when cutbacks are proposed in useless posts or mergers of favorite organizational entities. The gaps between an organization's rhetoric, decisions, and actions are often viewed as "hypocrisy," and complex international organizations within the UN system must struggle to resolve such contradictions; if they do not, their legitimacy if not survival is threatened.[47]

The UN's normative and convening role for the 2030 development agenda is accepted and appreciated. However, it is unclear what mechanisms the world organization will use to monitor performance independently or interact on the implementation of the new agenda.

The glass remains 90 percent empty, although some argue that it is 10 percent full. DaO was yet another missed opportunity to make the "system" more than a euphemism.

Conclusion

The annex to every textbook about the world organization contains a simple graphic of the so-called UN system, a two-dimensional depiction that is misleading. As hinted earlier, the characterization of the UN as a "family" has the distinct advantage of problematizing its ideational and operational behavior: like a family, the United Nations is in some respects harmonious but in far more numerous ways extremely dysfunctional; sometimes it stands united, but all too often divided.

It is worth repeating the acute difficulty in mobilizing consensus among the First UN's 193 member states. The world organization has a key convening function, serving as a platform, literally, to discuss virtually anything. We have encountered numerous examples of overlapping missions and competition for limited resources, which mean that UN organizations have similar pathologies to other institutions that seek to exclude rivals and expand market shares.

The relationship between UN headquarters and specialized agencies reflects the horizontal nature of authority in the system. Robert Jackson, in his customary outspoken and picturesque fashion, began the 1969 *Capacity Study* about the shape of the UN's development system as follows: "Governments created this machine which is ... unmanageable in the strictest use of the word ... like some prehistoric monster."[48] What is the result of adding almost a half-century to the age of a dinosaur?

The UN system is the opposite of a hierarchy – like those in professional armed forces or most Fortune 500 corporations. No sensible soldier or meticulous manager could survive on First Avenue in Manhattan. Many textbooks begin by declaring that the UN is *not* a world government – an institutional designer would not win an award for such a poor imitation of a national government with ministries that go begging for resources and are dispersed: the Ministry of Education in Paris (UNESCO), the Ministry of Defense in New York (Security Council and DPKO), the Ministry of Agriculture in Rome (FAO along with WFP and IFAD), the Treasury in Washington (the World Bank and IMF), and the Ministry of Environment in Nairobi (UNEP).

After seven decades, it would be hard to imagine relocating so many headquarters. At the same time, more centralized funding, consolidation, and top-down direction are not beyond intergovernmental imaginations and the capacities of international civil servants.

Or are they? In his address to ECOSOC in July 2017, António Guterres recommended essentially more of the same by moving "towards a Funding Compact." He pleaded for more core support but proposed no incentives to individual organizations to do anything more than go their own way.

9

LET'S BE SERIOUS – THE UN WE WANT (AND NEED) FOR THE WORLD WE WANT

Two counterfactuals anchor this book. Chapters 3 to 5 challenge the reader to go beyond the received wisdom that the planet would not be much worse off without the United Nations. Chapters 6 to 8 undermine the fatalistic conventional thinking that repairing the world organization is not only a fool's errand but would not make much of a difference anyway.

This final chapter explores some feasible initiatives during the first term of Secretary-General António Guterres, in office less than a year as this book goes to press. The planet and the UN survived the preceding decade with Secretary-General Ban Ki-moon, who relished being "invisible," a judgment that coincided with *The Economist*'s forthright evaluation: "the dullest – and among the worst."[1]

It is essential that Guterres rock the UN boat, and that other senior and junior officials make sizable, if not tidal, waves. While institutions are stronger than the individuals who direct them, another decade of mediocrity and low visibility could relegate the United Nations to the margins of world politics, if not oblivion.

This chapter emphasizes strategies for reform that are both desirable *and* possible. The initial shots across the bow by the Trump administration are likely to be followed by broadsides. They make even clearer why change is imperative if the world organization is not to become a relic. Comments are directed to the First UN and the Second UN, but the Third UN's weight must necessarily be thrown around to back successful changes.

We should recall that politics outside the UN are primary, while factors inside are secondary. For example, the end of the Cold War explained the UN's renaissance in the late 1980s, not the other way around. The end of the Cold War permitted the world body to engage with consensus, commitment, and vigor. Once empowered, UN personnel and entities have, however, exerted an independent influence on states and other actors; they could have done far more.

The United Nations has always blended lofty ideals with ugly realities. The Charter articulates the aspirations of an international society – a world of peace and justice with rights and prosperity for all. The world organization's daily operations, however, occupy the netherworld of foreign policies and national interests. The UN thus represents both the pursuit of a better world and the abject failure to achieve it. Squaring that circle is my task.

Sacrosanct Sovereignty and North–South Theater: Contemporary Challenges and the First UN

The UN has pursued reform, essentially since the ink dried on the Charter, but acutely over the last quarter-century. Reforming the First UN is tortuous. States do not readily give up their privileges or influence, and engineering political change is beyond the aspirations of any mortal, certainly this author. Consequently, this section reflects the reality that pleas are unlikely to penetrate the cultures and calculations of hermetically sealed foreign ministries before moving to discuss change that is more plausible.

Some fear that granting more collective authority to the First UN would make the world organization even more of a foreign policy tool of major powers. The Security Council was conceived as a variation of nineteenth-century "concert diplomacy"; and in the UN's principal security organ the great powers enjoy privileged status – a version of "high-table diplomacy."[2] Reform of the Security Council's permanent membership is a permanent agenda item in New York, but with no likelihood of movement anytime soon.[3] Possibilities for long-range reform involve more permanent members; shorter-range changes involve longer and more frequent terms for influential countries. However, each structural proposal threatens to pry open Pandora's box. Which developing countries should join the P-5 or assume more frequent and longer terms? Should they be the most powerful or populous? What about the voice of the small and powerless, or of traditional supporters of multilateralism from the Nordic countries? Should a splintered state retain its seat? Why should economic powers whose constitutions impede overseas military involvement (i.e., Germany and Japan) have a seat? Should there be three permanent European members? Why not just the EU and the

United Kingdom after Brexit? Which countries should wield vetoes? Should all regions have at least one permanent seat?

In 2004, the High-Level Panel on Threats, Challenges and Change provided two models, illustrating the pitfalls of reform – that is, even individual experts could not agree on a single proposal, and no one addressed how increased membership would not make council decision making even more problematic.[4] Both were based on regional representation, with new council seats (expanding from fifteen to twenty-four) distributed among Africa, Asia/Pacific, Europe, and the Americas. The models did not expand the veto among permanent members. They addressed several principles to circumnavigate thorny issues. The first was that all members have enhanced financial, military, and diplomatic responsibilities; the second was to add more countries from the Global South; the third was not to impair effectiveness; and the fourth was to increase democracy and accountability.

The best that member states could muster at the 2005 World Summit was recommending "that the Security Council continue to adapt its working methods so as to increase the involvement of States not members of the Council in its work, as appropriate, enhance its accountability to the membership and increase the transparency of its work."[5] The seemingly endless debates over the years have at least created a permissive environment that has facilitated pragmatic modifications in working methods. Charter Article 7 specifies that the council adopts its own rules of procedure, which have been called "provisional" since 1946. While structural reform is a fool's errand, more openness, accountability, and diverse inputs into its deliberations are not, and they could usefully expand.[6] Moreover, more informal settings in the G-20 and other forums undoubtedly have opened other avenues for complementary initiatives.

In 2008, the General Assembly attempted a different tack, "intergovernmental negotiations on Security Council reform in informal plenary of the General Assembly." Not surprisingly, no hint of progress was visible for the seventieth anniversary in 2015, nor has there been since. Disagreements on size, representation, and the veto persist. The present situation resembles a group of doctors who agree on the patient's illness but disagree on the remedy; and, for those who agree, no prescription is available. The Security Council is an anachronism in world politics, but no one can find a workable formula that satisfies the leading stakeholders.

These challenges clearly illustrate the difficulty of addressing the UN's primary ailment of state sovereignty. Yet, even here, modest movement took place with respect to R2P because at least mass atrocities are now considered unacceptable behavior by states; and thus sovereignty can be abrogated when a state is manifestly unwilling or unable to protect its citizens. A possible future and not insignificant application of past practice would be the extension of UPR-like procedures for other issues across the UN system. In this way, the principle that sovereigns are subject to peer review could serve to make their records more public and thus enhance accountability.

The ugly head of sovereignty also manifests itself in the counterproductive machinations of North versus the Global South. Here there is room to maneuver and move beyond the kitchen-sink approach to agenda-setting and the theatrical fireworks that pass for diplomacy. In order for states – in the North and in the Global South – to discuss seriously a policy option or an operational effort, the typical procedure is to include something for everyone. This approach necessarily condemns deliberations to remain on well-ploughed ground rather than addressing priorities or seeking new solutions to age-old problems.

There are, however, cases where alternatives have been tried with some success. For instance, the artificial fortifications between the North and the Global South were breached to reach successful agreements about the ICC and landmines. The key is to move beyond traditional roles by bringing new partners and counterparts into conversations; and to proceed even without some of the major powers.

The Global Compact is a another illustration that represented a radical departure from previous conventional wisdom – the leftover pipe-dream from the 1960s and 1970s of international regulation of transnational corporate behavior favored by the Global South – toward an active engagement with the private sector. More than 9,000 companies have accepted its ten core principles to guide best practices: support of internationally proclaimed human rights; uphold such labor rights as freedom of association and collective bargaining as well as eliminate compulsory, child, and discriminatory practices; promote environmental practices and eco-friendly technology; and work against corruption. These efforts at first brought knee-jerk criticisms from many diehards in the Global South and some NGOs that the UN had lost its soul.

Nonetheless, for more sober analysts, since 2000 the UN has distanced itself from an outmoded hostility about the market and transnational corporations (TNCs), seeking instead to advance responsible corporate citizenship so that business can be part of the solution to the challenges of globalization. "Cooperation with the private sector has become politically feasible and operationally desirable," wrote

Georg Kell, the director of the program.[7] The private sector – in partnership with other nongovernmental actors – should help realize a more sustainable and inclusive global economy. The main normative shift, in the words of its intellectual midwife, John Ruggie, was the shift away from efforts to regulate the private sector to a "learning model" of how to make the most of its potential.[8]

The Global Compact is a voluntary corporate initiative to catalyze actions in support of UN goals and to mainstream its human rights, labor, and environmental principles. It is not a regulatory instrument and thus does not police, enforce, or measure the behavior or actions of companies. Rather, it relies on public accountability, transparency, and the enlightened self-interest of companies, labor, and civil society. Unlike earlier initiatives, however, the Global Compact did not run aground on North–South rhetorical shoals.[9] Empty doctrinal squabbles gave way to finding desirable contributions and investments. Corporate social responsibility[10] for the 80,000 or so TNCs, as well as ten times that number of subsidiaries and millions of suppliers, is an esential normative element of global economic governance.[11]

If the UN is to begin to reflect the complexity of actors necessary to address global problems – and the for-profit sector's resources and energy dwarf those of non-profit NGOs – the world organization should consider the agenda-setting of the Global Compact not only as a substantial step in the right direction but in many ways a model. By aggressively building an array of partnerships with civil society and several thousand firms, the UN moved in largely uncharted international waters and could not rely on the non-functioning compass provided by North–South orthodoxy. With foreign direct investment and worker remittances now dwarfing ODA, the need is clear to move beyond the sterile performances guided by tired scriptwriters from the North and the Global South who guaranteed poor and hackneyed productions, and ultimately failure.

Proponents of enhanced international cooperation properly advocate that states should emphasize common interests and global public goods. Yet holding one's breath for that outcome is dangerous because governments are unlikely to set aside sacrosanct state sovereignty anytime soon. There is room to find palliatives for counterproductive North–South theatrics; also there is space in the immediate future for altering the Second UN. Here progress is actually possible, and so a specific emphasis should be placed on mobilizing member-state support for transforming UN structures and the performance of UN staff.

175

THE WORLD WITH A MORE CREATIVE AND EFFECTIVE UN?

Remedies for the Second UN and International Peace and Security

More effective peace operations are plausible by modifying how operations are conducted, placing greater emphasis on peacebuilding, and strengthening the international civil service and its leadership. Stumbling and fumbling peace operations, including hybrids with regional organizations, illustrate a general failure to distinguish between the military operations that the Second UN can manage (traditional and even muscular peacekeeping) and those that it cannot and should not (enforcement). As Michael Mandelbaum wrote, "the U.N. itself can no more conduct military operations on a large scale on its own than a trade association of hospitals can conduct heart surgery."[12] Enforcement is best left to the militaries of states that have UN authorization, although mechanisms for greater oversight by the Security Council of military operations conducted under its auspices are clearly required.

The Secretariat's, and thereby the Security Council's, ability to monitor subcontracted operations has long been ripe for rationalization.[13] The 1991 Persian Gulf War was the first military enforcement action of the post-Cold War era, but the secretary-general and the staff were on the sidelines for decisions about waging the ground war. Security Council authorizations were politically useful, but coalition forces were not accountable to the world organization in any way. This pattern has since been repeated in Mali, Libya, Kosovo, and Afghanistan. Charter Article 99 empowers the secretary-general to bring the council's attention to matters that could threaten international peace and security. Greater use of this article is, however, more attractive on paper than in reality. Raising sensitive geopolitical issues resisted by key countries risks alienating the very same powerful states whose support is necessary for addressing them in the first place; in particular, use of this article could not be effective if the P-5 are outraged.

Meanwhile, more vigorous follow-up is necessary for strengthening traditional and even muscular peacekeeping, stabilization, and transitional operations that began in 2000 when Secretary-General Annan appointed Lakhdar Brahimi to head a panel. The resulting report's blunt language focused on getting states to take their responsibilities seriously by creating clear mandates with reasonable objectives and providing properly trained and equipped troops. Meaningful consensus among member states remains elusive, and most of the report's

176

commonsensical recommendations have not been implemented. The secretary-general must go begging and start from scratch for each new peace operation and the renewed mandates of existing ones. The difficulty in fielding missions and getting them to full strength was repeated in recent operations in Darfur, Mali, and the CAR. UN peacekeeping, even the traditional type, remains unsystematic and ad hoc in composition and deployment.

This reality could and should change along the lines of the 2008 DPKO guidelines for effective peacekeeping – the "Capstone Document," which reiterated basic principles: consent of the parties, impartiality, and non-use of force except in self-defense (or defense of the mandate). It repeated that missions must have clear mandates and obtainable goals, and that the UN had no comparative advantage in peace enforcement. It cited Security Council support and adequate funding as prerequisites for mounting peace operations. The DPKO also properly turned the spotlight on itself, stressing the need for better planning and execution.

The central contradiction for most peacekeepers is that maintaining international peace and security involves tackling problems that states cannot, or do not, want to address. Contemporary operations often are "neither fish nor fowl" (neither peacekeeping nor peace enforcement), which cannot be finessed by a sleight of hand oxymoron, "enforcement peacekeeping."[14] In addition, contemporary operations require integrating activities across the UN system.[15] Member states often wish to "do something" (or convey that impression), but not badly enough to invest blood and treasure. As such, "success" consists of preventing a situation from getting worse or spiraling out of control. The Second UN lurches from crisis to crisis but takes too little time to learn lessons.

Meanwhile, the Security Council continues to authorize complex, multidimensional missions with robust mandates that authorize force to protect civilians but without adequate human and financial resources. A 2014 UN internal oversight report found that peacekeepers rarely use force to protect civilians, but they are not hesitant to use it to protect themselves in hazardous environs. It is worth noting that African peacekeepers have been willing to sustain higher casualties in UN and regional operations than would be sustainable for Western militaries and their publics.[16] Deep cleavages exist between the poorer countries that provide troops and the richer ones that fund them.[17] UN peacekeeping has become a Third World ghetto – in 2016, about 95 percent of troops were contributed by the Global South.[18] Poorer states complain that their peacekeepers have not received a raise in over a decade – they do not note, however, how much of UN payments go into state coffers rather than into peacekeepers' pockets. More accountability and transparency in reporting could alleviate some of these problems.

In October 2014, the secretary-general established the High-Level Independent Panel on Peace Operations.[19] The panel reiterated past recommendations (regarding political support and the resources); HIPPO also urged that peace operations avoid counterterrorism. Despite criticism, UN operations can protect civilians when sufficient political will and military muscle are available.[20] While peacekeepers have traditionally been reluctant to use force to protect civilians, often their mere presence can help deter attacks.

A structural advance by the 2005 World Summit was the Peacebuilding Commission, which requires higher and more predictable funding. As stabilization of war-torn societies is becoming the UN's main security activity, the entire peacebuilding process requires the kind of consolidation that has been indicated as desirable throughout this book. And the PBSO should be in a position to implement lessons from its own learning while integrating those of peacekeepers, peacemakers, humanitarians, and developmental specialists.

Reforming and strengthening the staff is essential for the UN to continue its operations, but that is no easy task because most reform starts at the top and often is interrupted when leadership changes.[21] When Secretary-General Annan unveiled his strategy for a "quiet revolution" in 1997, he initiated measures to improve the management of peace operations,[22] which continued subsequently during the Ban administration. One of the first steps by António Guterres was to co-locate parts of the senior staff previously working in separate locations on politics, peacekeeping, and logistics. He also was building upon a rationalized cabinet structure – consisting of the Senior Management Group (SMG) with division heads and an executive committee system – that facilitated more cooperation than had existed previously. Senior officials (including those based in Geneva and Vienna through teleconferencing) meet weekly with the secretary-general. In addition, the Executive Committee on Peace and Security holds bi-weekly discussions with senior officials whose units deal with peacekeeping. These processes were supplemented by a number of issue-specific task forces, including for each peace operation, as well as special meetings with other actors who serve as operational partners in the field, among them development and humanitarian agencies and international financial institutions.

The Executive Office of the Secretary-General (EOSG) has asked for permission to request advisory opinions from the International Court of Justice under Charter Article 96. Such action could clarify questionable situations that represent threats to the peace and suggest policy options that are politically and legally acceptable. One key to advisory opinions is getting a specific response. Like all courts, the ICJ often relies on procedural interpretations to set aside cases. Moreover, the court is not a crisis-driven body and rarely acts quickly – until recently, it decided, on average, only one or two cases per year. Washington has made clear that it does not want the ICC second-guessing decisions about its choice of weapons and targets, and so the United States – and Russia or China for that matter – would hardly welcome the secretary-general's posing similar questions to the ICJ. At the same time, answers are crucial; so why not try?

Agreement on standards and interpretations could also be helpful. The language of resolutions is purposefully vague to secure wide intergovernmental assent: "all necessary means" in the war against Iraq created a host of questions about proportionality; and "all measures necessary" was quintessential UN doublespeak that did not permit sufficient action to help Bosnia's Muslims. The language of international decisions is elliptical to allow latitude in determining which actions and procedures constitute legitimate follow-up. The secretary-general – and not just the General Assembly and the Security Council – should be authorized to request ICJ advisory opinions to help reduce the criticism of selective application of principles that guide decision making. Seeking the court's opinion could be harmful in the midst of a crisis; but if judgments were more routine they could be building blocks over the longer term in anticipating contingencies and establishing precedents in a timely fashion.

The Secretariat's fact-finding capabilities should improve so that the secretary-general has access to timely, unbiased, and impartial accounts. Special units currently focus on early warning and prevention – a top priority of Guterres – but they require greater access to classified information about volatile situations. The Secretariat's ability to launch preventive diplomacy and possibly recommend preventive deployments presently is too circumscribed.

Underlying issues here and below is that the Cold War's demise could have permitted the UN to revive old-fashioned ideals of an objective, independent, and competent international civil service. It did not. The organization's success begins and ends with its employees, and an ignored reality is the crying need to overhaul personnel – qualifications and competence have long been secondary to geographic and political considerations. In addition women have consistently

179

been overlooked,[23] which was evident in calculations by one former senior staffer, Karin Landgren, that in 2015 men were appointed to 92 percent of senior positions.[24]

The need for protecting and providing incentives for whistle-blowers was evident earlier in the analysis of sexual scandals by peacekeepers. Before that, the Oil-for-Food Programme debacle in Iraq documented serious flaws in management and judgment. The fourth report from a team headed by Paul Volcker used apt language for an inefficient and politicized administration in desperate need of repair: "The inescapable conclusion from the Committee's work is that the United Nations Organization needs thoroughgoing reform – and it needs it urgently."[25] Member states simply must provide the secretary-general with the leeway to reshape the staff, or at least they must stop grumbling about its shortcomings.

Remedies for the Second UN in Human Rights, Humanitarian Action, and Sustainable Development

Before putting forward three overarching proposals, it would be helpful to list some acute challenges facing the humanitarian and development parts of the United Nations, ones that could trigger transformations or, if ignored, the further marginalization of the system. While adaptations have taken place over the years, radical reform has been elusive and change piecemeal. Can the UN system become fitter for purpose, as this book argues, or will it become increasingly irrelevant? The answer depends on whether the system successfully confronts, rather than ignores, five challenges: competition, coherence, co-optation, capacity, and complacency.

- Competition means that the UN system is increasingly becoming marginal, which is disbursing less than 5 percent of total global ODA, instead of the 20 percent that it had two decades ago. The UN's operations are financed by grants, which are becoming less important in comparison with alternative sources and expertise – ranging from foundations such as Gates's to NGOs of rival size, to foreign direct investment that globally is five to six times larger than total ODA, and to remittances that are two and a half times that size.
- Coherence, or the lack thereof, is lamented throughout these pages; but the decibel levels of criticism are increasing along with growing impatience over proliferation, decentralization, rivalry,

turf battles, and redundancy. Complaints about such shortcomings raise hackles, not just in Trump's Washington but also in the capitals of the "good guys" in Northern Europe as well.

- Co-optation, or the use of the multilateral system as an adjunct to bilateral assistance, has essentially turned UN organizations into subcontractors for donor priorities. The growth in non-DAC aid is encouraging and signals the end of the simplistic world of Western aid providers and Southern recipients; but resources from new donors are overwhelmingly bilateral, with those for the UN system so narrowly earmarked for non-core purposes that they should not be categorized as ODA. The UN system is no longer composed of organizations; rather, it consists of contractors.
- Capacity is another variable. What exactly can the system do? How robust is the expertise within it? What are its comparative advantages? How can they be maximized? Merely replicating past activities is unviable – inertia does not constitute a strategy.
- Complacency characterizes the attitude of too many international civil servants who do not admit the world organization's critical condition. Something drastic ("transformation" is not too strong a word) must be done to save the UN system from becoming an anachronism.

Three strategies could confront head-on these challenges. They reflect lessons from the previous chapters and would help make the UN more central rather than peripheral to global problem-solving.

Fewer Moving Parts and Operations in Fewer Countries

The above alliteration should continue with "consolidation" or "centralization" as obvious solutions, but they are anathema to officials who rationalize futile complexity and react to incentives from donors to go their own way. The UN's structure (see figure 2.1, pp. 30–1) would have puzzled the US cartoonist Rube Goldberg, whose elaborate contraptions symbolized the human capacity for exerting maximum effort to achieve minimal results.

The so-called UN system has become increasingly disjointed and inadequately adapted to contemporary needs, often being sidelined by other, more effective development and humanitarian organizations and initiatives along with alternative sources of finance, expertise, and oversight. While the need for concentration on comparative advantages by fewer organizations in a more concerted fashion has never been more obvious, the UN system has never had more entities or been more fragmented. New organizations and new sub-units have been added, but outmoded and overlapping ones have virtually never been disbanded, rationalized, or combined. One immediate remedy would be for the UN system to be operational in only fifty or so – whatever euphemism is preferred – "least developed" and "fragile" or "failed" or "conflict-prone" or "post-conflict" states rather than spread thin over almost three times that number of developing countries.

Tough love is in order. The UN should not be operational everywhere. Concentration is justified for two reasons: First, limited resources dictate that it should focus on those countries most in need of its assistance. Second, the UN system, on paper and often in reality, is the only institution that can deploy a full range of necessary services, from security to humanitarian relief, from peacebuilding to sustainable development.

There also should be fewer moving parts of the UN system. After chairing a panel on the future of multilateralism, Kevin Rudd was persuaded that the top priority was a "Team UN" that could overcome "rigid institutional silos by moving increasingly to integrated, multi-disciplinary teams ... driven by fully-empowered directors of local UN operations."[26]

The perpetual call for "coordination" not only makes eyes glaze over but also obfuscates the extent to which atomization serves UN organizations and their staffs rather than beneficiaries – "United Nations Management – an Oxymoron?" asked one puzzled former senior staffer after thirty-five years of service.[27] With the exception of the consolidation that produced UN Women, the system has never eliminated a major entity. Donors must cease talking out of two sides of their mouths and insist on consolidation and centralization. Coordination is a time-tested, vacuous recipe to leave bureaucratic things as they are. The previous reform effort was euphemistically labelled "delivering as one," but it is not that distinct from earlier effforts and could be more accurately labeled "competing as many."

Secretary-General Guterres should make streamlining a priority. There is no better, or more achievable, legacy.

More Big Ideas and Independent Monitoring

While the operational UN need not be everywhere, the world organization has a comparative advantage in being everywhere for norm- and standard-setting. Universal norms are, well, universal. So it is fitting to examine the evidence from the independent United Nations

Intellectual History Project (UNIHP) about the world body's most distinctive contributions as a purveyor of ideas. International organizations live or die by the quality and relevance of their policies. The UN has no real competitor in convening power and idea-mongering. After seven decades, one of the UN's central contributions and legacies is that we know what we know; and we know what we do not know.

We should neither exaggerate nor understate the UN's contributions. The balance sheet, however, shows a surplus with a value-added for eight steps: providing a forum for debate; generating ideas and policies; giving them international legitimacy; promoting their adoption for policy; implementing or testing them at country level; generating resources to pursue them; monitoring progress; and burying bad ideas. Margaret Joan Anstee used alliteration to label them: forum, fount, font, fanfare, framing, funding, following – and funeral.

UNIHP's books and oral histories constitute a foundation on which senior officials, and certainly the ninth secretary-general, should build. The United Nations has added significant value to policy ideas, normative priorities, and standard-setting. One can imagine a world without many of the concerns elaborated in the preceding pages, or with preoccupations or possible solutions having come on stream later than they did. But it would be an even poorer and less humane planet than the one that we inhabit.

Monitoring the SDGs from 2016 to 2030, for instance, provides the opportunity to demonstrate anew the UN system's capacities to call a spade at least a shovel. It could counterbalance the painful process of formulating the SDGs, an illustration of the non-system at work because the sum of the parts was less than what the whole could have been. Not only were member states acting on their predictable narrow national interests, but UN organizations were joined by civil society allies to lobby intensely for their hobby horses. Optimists called them "aspirational," whereas skeptics such as Bjørn Lomborg noted, "Having 169 priorities is the same as having none."[28] An unkind William Easterly suggested an alternative acronym: "senseless, dreamy, garbled."[29]

If the SDGs are to realize their potential as universal aspirations that are meaningful across sectors and for multiple partners, the UN system should add value with tough love. Allowing governments to report on their own misbehavior is a lethal mistake. Following the UNDP's *Human Development Report*, the UN system's independent monitoring of SDGs could establish a sense of proper sequencing and priorities. This effort would not be a stretch for a Second UN with a spine.

Better Use of Better People

Mediocre officials hide behind the convenient excuse that political correctness prevents initiatives, or that senior officials make creativity impossible for more junior staff. In reality, the United Nations could and should rediscover the idealism, independence, competence, and dedication of the international civil service, make room for original minds, and create more mobile personnel and career development paths for a twenty-first-century secretariat. And whistleblowers deserve commendations rather than criticisms. Perhaps most importantly, Guterres's record as UNHCR manager bears emulating more broadly – over a decade, he reduced headquarters costs as a percentage of total costs by over 50 percent, and staff costs by almost that much.[30]

The Second UN is desperately in need of repair. It can be reinvigorated to alter the way that international secretariats do business. In field operations and headquarters, autonomous officials have provided and should provide crucial and autonomous inputs into policy formulation, advocacy, project implementation, and monitoring. People matter.

While everyone cannot win international prizes, nonetheless secretariats should aim to recruit the best and the brightest. For instance, ten individuals with substantial UN experience have won the Nobel Prize in economic sciences – Jan Tinbergen, Wassily Leontief, Gunnar Myrdal, James Meade, W. Arthur Lewis, Theodore W. Schultz, Lawrence R. Klein, Richard Stone, Amartya Sen, and Joseph Stiglitz (a former World Bank chief economist now closely associated with the UN). Another fourteen have won the Nobel Peace Prize as UN officials or as organizations staffed by international personnel: John Boyd Orr, Ralph Bunche, the UNHCR (twice), Dag Hammarskjöld, UNICEF, the ILO, Alva Myrdal, UN peacekeepers, the UN itself (shared with Kofi Annan), the IAEA (shared with Mohamed ElBaradei), the IPCC, and Martti Ahtissari.

Ignoring standard operating procedures (SOPs) is essential to break down organizational silos or at least build bridges between them. For instance, former US congressman and later UNDP administrator Bradford Morse, together with Canadian businessman Maurice Strong, ignored the feudal system's rules when they headed the Office of Emergency Operations in Africa in the mid-1970s. Thanks to their experience, reputation, and independence, Morse and Strong overrode the UN's SOPs just as Jackson had ignored them in order to shake up the system. He applied the military skills and hierarchical command structure from defending Malta and leading the Middle East Supply Centre to the UNRRA in postwar Europe, Africa, and Asia. Later, he did the same for the biggest UN relief operation to date at that time, in Bangladesh in 1971.

Such personalities and approaches are essential at senior *and* junior levels if the Second UN is to function as it could and should. International civil servants would not exist without the member states of the First UN, of course, but what would member states accomplish without a secretariat? Old-timers, especially the idealistic first generation recruited in the 1940s and 1950s, are appalled at the extent to which nationality has come to trump competence and obsequiousness overshadows courage.

Recruitment should return to the origins of the League of Nations and early UN secretariats. The highest consideration should be competence rather than a variety of quotas – geography, ideology, gender, or age, which are used to justify shameless cronyism in hiring for senior and junior posts. If government nominations for posts continue in preference to open competition, only the most professionally qualified and experienced candidates should be considered. And in contrast with the take-it-or-leave-it approach of the posts "reserved" for particular nationalities, several candidates should be nominated and the choice left to UN administrators. For senior appointments – to his cabinet, inner circle, or special representatives – it is time that the secretary general should cease asking, formally or informally, for P-5 approval and promising posts as part of campaigning.

Many interpret Dag Hammarskjöld's first year as an unmatchable attempt at the Sisyphean task of reforming the Secretariat,[31] an especially crucial effort after the McCarthy-era attacks. However, security crises have invariably distracted secretaries-general from such efforts. Quality, independence, and representation can be balanced. Special recruitment and promotion efforts can be given to underrepresented regions or language groups (not countries) by casting the net to attract world-class candidates of both genders. Pressures are exerted by governments, friends, and family members for candidates from industrialized and developing countries alike; but crass cronyism and outside lobbying for influence and patronage can and should be squelched.

Several reports have proposed, and the 2005 World Summit actually agreed, to cut deadwood and reduce the staff's average age.

185

Nothing happened. But this long-standing proposal would not necessarily improve matters – enterprising staff could take a payment and seek alternative employment while the most unproductive would remain because they have few options. The more pertinent challenge is gathering *new* timber for the secretariat of the twenty-first century and ensuring that the most competent and productive be retained and promoted.

Final Thoughts

The previous pages contain plausible and feasible directions for the future United Nations. They suggest palliatives if not cures for what ails the world body. They would make a difference in creating a less violent world with enhanced international peace and security; a less repressive and unkind world with enhanced human rights and humanitarian action; and a less impoverished and polluted world with enhanced justice and development.

In 1942–5, when considering the UN's point of departure, those who defeated Nazi Germany and Imperial Japan wished to turn back the clock not to 1913 but, rather, to 1918. The founders sought to finesse the weaknesses and build on the strengths of the League of Nations. One undoubtedly can imagine a world without concerns for peace, stability, and prosperity, and without the ongoing experiment in institutionalized universal cooperation that is the United Nations. But as chapters 3–5 demonstrated, such a world would be poorer and more violent, repressive, and polluted than the one to which the world organization aspires and, at its best, contributes. At the same time, the UN could and should have performed better and done more; and chapters 6–8 pointed to concrete ways that the world body could have done so.

There is time to make the UN fitter for purpose. We are not starting from scratch; current UN structures are building blocks for a better future. Despite gridlock, many of today's global problems ironically reflect previous multilateral successes in which the United Nations has made essential contributions – for instance, more states as a result of decolonization; more globalization as a result of trade liberalization; more institutions as a result of collaboration and specialization; and more environmental degradation as a result of growth.[32]

We should recall that Charles de Gaulle famously dubbed the United Nations "*le machin*" ("the thing"), thereby dismissing international cooperation as frivolous in comparison with the real red meat of foreign policy, *Realpolitik*. He conveniently ignored that "the thing" had rescued occupied France. It began in Washington in January 1942 with signing the "Declaration by United Nations." Representatives of the twenty-six countries that subsequently crushed fascism anticipated the UN's formal establishment as an extension of their wartime commitments. They were not pie-in-the-sky utopians. The Trump administration would do well to recall that the United Nations was viewed not as a liberal plaything to be tossed aside when the going got tough but, rather, as a vital necessity for postwar peace and prosperity. It could only have been forged after a cataclysm on the scale of World War II's 50 million dead.

Brian Urquhart was the second UN official recruited in 1946 after combat in the European theater, and he recalled that the "remarkable generation of leaders and public servants" during and after the war were "more concerned about the future of humanity than the outcome of the next election."[33] The current generation of presidents and prime ministers has no such vision. But if the first half of this book is modestly persuasive – that the world without even the limping United Nations would have been far more violent, repressive, unkind, impoverished, and polluted – their myopia must mutate.

For most politicians, pundits, and the public, the United Nations is an afterthought, if a thought at all. Meanwhile, scholars and diplomats focus on the global sprawl of networks and informal institutions rather than on the requirements for strengthened intergovernmental institutions, most especially those of the UN. The contrast is stark with the approach and operations of the wartime United Nations – today we suffer from a misplaced enthusiasm for ad hoc pluralism rather than systematic multilateralism.

"Minilateralism" is another fad – for example, the G-20 or G-7 – whose proponents advocate assembling "the smallest possible number of countries needed to have the largest possible impact."[34] Infatuation also grew after Anne-Marie Slaughter's *A New World Order*, which viewed networks rather than actual organizations as the key to problem-solving.[35] Dan Drezner, in a *Foreign Policy* blog, and Stewart Patrick, in *Foreign Affairs*, lauded the sum of alternative arrangements and dismissed the universal-membership UN as hopeless and hapless. Apparently, we can only aspire to a variegated institutional sprawl – or what they dubbed "good-enough global governance."[36]

The hopes for "international volunteerism,"[37] or what the UNDP's *Human Development Report 2013* called "coherent pluralism," discount the necessity for and possibilities of the universal United Nations. A diminished role for the world organization is based on two propositions. Networks and partnerships are either better able to solve twenty-first-century problems, or alternatively they are viewed as all that is possible in a politically divided world. Both propositions are wrong, even if fragmentation opens possibilities for action and partnerships.[38] The UN's wartime precedents, achievements, and visions suggest that today's world order is a second-best surrogate for robust multilateralism. In brief, good-enough global governance ain't good enough.[39]

In evaluating the credits and debits on the UN's balance sheet, we can take a maximalist or minimalist position. If we compare the record of achievement against the Charter's lofty goals, the record invariably disappoints. The UN has fallen far short of its lofty ideals, but it would be utterly wrong to underestimate the successes wrought by that same UN. If we acknowledge that its actions depend on state foreign policies, which reflect narrowly conceived national interests, and that the Second UN often is not up to the task after states hand over seemingly intractable problems, then derision has to be moderated. "SG" is an accepted abbreviation for the UN's head, but it also stands for "scapegoat," a prevalent function in world politics for both the secretary-general and his organization.

If global problems require global solutions, they also require strengthened intergovernmental organizations, chief among which are those that compose the UN system. Ironically, foreign ministries worldwide commonly lament that the demand for global governance increases daily while its supply dwindles; that the gap is growing between the need for global solutions and the waning ability of multilateral organizations to meet them.

Warts and all, the United Nations matters. As a crucial, albeit sometimes unacknowledged component of our fragile international system, the danger is that the UN could fade away and further erode the stability of even our tenuous world order. Donald Trump's short-sighted and lamentable early decisions are unsettling to be sure. While the vituperative words of the forty-fifth US president's inauguration still poison the air, it is worth repeating what John F. Kennedy said in his first State of the Union Address on January 11, 1962:

> Our instrument and our hope is the United Nations – and I see little merit in the impatience of those who would abandon this imperfect world instrument because they dislike our imperfect world. For the troubles of a world organization merely reflect the troubles of the world itself. And if the organization is weakened, these troubles can only increase. We may not always agree with every detailed action taken by every officer of the United Nations, or with every voting majority. But

188

as an institution, it should have in the future, as it has had in the past since its inception, no stronger or more faithful member than the United States of America.[40]

This book ends without knowing exactly how the disruption caused by the Trump administration will affect the United Nations. Trump himself has made clear that the pursuit of narrow national interests is the only trustworthy guide, no matter what the result for the liberal order, including the UN, which the United States has championed since 1945. In particular, he menaced massive cuts in payments – assessments (or dues) and voluntary contributions. The first major target was the UNFPA, for which in April the administration took steps to stop payments.

How his threats will play out exactly is impossible to gauge, and the payments come from the budgets of the State Department and other government entities. Various advocacy groups – for refugees or reproductive health, for instance – will campaign against such cuts, as will other parts of the government and Congress, where proposals will be considered by members who are not compelled to agree.

Nonetheless, the news certainly will not be good. In the context of growing nationalism and increasingly inward-looking stances vis-à-vis multilateral institutions, the contents of this book also suggest that Secretary-General Guterres could use financial stringency and even crisis to implement a long-overdue transformation in the world organization's management. Whether or not he is a fan of Chinese characters, he necessarily will have to discover the double meaning of a crisis as opportunity – to make the world organization leaner if not meaner. Possible cuts in UN funding, however egregious the rationale, could provide the impetus for a long-postponed and desperately needed change in how the world organization does business. In particular, Guterres will need to evaluate the UN's comparative advantages; and he will need to apply a scalpel to units that could be trimmed or eliminated rather than the typical bureaucratic meat cleaver to across-the-board reductions.

Numerous UN and NGO documents, as well as academic analyses, concur that transformation is desperately required. At the same time, even sympathetic critics get bogged down with the daunting task of overcoming an international political status quo that serves the interests of the powers that be along with the bureaucratic status quo of individual UN entities. If past is prelude, transformation in international organizations comes only after international tectonic shocks like world wars. That idea alone should serve as a wake-up

189

call. Surely there is a better way to move toward a more stable and just world order than waiting for a global catastrophe?

The driving motivation behind this book is that the states that compose the UN's membership and the human beings who work for it are capable of learning and not only spurning lessons. The way that the history of the UN is dispensed often leaves the false impression that what happened could not have happened in any other way. Very little in history is inevitable. What governments and intergovernmental organizations and people do and opt not to do can make and has made a difference.

Like any counterfactual, the question on this book's cover can have no unequivocal reply. But it is worth giving an honest answer to an honest question – "What if?"

No, the world would not be better without the United Nations.

Yes, the world could be better with a more creative and robust United Nations.

NOTES

ACKNOWLEDGEMENTS

1 Thomas G. Weiss, *Thinking about Global Governance: Why People and Ideas Matter* (London: Routledge, 2011), pp. xiii–xv.
2 Thomas G. Weiss, *What's Wrong with the United Nations and How to Fix It*, 3rd edn (2016); *Humanitarian Intervention: Ideas in Action*, 3rd edn (2016); and *Global Governance: Why? What? Whither?* (2013).
3 Thomas G. Weiss, David P. Forsythe, Roger A. Coate, and Kelly-Kate Pease, *The United Nations and Changing World Politics*, 8th edn (Boulder, CO: Westview Press, 2017).
4 Thomas G. Weiss and Sam Daws (eds), *The Oxford Handbook on the United Nations*, 2nd edn (Oxford: Oxford University Press, forthcoming 2018).
5 Thomas G. Weiss and Ramesh Thakur, *Global Governance and the UN: An Unfinished Journey* (Indianapolis: Indiana University Press, 2010); and Thomas G. Weiss and Rorden Wilkinson (eds), *International Organization and Global Governance*, 2nd edn (London: Routledge, 2018).
6 Louis Emmerij, Richard Jolly, and Thomas G. Weiss, *Ahead of the Curve? UN Ideas and Global Challenges* (Bloomington: Indiana University Press, 2001); Thomas G. Weiss, Tatiana Carayannis, Louis Emmerij, and Richard Jolly, *UN Voices: The Struggle for Development and Social Justice* (Bloomington: Indiana University Press, 2005); and Richard Jolly, Louis Emmerij, and Thomas G. Weiss, *UN Ideas That Changed the World* (Bloomington: Indiana University Press, 2009).
7 Dan Plesch and Thomas G. Weiss (eds), *Wartime Origins and the Future United Nations* (London: Routledge, 2015).
8 Stephen Browne and Thomas G. Weiss (eds), *Post-2015 UN Development: Making Change Happen?* (London: Routledge, 2014).
9 ICISS, *The Responsibility to Protect* (Ottawa: ICISS, 2001); and Thomas G. Weiss and Don Hubert, *The Responsibility to Protect: Research, Bibliography, and Background* (Ottawa: ICISS, 2001).
10 Peter J. Hoffman and Thomas G. Weiss, *Sword & Salve: Confronting New Wars and Humanitarian Crises* (Lanham, MD: Rowman & Littlefield, 2006);

and *Humanitarianism, War, and Politics: Solferino to Syria and Beyond* (Lanham, MD: Rowman & Littlefield, 2018).

11 Michael J. Barnett and Thomas G. Weiss (eds), *Humanitarianism in Question: Politics, Power, Ethics* (Ithaca, NY: Cornell University Press, 2008); and Michael J. Barnett and Thomas G. Weiss, *Humanitarianism Contested: Where Angels Fear to Tread* (London: Routledge, 2011).

INTRODUCTION

1 "Ban Ki-moon's Thankless Position," *New York Times*, June 11, 2016.
2 Kofi A. Annan, "What Is the International Community? Problems without Passports," *Foreign Policy*, no. 132 (September–October 2002): 30–1.
3 Kevin Rudd, "My 10 Principles to Reform the United Nations, before It's Too Late," *The Guardian*, August 8, 2016.
4 Richard Haass, *A World in Disarray: American Foreign Policy and the Crisis of the Old Order* (New York: Penguin, 2017).
5 Mark Malloch Brown, *The Unfinished Global Revolution* (New York: Penguin, 2011), p. 190.
6 Dag Hammarskjöld, *The International Civil Servant in Law and in Fact* (Oxford: Clarendon Press, 1961) [lecture given at Oxford University, May 30, 1961].
7 Quoted by Robert Cowley, "Introduction," in *What If? Eminent Historians Imagine What Might Have Been*, ed. Robert Cowley (New York: Putnam, 2001), p. xiii.
8 James D. Fearon, "Counterfactuals and Hypothesis Testing in Political Science," *World Politics* 43(2) (1991): 170.
9 Philip E. Tetlock and Aaron Belkin (eds), *Counterfactual Thought Experiments in World Politics: Logical, Methodological, and Psychological Perspectives* (Princeton, NJ: Princeton University Press, 1996), p. 6.
10 Brian Skyrms (ed.), *The Dynamics of Rational Deliberation* (Cambridge, MA: Harvard University Press, 1990).
11 Alan Weisman, *The World without Us* (New York: St Martin's Press, 2006).

CHAPTER 1 "THREE" UNITED NATIONS

1 Thomas G. Weiss, Tatiana Carayannis, and Richard Jolly, "The Third UN," *Global Governance* 14(1) (2009): 123–42.
2 Quoted by James Traub, *The Best Intentions: Kofi Annan and the UN in the Era of American World Power* (New York: Farrar, Straus & Giroux, 2006), p. 266.
3 Inis L. Claude, Jr, *Swords into Plowshares: The Problems and Prospects of International Organization* (New York: Random House, 1956).
4 Robert W. Cox and Harold K. Jacobson (eds), *The Anatomy of Influence: Decision Making in International Organization* (New Haven, CT: Yale University Press, 1973).
5 Michael Barnett and Martha Finnemore, "Political Approaches," in *The Oxford Handbook on the United Nations*, ed. Thomas G. Weiss and Sam Daws (Oxford: Oxford University Press, 2007), p. 42.

6 Thant Myint-U and Amy Scott, *The UN Secretariat: A Brief History (1945–2006)* (New York: International Peace Academy, 2007), pp. 126–8.
7 Roland Rich, *The Three UNs at Three Score Years and Ten*, Global Futures Occasional Paper 1 (Trenton, NJ: Rutgers University, 2016).
8 *Foreign Policy*, no. 132 (September–October 2002): 28–46.
9 Barry Carin et al., "Global Governance: Looking Ahead," *Global Governance* 12(1) (2006): 1–6; Geoffrey Wiseman, *"Polylateralism" and New Modes of Global Dialogue*, Discussion Paper no. 59 (Leicester: Leicester Diplomatic Studies Programme, 1999); and Philip G. Cerny, "Plurilateralism: Structural Differentiation and Functional Conflict in the Post-Cold War World Order," *Millennium: Journal of International Studies* 22(1) (1993): 27–51.
10 Thomas G. Weiss and Leon Gordenker (eds), *NGOs, the UN, and Global Governance* (Boulder, CO: Lynne Rienner, 1996); and Peter Willetts (ed.), *The "Conscience" of the World: The Influence of Non-Governmental Organisations in the UN System* (Washington, DC: Brookings Institution Press, 1996).

CHAPTER 2 FOUR UN AILMENTS

1 Readers interested in this chapter should consult the volume by Thomas G. Weiss, *What's Wrong with the United Nations and How to Fix It*, 3rd edn (Cambridge: Polity, 2016).
2 Jack Donnelly, "Sovereign Inequality and Hierarchy in Anarchy: American Power and International Society," in *American Foreign Policy in a Globalized World*, ed. David P. Forsythe, Patrice C. McMahon, and Andy Wedeman (New York: Routledge, 2006), pp. 81–104.
3 Stephen Krasner, *Sovereignty: Organized Hypocrisy* (Princeton, NJ: Princeton University Press, 1999), pp. 1–42.
4 Quoted by Kathleen Newland with Erin Patrick and Monette Zard, *No Refuge: The Challenge of Internal Displacement* (New York: Office for the Coordination of Humanitarian Assistance, 2003), p. 37.
5 Richard N. Haass, *The Opportunity: America's Moment to Alter History's Course* (New York: Public Affairs, 2005), p. 41.
6 Hedley Bull, *The Anarchical Society: A Study of Order in World Politics* (New York: Columbia University Press, 1977).
7 Barry Buzan, *From International to World Society* (Cambridge: Cambridge University Press, 2004); and Robert Jackson, *The Global Covenant: Human Conduct in a World of States* (Oxford: Oxford University Press, 2000).
8 David Hulme, *Should Rich Nations Help the Poor?* (Cambridge: Polity, 2016), p. 6.
9 Daniel Deudney, "The Great Descent: 'Global Governance' in Historical and Theoretical Perspective," in *Why Govern? Rethinking Demand and Progress in Global Governance*, ed. Amitav Acharya (Cambridge: Cambridge University Press, 2016), p. 31.
10 Conor Cruise O'Brien, *United Nations: Sacred Drama* (London: Hutchinson, 1968).
11 Georges Balandier and Alfred Sauvy, *Le "Tiers-monde": sous-développement et développement* (Paris: Presses Universitaires de France, 1961).

12 Jacqueline Ann Braveboy-Wagner, *Institutions of the Global South* (London: Routledge, 2008).
13 Richard Wright, *The Color Curtain* (Jackson, MS: Banner Books, 1956), pp. 13–14.
14 Mark T. Berger, "After the Third World? History, Destiny and the Fate of Third Worldism," *Third World Quarterly* 25(1) (2004): 13; the issue reviews the history. See also Carlos P. Romulo, *The Meaning of Bandung* (Chapel Hill: University of North Carolina Press, 1956); Peter Worsley, *The Third World* (London: Weidenfeld & Nicolson, 1964); Geir Lundestad, *East, West, North, South: Major Developments in International Politics since 1945* (New York: Oxford University Press, 1999); and Vijay Prashad, *The Poorer Nations: A Possible History of the Global South* (London: Verso Books, 2013).
15 Joseph S. Nye, "UNCTAD: Poor Nations' Pressure Group," in *The Anatomy of Influence: Decision Making in International Organization*, ed. Robert W. Cox and Harold K. Jacobson (New Haven, CT: Yale University Press, 1973), pp. 334–70.
16 Ian Taylor and Karen Smith, *United Nations Conference on Trade and Development (UNCTAD)* (London: Routledge, 2007); and John Toye and Richard Toye, *The UN and Global Political Economy: International Trade, Finance, and Development* (Bloomington: Indiana University Press, 2004).
17 Martha Finnemore and Kathryn Sikkink, "International Norm Dynamics and Political Change," *International Organization* 52(4) (1998): 887–917.
18 Harold K. Jacobson, *Networks of Interdependence: International Organizations and the Global Political System*, 2nd edn (New York: Knopf, 1984); and Christer Jönsson, "Interorganizational Theory and International Organization," *International Studies Quarterly* 30(1) (1986): 39–57.
19 Erskine Childers with Brian Urquhart, *Renewing the United Nations System* (Uppsala: Dag Hammarskjöld Foundation, 1994), p. 32.
20 Andrew Mack, "Conflicts and Security," in *Why Govern?* ed. Acharya, p. 117.
21 Dag Hammarskjöld Foundation, *Financing the United Nations Development System: Current Trends and New Directions* (New York and Stockholm: DHF, 2016).
22 *Budgetary and Financial Situation of the Organizations of the United Nations System, Note by the Secretary-General*, UN document A/71/583, 28 October 2016, table 3.
23 Quoted by Thomas G. Weiss, Tatiana Carayannis, Louis Emmerij, and Richard Jolly, *UN Voices: The Struggle for Development and Social Justice* (Bloomington: Indiana University Press, 2005), p. 205.
24 UN, *Delivering as One: The Report of the Secretary-General's High-Level Panel* (New York: UN, 2006).
25 Margaret Joan Anstee, "UN Reform: Top of the Agenda for the Next SG?" FUNDS Briefing 24, December 2014, p. 4; www.futureun.org/en/Publica tions-Surveys/Article?newsid=60.
26 Stephen Browne and Thomas G. Weiss, *Supporting the 2030 Agenda for Sustainable Development: Lessons from the MDG Fund* (New York: FUNDS, 2016).
27 Thomas G. Weiss, "United Nations – Before, During, and After 1945," *International Affairs* 90(6) (2015): 1221–35.

28 Anne-Marie Slaughter, "How to Succeed in the Networked World," *Foreign Affairs* 95(6) (2016): 85.

29 UN and Dag Hammarskjöld Foundation, *Financing the United Nations Development System: Current Trends and New Directions* (Stockholm: Dag Hammarskjöld Foundation, June 2016).

30 ECOSOC Independent Team of Advisors, "The Future We Want – the UN We Need," informal document dated June 16, 2016, for ECOSOC Dialogue Workshop no. 8, June 22–3, 2016, pp. 9–10.

31 Simon Chesterman (ed.), *Secretary or General? The UN Secretary-General in World Politics* (Cambridge: Cambridge University Press, 2007).

32 Egon Ranshofen-Wertheimer, *The International Secretariat: A Great Experiment in International Administration* (Washington, DC: Carnegie Endowment for International Peace, 1945); Thomas G. Weiss, *International Bureaucracy: An Analysis of the Operation of Functional and Global International Secretariats* (Lexington, MA: D. C. Heath, 1975); Leon Gordenker, *The UN Secretary-General and Secretariat*, 2nd edn (London: Routledge, 2009); and James O. C. Jonah, "Secretariat: Independence and Reform," in *The Oxford Handbook on the United Nations*, ed. Thomas G. Weiss and Sam Daws (Oxford: Oxford University Press, 2007), pp. 160–74.

33 Dag Hammarskjöld, *The International Civil Servant in Law and in Fact* (Oxford: Clarendon Press, 1961), p. 329 [lecture given at Oxford University, May 30, 1961].

34 Francesco Mezzalama, *Young Professionals in Selected Organizations of the United Nations System: Recruitment, Management and Retention* (Geneva: Joint Inspection Unit, 2000), quotations at pp. v–vi.

35 Michael Barnett and Martha Finnemore, *Rules for the World: International Organizations in Global Politics* (Ithaca, NY: Cornell University Press, 2004).

36 Mark Malloch Brown, "Can the UN Be Reformed?" *Global Governance* 14(1) (2008): 7–8.

CHAPTER 3 A MORE VIOLENT WORLD WITH DIMINISHED INTERNATIONAL PEACE AND SECURITY?

1 Max Harrelson, *Fires All around the Horizon: The UN's Uphill Battle to Preserve the Peace* (New York: Praeger, 1989), p. 89.

2 Boutros Boutros-Ghali, *An Agenda for Peace: Preventive Diplomacy, Peacemaking and Peace-Keeping* (New York: United Nations, 1992), para. 46.

3 Marrack Goulding, "The Changing Role of the United Nations in Conflict Resolution and Peace-Keeping," speech given at the Singapore Institute of Policy Studies, March 13, 1991, p. 9; see also "The Evolution of Peacekeeping," *International Affairs* 69(3) (1993): 451–64 and *Peacemonger* (London: John Murray, 2002).

4 John Mackinlay, *The Peacekeepers: An Assessment of Peacekeeping Operations at the Arab–Israel Interface* (London: Unwin Hyman, 1989); William J. Durch (ed.), *The Evolution of UN Peacekeeping* (New York: St Martin's Press, 1993); Paul F. Diehl and Alexandru Balas, *Peace Operations*, 2nd edn (Cambridge: Polity, 2014); and Adekeye Adebajo, *UN Peacekeeping*

in Africa: From the Suez Crisis to the Sudan Conflicts (Boulder, CO: Lynne Rienner, 2011).

5 Richard Gowan, "For U.N. and Europe, a Peacekeeping Crisis in Lebanon," *World Politics Review* (March 25, 2013): 1.

6 Brian Urquhart, "Beyond the 'Sheriff's Posse,'" *Survival* 32(3) (1990): 198; and *A Life in Peace and War* (New York: Harper & Row, 1987).

7 S. Neil MacFarlane, *Superpower Rivalry and Third World Radicalism* (Baltimore: Johns Hopkins University Press, 1985); Elizabeth Valkenier, *The Soviet Union and the Third World* (New York: Praeger, 1985); and Jerry Hough, *The Struggle for the Third World* (Washington, DC: Brookings Institution Press, 1986).

8 Steven Pinker, *The Better Angels of Our Nature: Why Violence Has Declined* (New York: Viking, 2011); and Joshua S. Goldstein, *Winning the War on War: The Decline of Armed Conflict Worldwide* (New York: Dutton, 2011).

9 Human Security Report Project, *Human Security Report 2009–2010: The Causes of Peace and the Shrinking Costs of War* (New York: Oxford University Press, 2011).

10 Avalon Project, "The Cuban Missile Crisis: Editorial Note," http://avalon. law.yale.edu/20th_century/msc_cuba263.asp.

11 Bertrand G. Ramcharan, *Preventive Diplomacy at the UN* (Bloomington: Indiana University Press, 2008).

12 Francis O. Wilcox, "Regionalism and the United Nations," *International Organization* 19(3) (1965): 789–811; and Tom J. Farer, "The Role of Regional Collective Security Arrangements," in *Collective Security in a Changing World*, ed. Thomas G. Weiss (Boulder, CO: Lynne Rienner, 1993), pp. 153–89.

13 William T. Tow, *Subregional Security Cooperation in the Third World* (Boulder, CO: Lynne Rienner, 1990).

14 S. Neil MacFarlane and Thomas G. Weiss, "Regional Organizations and Regional Security," *Security Studies* 2(1) (1992): 6–37; and Alexander Orakhelashvili, *Collective Security* (Oxford: Oxford University Press, 2011).

15 Mohammed Ayoob, *The Third World Security Predicament: State Making, Regional Conflict, and the International System* (Boulder, CO: Lynne Rienner, 1995); and Brian Job (ed.), *The Insecurity Dilemma: National Security of Third World States* (Boulder, CO: Lynne Rienner, 1992).

16 Jarat Chopra and Thomas G. Weiss, "Prospects for Containing Conflict in the Former Second World," *Security Studies* 4(3) (1995): 552–83; Lena Jonson and Clive Archer (eds), *Peacekeeping and the Role of Russia in Eurasia* (Boulder, CO: Westview Press, 1996); and Alan K. Henrikson, "The Growth of Regional Organizations and the Role of the United Nations," in *Regionalism in World Politics: Regional Organizations and World Order*, ed. Louise Fawcett and Andrew Hurrell (Oxford: Oxford University Press, 1995), pp. 122–68.

17 Thomas J. Bassett and Scott Straus, "Defending Democracy in Côte d'Ivoire," *Foreign Affairs* 90(4) (2011): 130–40.

18 Nina Tannenwald, "The UN and Debates Over Weapons of Mass Destruction," in *The United Nations and Global Security*, ed. Richard M. Price and Mark W. Zacher (New York: Palgrave Macmillan, 2004), pp. 3–20.

19 Jane Boulden, Ramesh Thakur, and Thomas G. Weiss (eds), *The United Nations and Nuclear Orders* (Tokyo: UN University Press, 2009).
20 John G. Ruggie, *Winning the Peace: America and World Order in the New Era* (New York: Columbia University Press, 1996), and *Constructing the World Polity: Essays on International Institutionalization* (New York: Routledge, 1998); and G. John Ikenberry, *After Victory: Institutions, Strategic Restraint, and the Rebuilding of Order after Major Wars* (Princeton, NJ: Princeton University Press, 2001), and *Liberal Order and Imperial Ambition: American Power and International Order* (Cambridge: Polity, 2006).
21 John G. Ruggie, "Doctrinal Unilateralism and its Limits: America and Global Governance in the New Century," in *American Foreign Policy in a Globalized World*, ed. David P. Forsythe, Patrice C. MacMahon, and Andrew Wedeman (New York: Routledge, 2006), pp. 31–50.
22 Rosemary Foot, S. Neil MacFarlane, and Michael Mastanduno (eds), *U.S. Hegemony and International Organizations: The United States and Multilateral Institutions* (Oxford: Oxford University Press, 2003).
23 *Comprehensive Report of the Special Advisor to the DCI on Iraq's WMD, with Addendums (Duelfer Report)*, 3 vols, www.gpo.gov/fdsys/pkg/GPO-DUELFERREPORT/content-detail.html.
24 Kelly-Kate Pease, *International Organizations: Perspective on Governance in the Twenty-First Century*, 5th edn (New York: Longman, 2012), pp. 144–6.
25 Maria Rost-Rublee, "Taking Stock of the Nuclear Proliferation Regime: Using Social Psychology to Understand Regime Change," *International Studies Review* 10(3) (2008): 421.
26 N. Jansen Calamita, "Sanctions, Countermeasures and the Iranian Nuclear Issue," *Vanderbilt Journal of Transnational Law* 42 (November 2009): 1393–442.
27 The IAEA stated that it "has no credible indications of activities in Iran relevant to the development of a nuclear explosive device after 2009" and found "no credible indications of the diversion of nuclear material in connection with the possible military dimensions to Iran's nuclear programme." See *Final Assessment on Past and Present Outstanding Issues regarding Iran's Nuclear Programme*, IAEA document GOV/2015/68, December 2, 2015, p. 15.
28 "Don't Let Iran's Progress on the Nuclear Deal Go to Waste," *New York Times*, July 5, 2016.
29 Quoted by David E. Sanger, "A Year Later, a Mixed Record for the Iran Accord," *New York Times*, July 14, 2016.
30 "Central America – ONUCA: Background," www.un.org/en/peacekeeping/missions/past/onucabackgr.html.
31 Karim Makdisi and Coralie Pisan Hindawi, *Creative Diplomacy amidst a Brutal Conflict: Analyzing the OPCW–UN Joint Mission for the Elimination of the Syrian Chemical Weapons Program* (Beirut, Lebanon: American University in Beirut, 2016).
32 Stephen Browne and Thomas G. Weiss (eds), *Peacebuilding Challenges for the UN Development System* (New York: FUNDS, 2015).
33 Kofi A. Annan, "Secretary-General's Speech to the 54th Session of the General Assembly," September 20, 1999.
34 Adam Roberts, "NATO's 'Humanitarian War' in Kosovo," *Survival* 41(3) (1999): 102–23.

35 Human Rights Watch, "Kosovo: Failure of NATO, U.N. to Protect Minorities," July 27, 2004, www.hrw.org/english/docs/2004/07/27/serbia 9136.htm.
36 Matthew Brunwasser, "Kosovo and Serbia Reach Key Deal," *New York Times*, February 24, 2012.

CHAPTER 4 A MORE REPRESSIVE AND UNKIND WORLD WITH DIMINISHED HUMAN RIGHTS AND HUMANITARIAN ACTION?

1 Roger Normand and Sarah Zaidi, *Human Rights at the UN: The Political History of Universal Justice* (Bloomington: Indiana University Press, 2008).
2 David A. Kay, *The New Nations in the United Nations 1960–1967* (New York: Columbia University Press, 1970). For the changing conversation about imperialism in the League of Nations, see Susan Pedersen, *The Guardians: The League of Nations and the Crisis of Empire* (Oxford: Oxford University Press, 2015); and Steven L.B. Jensen, *The Making of International Human Rights* (Cambridge: Cambridge University Press, 2016).
3 Quoted by Thomas G. Weiss, Tatiana Carayannis, Louis Emmerij, and Richard Jolly, *UN Voices: The Struggle for Development and Social Justice* (Bloomington: Indiana University Press, 2005), p. 171.
4 Robert Aldrich and John Connell, *The Last Colonies* (Cambridge: Cambridge University Press, 1998).
5 Julius Nyerere, "Foreword," in Chakravarti Raghavan, *Recolonization: GATT, the Uruguay Round & the Third World* (London: Zed Books, 1990), p. 19.
6 Paul Kennedy, *The Parliament of Man: The Past, Present, and Future of the United Nations* (New York: Random House, 2006).
7 Bertrand G. Ramcharan, "Norms and Machinery," in *The Oxford Handbook on the United Nations*, ed. Thomas G. Weiss and Sam Daws (Oxford: Oxford University Press, 2007), p. 441.
8 Johannes Morsink, *The Universal Declaration of Human Rights: Origins, Drafting and Intent* (Philadelphia: University of Pennsylvania Press, 1999); and Mary Ann Glendon, *A World Made New: Eleanor Roosevelt and the Universal Declaration of Human Rights* (New York: Random House, 2001).
9 Normand and Zaidi, *Human Rights at the UN*, pp. 8 and xiii.
10 Ibid., p. 2.
11 Bertrand G. Ramcharan, *Contemporary Human Rights Ideas* (London: Routledge, 2008); Julie Mertus, *The United Nations and Human Rights*, 2nd edn (London: Routledge, 2009); and Philip Alston and Frederic Megret (eds), *The United Nations and Human Rights: A Critical Appraisal*, 2nd edn (Oxford: Oxford University Press, 2005).
12 Quoted by Normand and Zaidi, *Human Rights and the UN*, pp. 83 and 88.
13 Quoted by William Korey, *NGOs and the Universal Declaration of Human Rights: "A Curious Grapevine"* (New York: St Martin's Press, 1998), p. 9.
14 Johannes Morsink, *The Universal Declaration of Human Rights: Origins, Drafting and Intent* (Philadelphia: University of Pennsylvania Press, 1999).
15 *World Conference on Human Rights: The Vienna Declaration and Programme of Action* (New York: UN, 1993).
16 Bertrand G. Ramcharan, *The UN High Commissioner for Human Rights:*

The Challenges of International Protection (Leiden, Netherlands: Martinus Nijhoff, 2002); and Bertrand G. Ramcharan (ed.), *Human Rights Protection in the Field* (Leiden, Netherlands: Martinus Nijhoff, 2006).

17 "Displacement Studies and the Role of Universities," lecture by Francis Deng to a Conference of the German Academic Exchange Service, University of Kassel, Germany, June 2002.
18 ICISS, *The Responsibility to Protect* (Ottawa: ICISS, 2001); and Thomas G. Weiss and Don Hubert, *The Responsibility to Protect: Research, Bibliography, and Background* (Ottawa: ICISS, 2001).
19 Thomas G. Weiss, *Military–Civilian Interactions: Humanitarian Crises and the Responsibility to Protect*, 2nd edn (Lanham, MD: Rowman & Littlefield, 2005).
20 Contrary interpretations are Rajan Menon, *The Conceit of Humanitarian Intervention* (Oxford: Oxford University Press, 2016); and Graham Harrison, "Onwards and Sidewards? The Curious Case of the Responsibility to Protect and Mass Violence in Africa," *Journal of Intervention and Statebuilding* 10(2) (2016): 143–61.
21 Kofi A. Annan, *The Question of Intervention: Statements by the Secretary-General* (New York: UN, 1999), p. 7.
22 Frances M. Deng et al., *Sovereignty as Responsibility: Conflict Management in Africa* (Washington, DC: Brookings Institution Press, 1996); and Kofi Annan, *The Question of Intervention* and *"We the Peoples": The United Nations in the 21st Century* (New York: UN, 2000).
23 UN, *2005 World Summit Outcome*, General Assembly resolution A/Res/60/1, October 24, 2006, paras. 138–9.
24 Interpretations by commissioners are Gareth Evans, *The Responsibility to Protect: Ending Mass Atrocity Crimes Once and For All* (Washington, DC: Brookings Institution Press, 2008); and Ramesh Thakur, *The United Nations, Peace and Security: From Collective Security to the Responsibility to Protect*, 2nd edn (Cambridge: Cambridge University Press, 2017). See also Alex J. Bellamy, *Responsibility to Protect: The Global Effort to End Mass Atrocities* (Cambridge: Polity, 2009); Anne Orford, *International Authority and the Responsibility to Protect* (Cambridge: Cambridge University Press, 2011); Aidan Hehir, *The Responsibility to Protect: Rhetoric, Reality and the Future of Humanitarian Intervention* (Basingstoke: Palgrave Macmillan, 2012); and Thomas G. Weiss, *Humanitarian Intervention: Ideas in Action*, 3rd edn (Cambridge: Polity, 2016).
25 Anthony Lewis, "The Challenge of Global Justice Now," *Daedalus* 132(1) (2003): 8.
26 Mohammed Ayoob, "Humanitarian Intervention and International Society," *International Journal of Human Rights* 6(1) (2002): 84.
27 Thomas G. Weiss and Barbara Crossette, "The United Nations: Post-Summit Outlook," in *Great Decisions 2006* (New York: Foreign Policy Association, 2006), pp. 9–20.
28 José E. Alvarez, *International Organizations as Law-Makers* (Oxford: Oxford University Press, 2005), p. 591.
29 Alexander J. Bellamy, "What Will Become of the Responsibility to Protect?" *Ethics & International Affairs* 20(2) (2006): 143–69.
30 Summaries from the Global Centre for the Responsibility to Protect, www.globalr2p.org/resources/897.

31 Rama Mani and Thomas G. Weiss (eds), *The Responsibility to Protect: Cultural Perspectives in the Global South* (London: Routledge, 2011).
32 Gareth Evans, "The Limits of Sovereignty: The Case of Mass Atrocity Crimes," *Prism* 5(3) (2015): 3.
33 Thomas G. Weiss, "RtoP Alive and Well After Libya," *Ethics & International Affairs* 25(3) (2011): 287–92.
34 "Letter Dated 9 November 2011 from the Permanent Representative of Brazil to the United Nations Addressed to the Secretary-General," UN document A/66/551-S/2011/701, p. 1.
35 Laura Landolt, "Externalizing Human Rights: From Commission to Council, the Universal Periodic Review and Egypt," *Human Rights Review* 14(2) (2013): 107–29.
36 Bertrand G. Ramcharan, *The Human Rights Council* (London: Routledge, 2011), p. 64.
37 *Interim Report of the Commission of Experts Established Pursuant to Security Council Resolution 780*, UN doc. S/25274, 10 February 1993, para. 72.
38 *Report of the Secretary-General Pursuant to Paragraph 2 of Security Council Resolution 808 (1993)*, UN document S/25704, May 3, 1993. Statute of the International Criminal Tribunal for the Prosecution of Persons Responsible for Serious Violations of International Humanitarian Law Committed in the Former Yugoslavia Since 1991, annex to UN doc. S/25704, 36–48.
39 UN document S/PRST/1994/21, April 30, 1994.
40 UN document S/1994/546, May 6, 1994. The response is *The Report of the Secretary-General on the Situation in Rwanda*, UN document S/1994/565, May 13, 1994.
41 *Report of the Commission on Human Rights on its Third Special Session*, UN document E/1994/24/Add.2, May 25, 1994.
42 *Preliminary Report of the Independent Commission of Experts Established in Accordance with S.C. Res. 935*, UN document S/1994/1125, October 4, 1994.
43 Fanny Benedetti and John L. Washburn, "Drafting the International Criminal Court Treaty," *Global Governance* 5(1) (1999): 1–38.
44 Teresa Whitfield, *Friends Indeed? The United Nations, Groups of Friends, and the Resolution of Conflict* (Washington, DC: US Institute of Peace Press, 2007), pp. 9 and 2.
45 Program in Law and Public Affairs, *The Princeton Principles on Universal Jurisdiction* (Princeton, NJ: Princeton University Press, 2001); Council on Foreign Relations, *Toward an International Criminal Court?* (New York: Council on Foreign Relations, 1999); and Steven R. Ratner and James L. Bischoff (eds), *International War Crimes Trials: Making a Difference?* (Austin: University of Texas Law School, 2004).
46 David Bosco, *Rough Justice: The International Criminal Court in a World of Power Politics* (Oxford: Oxford University Press, 2014).
47 Benjamin Ferencz, "Misguided Fears about the International Criminal Court," *Pace International Law Review* 15 (Spring 2003): 223–46.
48 US Department of State, "US Signs 100th Article 98 Agreement," press statement 2005/463 by Richard Boucher, Spokesman, Washington, DC, May 3, 2005; https://2001-2009.state.gov/r/pa/prs/ps/2005/45573.htm.
49 Barack Obama, *National Security Strategy* (Washington, DC: White House, 2010), http://nssarchive.us/national-security-strategy-2010/.

50 William Schabas, *The International Criminal Court: A Commentary on the Rome Statute* (New York: Oxford University Press, 2010).

51 Yuval Shany, "Assessing the Effectiveness of International Courts: A Goal-Based Approach," *American Journal of International Law* 106(2) (2012): 225–70.

52 David Rieff, *In Praise of Forgetting: Historical Memory and its Ironies* (New Haven, CT: Yale University Press, 2016).

53 Martin J. Burke and Thomas G. Weiss, "The Security Council and Ad Hoc Tribunals: Law and Politics, Peace and Justice," in *The Security Council as Global Legislator*, ed. Vesselin Popovksi and Trudy Fraser (London: Routledge, 2014), pp. 241–65.

54 *Global Humanitarian Assistance Report 2014* (Bristol: Development Initiatives, 2014), pp. 4–5; www.globalhumanitarianassistance.org/wp-content/uploads/2014/09/GHA-Report-2014-interactive.pdf.

55 High-Level Panel on Humanitarian Financing, *Too Important to Fail—Addressing the Humanitarian Financing Gap* (New York: UN, 2016); www.regeringen.se/contentassets/7c58cbe54ef9435db005aca302e8cd25/high-level-panel-on-humanitarian-financing-report-to-the-secretary-general.

56 Drawn from a 2003 OCHA roster, which is no longer updated.

57 Linda Polman, *The Crisis Caravan: What's Wrong with Humanitarian Aid?* (New York: Henry Holt, 2010), p. 10.

58 John Arquilla and David Ronfeldt, *Swarming and the Future of Conflict* (Washington, DC: Rand Corporation, 2000).

59 Rachel McCleary, *Global Compassion: Private Voluntary Organizations and U.S. Foreign Policy since 1939* (Oxford: Oxford University Press, 2009), p. 16.

60 Abby Stoddard, Adele Harmer, and Katherine Haver, *Providing Aid in Insecure Environments: Trends in Policy and Operations*, HPG Report 23 (London: Overseas Development Institute, 2006).

61 Peter Walker and Catherine Ross, *Professionalizing the Humanitarian Sector: A Scoping Study*, Report Commissioned by the Enhancing Learning and Research for Humanitarian Assistance, April 2010, pp. 11–12.

62 Benedict Anderson, *Imagined Communities* (London: Verso, 1983).

63 Michael Klein, *The Market for Aid* (Washington, DC: World Bank, 2005).

64 Martin Luther King, Jr., "Our God Is Marching On!," March 25, 1965; https://kinginstitute.stanford.edu/our-god-marching.

CHAPTER 5 A MORE IMPOVERISHED AND POLLUTED WORLD WITH
DIMINISHED DEVELOPMENT?

1 Thomas G. Weiss and Anthony Jennings, *More for the Least? Prospects for Poorest Countries in the Eighties* (Lexington, MA: D. C. Heath, 1983).

2 Michael Ward, *Quantifying the World: UN Ideas and Statistics* (Bloomington: Indiana University Press, 2004), p. 4.

3 Ibid.

4 UNSO, *A System of National Accounts and Supporting Tables* (New York: UN, 1953).

5 Ward, *Quantifying the World*, p. 49. See also Devaki Jain, *Women,*

Development, and the UN: A Sixty-Year Quest for Equality and Justice (Bloomington: Indiana University Press, 2005).

6 D. V. McGranahan et al., *Contents and Measurement of Socio-Economic Development* (New York: Praeger, 1972).

7 UN, *United Nations Development Decade: Proposals for Action* (New York: UN, 1962), p. 5.

8 ILO, *Employment, Growth and Basic Needs: A One-World Problem* (Geneva: ILO, 1976).

9 UNDP, *Human Development Report 1990* (Oxford: Oxford University Press, 1990), p. 1.

10 Amartya Sen, *Poverty and Famines: An Essay on Entitlement and Deprivation* (Oxford: Oxford University Press, 1982); *Inequality Re-examined* (Oxford: Oxford University Press, 1992); and *Development as Freedom* (New York: Knopf, 1999).

11 Quoted by Sakiko Fukuda-Parr and A. K. Shiva Kumar, *Readings in Human Development* (Oxford: Oxford University Press, 2003), p. vii.

12 UNDP, *Human Development Report 1999* (New York: Oxford University Press, 1999), p. 23.

13 Paul Streeten, "Human Development: Means and Ends," *American Economic Review* 84(2) (1994): 236.

14 UNDP, *Human Development Report 1990*, p. 1.

15 Frank Fenner et al., *Smallpox and its Eradication* (Geneva: WHO, 1988).

16 WHO, "SARS – How WHO's Western Pacific Regional Office Responded to the Threat of a Global Health Crisis," January 4, 2005.

17 WHO, "Frequently Asked Questions on Human Infection Caused by the Avian Influenza A (H7N9) Virus," February 14, 2014, www.who.int/influenza/human_animal_interface/faq_H7N9/en/.

18 Scott Barrett, *Why Cooperate? The Incentive to Supply Global Public Goods* (Oxford: Oxford University Press, 2007), p. 3.

19 Stephen Browne and Thomas G. Weiss, "The UN's Post-2015 Development Agenda – New Goals, New Leadership," in *Great Decisions 2016* (New York: Foreign Policy Association, 2016), pp. 63–74.

20 Richard Jolly, Louis Emmerij, Dharam Ghai, and Frederic Lapeyre, *UN Contributions to Development Thinking and Practice* (Bloomington: Indiana University Press, 2004), pp. 247–75; Stephen Browne, *Sustainable Development Goals and UN Goal-Setting* (London: Routledge, 2017); and Sakiko Fukuda-Parr, *Millennium Development Goals: Ideas, Interests and Influence* (London: Routledge, 2017).

21 UN, *The Millennium Development Goals Report 2015* (New York: UN, 2015); www.un.org/millenniumgoals/2015_MDG_Report/pdf/MDG%20 2015%20rev%20(July%201).pdf.

22 Mahbub ul Haq, Richard Jolly, and Paul Streeten (eds), *The UN and the Bretton Woods Institutions: New Challenges for the Twenty-First Century* (Basingstoke: Macmillan, 1995).

23 UN, *2005 World Summit Outcome*, UN General Assembly resolution 60/1, October 24, 2006. See Millennium Project, *Investing in Development: A Practical Plan to Achieve the Millennium Development Goals*, ed. Jeffrey D. Sachs (New York: UNDP, 2005); and Jeffrey Sachs, *The End of Poverty: Economic Possibilities for Our Time* (New York: Penguin, 2005).

24 Four documents were published between September 2013 and November 2014 in preparation for COP21, including *Climate Change 2014: Synthesis Report* (Geneva: IPCC, 2014), available at www.ipcc.ch.

25 "IPCC Agrees Special Reports, AR6 Workplan," Press Release, April 14, 2016, https://www.ipcc.ch/news_and_events/pdf/press/160414_pr_p43.pdf.

26 Nigel Lawson, *An Appeal to Reason: A Cool Look at Global Warming* (London: Duckworth Overlook, 2008).

27 Stephen J. Macekura, *Of Limits and Growth: The Rise of Global Sustainable Development in the Twentieth Century* (Cambridge: Cambridge University Press, 2015).

28 UN, "Adoption of the Paris Agreement," UN document FCCC/CP/2015/L.9/ Rev. 1, December 12, 2015; http://unfccc.int/resource/docs/2015/cop21/eng/ l09r01.pdf.

29 Quoted by Laurie Goering, "Paris Deal 'Departing Station' for Climate Action – UN's Figueres," Thomson Reuters Foundation, October 27, 2015, www.trust.org/item/20151027110443-bd1lm/?source=jtDontmiss.

30 Robert O. Keohane, "International Institutions: Can Interdependence Work?" *Foreign Policy* (Spring 1998): 82–96.

PART III THE WORLD WITH A MORE CREATIVE AND EFFECTIVE UN

1 *Functioning of the Office of the President of the General Assembly Observations and recommendations of the Secretary-General's Task Force,* UN document A/70/783, March 23, 2016, www.un.org/ga/search/view_doc. asp?symbol=A/70/783.

2 Anthony Banbury, "I Love the U.N., But It Is Failing," *New York Times,* March 18, 2016.

3 Human Rights Advisory Panel, N.M. and Others v. UNMIK: Case No. 26/08, Opinion of 26 February 2016; www.unmikonline.org/hrap/Eng/Cases%20 Eng/26-08%20NM%20etal%20Opinion%20FINAL%2026feb16.pdf.

4 Transparency International, *Corruption & Peace Operations: Risks and Recommendations for Troop Contributing Countries and the United Nations,* Defence & Security, March/April 2016; http://ti-defence.org/wp-content/uploads/2016/04/160330CorruptionRiskTCCsTIIDSPFIN.pdf.

5 UN, *Final Report of the Independent Panel of Experts on the Cholera Outbreak in Haiti,* May 4, 2011, p. 4; www.ijdh.org/2011/05/topics/health/ final-report-of-the-independent-panel-of-experts-on-the-cholera-outbreak-in -haiti-u-n-independent-panel/.

CHAPTER 6 A LESS VIOLENT WORLD WITH ENHANCED INTERNATIONAL PEACE AND SECURITY?

1 Devesh Kapur, John P. Lewis, and Richard Webb, *The World Bank: Its First Half Century* (Washington, DC: Brookings Institution Press, 1997), vol. 1: *History*, p. 533.

2 UN, *The United Nations Development Decade: Proposals for Action* (New York: UN, 1962), pp. 12–13, 24–5.

3 "Net ODA," https://data.oecd.org/oda/net-oda.htm.

4 Quoted by Richard MacGraham et al., *Disarmament and World Development* (Oxford: Pergamon Press, 1986), p. 235.
5 Joseph E. Stiglitz, *The Roaring Nineties* (New York: W. W. Norton, 2003).
6 Sam Perlo-Freeman, Aude Fleurant, Pieter Wezeman, and Siemon Wezeman, "SIPRI Fact Sheet: Trends in World Military Expenditure, 2015," Stockholm International Peace Research Institute, April 2016, p. 2.
7 UNDP, *Human Development Report 1994: New Dimensions of Human Security* (New York: Oxford University Press, 1994), pp. 22–4.
8 Mary Kaldor, *New and Old Wars: Organized Violence in a Global Era*, 3rd edn (Cambridge: Polity, 2012). See also Mats Berdal and David M. Malone (eds), *Greed and Grievance: Economic Agendas in Civil Wars* (Boulder, CO: Lynne Rienner, 2000).
9 S. Neil MacFarlane and Yuen Foong Khong, *Human Security and the UN: A Critical History* (Bloomington: Indiana University Press, 2006).
10 Adam Roberts and Richard Guelff (eds), *Documents and Laws of War*, 3rd edn (Oxford: Oxford University Press, 2000); and Michael Byers, *Law War: Understanding International Law and Armed Conflict* (New York: Grove Press, 2005).
11 Department of Foreign Affairs and International Trade, *Human Security: Safety for People in a Changing World* (Ottawa: Government of Canada, 1999).
12 *Report of the Secretary General to the Security Council on the Protection of Civilians in Armed Conflict*, UN document S/1999/957, September 8, 1999.
13 Quoted by Thomas G. Weiss, Tatiana Carayannis, Louis Emmerij, and Richard Jolly, *UN Voices: The Struggle for Development and Social Justice* (Bloomington: Indiana University Press, 2005), p. 302.
14 *Prevention of Armed Conflict: Report of the Secretary General*, UN document A/55/985-S/2001/574, June 7, 2001.
15 Commission on Human Security, *Human Security Now* (New York: UN, 2003).
16 Secretary General's High-Level Panel on Threats, Challenges and Change, *A More Secure World: A Shared Responsibility* (New York: UN, 2004).
17 Independent Commission on International Development Issues, *North–South: A Programme for Survival* (London: Pan Books, 1980).
18 Andrew Mack, "Human Security in the New Millennium," *Work in Progress: A Review of Research of the United Nations University* 16 (2002): 4.
19 UNDP, *Human Development Report 1994*, p. 59.
20 Bruno Simma (ed.), *The Charter of the United Nations: A Commentary*, 2nd edn (Oxford: Oxford University Press, 2002).
21 F. H. Hinsley, *Power and the Pursuit of Peace* (Cambridge: Cambridge University Press, 1963); S. J. Hemleben, *Plans for World Peace through Six Centuries* (Chicago: University of Chicago Press, 1943); and F. P. Walters, *A History of the League of Nations*, 2 vols (London: Oxford University Press, 1952).
22 Robert Riggs and Jack Plano, *The United Nations: International Organization and World Politics*, 2nd edn (Belmont, CA: Wadsworth, 1994), p. 100.
23 Jane Boulden, Ramesh Thakur, and Thomas G. Weiss (eds), *The United Nations and Nuclear Orders* (Tokyo: UN University Press, 2009).
24 Justin Gruenberg, "An Analysis of the United Nations Security Council Resolutions: Are All Countries Treated Equally?" *Case Western Reserve Journal of International Law* 41 (2009): 469–511.

25 Michael G. Smith, "Review of the UN High Level Independent Panel on Peace Operations, *Uniting Our Strengths for Peace: Politics, Partnership and People*," *Global Governance* 22(2) (2016): 179.

26 Michael Lipson, "Peacekeeping: Organized Hypocrisy?" *European Journal of International Relations* 13(1) (2007): 5–34.

27 Boutros Boutros-Ghali, *An Agenda for Peace* (New York: UN, 1992) and *Supplement to "An Agenda for Peace"* (New York: UN, 1995).

28 Panel on United Nations Peace Operations, *Report of the Panel on United Nations Peace Operations*, UN document A/55305-S/2000/809, August 21, 2000.

29 High-Level Panel on Threats, Challenges and Change, *A More Secure World: Our Shared Responsibility* (New York: UN, 2004).

30 Alain Le Roy and Susana Malcorra, *A New Partnership Agenda: Charting a New Horizon for UN Peacekeeping*, UNDPKO-DFS (New York: UN, 2009); see also UN, *Report of the Special Committee on Peacekeeping Operations and its Working Group* (New York: UN, 2009); and Ban Ki-moon, *Implementation of the Recommendations of the Special Committee on Peacekeeping Operations*, UN document A/64/573, December 22, 2009.

31 UN, *Uniting Our Strengths for Peace: Politics, Partnership and People* (New York: UN, 2015).

32 "General Assembly Authorizes $8.3 billion for 15 Peacekeeping Operations in 2015/16 as It Adopts 25 Resolutions, 1 Decision in Reports of Fifth Committee," UN document A/11657, June 25, 2015.

33 Alexandra Novosseloff, *The UN Military Staff Committee: Recreating a Missing Capacity* (London: Routledge, forthcoming).

34 Trygve Lie, *Memorandum of Points for Consideration in the Development of a Twenty-Year Programme for Achieving Peace through the United Nations*, UN document A/1304, 1950.

35 Patrick McCarthy, "Building a Reliable Rapid-Reaction Capability for the United Nations," *International Peacekeeping* 7(2) (2000): 139–54.

36 Stephanie Nebehay, "UN Plans Rapid Reaction Aid Force," *Reuters*, March 18, 2005; www.globalpolicy.org/security/pcacckpg/reform/2005/0318announce. htm.

37 Robert C. Johansen (ed.), *A United Nations Emergency Peace Service to Prevent Genocide and Crimes against Humanity* (New York: World Federalist Movement, 2006).

38 "United Nations Emergency Peace Service," Global Action to Prevent War, May 2009, www.globalactionpw.org/wp/wp-content/uploads/uneps-broch ure-may-09-final.pdf.

39 International Consultative Group chaired by Brian Urquhart and John C. Polanyi, *Towards a Rapid Reaction Capability for the UN* (Ottawa: Government of Canada, 1995), p. 62.

40 Annie Herro, Wendy Lambourne and David Penklis, "Peacekeeping and Peace Enforcement in Africa: The Potential Contribution of a UN Emergency Peace Service," *African Security Review* 18(1) (2009): 58–9.

41 Ban Ki-moon, *Implementing the Responsibility to Protect, Report of the Secretary-General*, UN document A/63/677, January 12, 2009, para. 64.

42 UN, *Report of the High-Level Independent Panel on United Nations Peace Operations*, UN document A/70/95-S/2015/446, June 17, 2015, para. 199.

43 Samantha Power, *"A Problem from Hell": America and the Age of Genocide*

(New York: Harper Perennial, 2003); and Michael Barnett, *Eyewitness to Genocide: The United Nations and Rwanda* (Ithaca, NY: Cornell University Press, 2003).

44 Roméo Dallaire, *Shake Hands with the Devil: The Failure of Humanity in Rwanda* (New York: Carroll & Graf, 2004).

45 Alan J. Kuperman, *The Limits of Humanitarian Intervention: Genocide in Rwanda* (Washington, DC: Brookings Institution Press, 2001).

46 Thomas G. Weiss, "Humanitarian Intervention and US Policy," in *Great Decisions 2012* (New York: Foreign Policy Association, 2012), pp. 59–70.

47 Graciana del Castillo, *Rebuilding War-Torn States: The Challenge of Post-Conflict Economic Reconstruction* (Oxford: Oxford University Press, 2008), and *Obstacles to Peacebuilding* (London: Routledge, 2017).

48 Quoted by Mimi Hall, "Obama Cites U.S. 'Responsibility' in Libya Intervention," *USA Today*, March 28, 2011.

49 Helene Cooper and Steven Lee Myles, "Obama Takes Hardline with Libya after Shift by Clinton," *New York Times*, March 18, 2011.

50 Jean-Baptiste Jeangène Vilmer, "Ten Myths about the 2011 Intervention in Libya," *Washington Quarterly* 39(2) (2016): 23–43.

51 OCHA, "2017 Libya Humanitarian Needs Overview – November 2016," http://reliefweb.int/report/libya/2017-libya-humanitarian-needs-overview-november-2016.

52 Roland Paris, *At War's End: Building Peace after Civil Conflict* (Cambridge: Cambridge University Press, 2013).

53 Rob Jenkins, *Peacebuilding: From Concept to Commission* (London: Routledge, 2013); and Cedric de Coning and Eli Stamnes (eds), *UN Peacebuilding Architecture* (London: Routledge, 2016).

54 "Trust Fund Fact Sheet," http://mptf.undp.org/factsheet/fund/PB000.

55 Advisory Group of Experts for the 2015 Review of United Nations Peacebuilding Architecture, *The Challenge of Sustaining Peace*, UN document A/69/968–S/2015/490, June 29, 2015.

56 Alberto Cutillo, *International Assistance to Countries Emerging from Conflict: A Review of Fifteen Years of Interventions and the Future of Peacebuilding*, International Peace Academy, Security–Development Nexus Program, February 2006, p. 60.

57 OECD, *Fragile States 2014: Domestic Resource Mobilisation in Fragile States* (Paris: OECD, 2014), p. 24.

58 Stephen Browne and Thomas G. Weiss (eds), *Peacebuilding Challenges for the UN Development System* (New York: FUNDS, 2015).

59 "Exclusive: President Barack Obama on 'Fox News Sunday,'" April 10, 2016, www.foxnews.com/transcript/2016/04/10/exclusive-president-barack-obama-on-fox-news-sunday.html.

60 Carsten Stahn, "R2P and *Jus Post Bellum*: Toward a Polycentric Approach," in *Jus Post Bellum: Mapping the Normative Foundations*, ed. Carsten Stahn, Jennifer Easterday, and Jens Iverson (Oxford: Oxford University Press, 2014), pp. 102–22. See also Antonia Chayes, "Chapter VII½: Is *Jus Post Bellum* Possible?" *European Journal of International Law* 24(1) (2013): 291–305; Gary J. Bass, "Jus Post Bellum," *Philosophy and Public Affairs* 45(3) (2004): 384–412; and Jean Bethke Elshtain, "The Ethics of Fleeing: What America Still Owes Iraq," *World Affairs* 170(4) (2008): 91–8.

61 Mohammed Sahnoun, "Foreword," in *Responsibility to Protect: Cultural*

Perspectives in the Global South, ed. Rama Mani and Thomas G. Weiss (London: Routledge, 2011), pp. xx–xxii; Albrecht Schnabel, "The Responsibility to Rebuild," in *The Routledge Handbook on the Responsibility to Protect*, ed. W. Andy Knight and Frazer Egerton (London: Routledge, 2012), pp. 50–63; and Outi Keranen, "What Happened to the Responsibility to Rebuild?" *Global Governance* 22(3) (2016): 331–48.

CHAPTER 7 A LESS REPRESSIVE AND UNKIND WORLD WITH ENHANCED HUMAN RIGHTS AND HUMANITARIAN ACTION?

1 Jan Herman Burgers, "The Road to San Francisco: The Revival of the Human Rights Idea in the Twentieth Century," *Human Rights Quarterly* 14(2) (1992): 447–78; and Samuel Moyn, *The Last Utopia: Human Rights in History* (Cambridge, MA: Harvard University Press, 2012).
2 David P. Forsythe, "Human Rights and Peace," in *Encyclopedia of Human Rights*, 3rd edn (New York: Oxford University Press, 2009), pp. 187–96.
3 Cathal J. Nolan, *Principled Diplomacy: Security and Rights in U.S. Foreign Policy* (Westport, CT: Greenwood Press, 1993).
4 Daniel C. Thomas, *The Helsinki Effect: International Norms, Human Rights, and the Demise of Communism* (Princeton, NJ: Princeton University Press, 2001); and William Korey, *The Promises We Keep: Human Rights, the Helsinki Process, and American Foreign Policy* (New York: St Martin's Press, 1993).
5 Christopher N. J. Roberts, *The Contentious History of the International Bill of Human Rights* (Cambridge: Cambridge University Press, 2015), p. 50.
6 Sakiko Fukada-Parr, Terra Lawson-Remer, and Susan Randolph, *Fulfilling Social and Economic Rights* (Oxford: Oxford University Press, 2015).
7 William F. Felice, *The Global New Deal: Economic and Social Human Rights in World Politics*, 2nd edn (Lanham, MD: Rowman & Littlefield, 2010); and A. Belden Fields, *Rethinking Human Rights for the New Millennium* (New York: Palgrave Macmillan, 2003).
8 Roger Normand and Sarah Zaidi, *Human Rights at the UN: The Political History of Universal Justice* (Indianapolis: Indiana University Press, 2008), pp. 211–12. Stephen Hopgood argues otherwise in *The Endtimes of Human Rights* (Ithaca, NY: Cornell University Press, 2013).
9 Quoted in *Foreign Policy* (November–December 2015), p. 49.
10 Zeid Ra'ad Zeid Al-Hussein, *A Comprehensive Strategy to Eliminate Future Sexual Exploitation and Abuse in UN Peacekeeping Operations*, UN document A/59/710, March 24, 2005.
11 "Statement of Commitment on Eliminating Sexual Exploitation and Abuse by UN and non-UN Personnel," https://interagencystandingcommittee.org/focal-points/documents-public/statement-commitment-eliminating-sexual-exploitation-and-abuse-un-and.
12 Neil MacFarquhar, "Peacekeepers' Sex Scandals Linger, On Screen and Off," *New York Times*, September 7, 2011.
13 Muna Ndulo, "The United Nations Response to Sexual Abuse and Exploitation of Women and Girls by Peacekeepers during Peacekeeping Missions," *Berkeley Journal and International Law* 27(1) (2009): 147.

14 Warren Hoge, "Report Finds U.N. Isn't Moving to End Sex Abuse by Peacekeepers," *New York Times*, October 19, 2005.

15 Maggie Farley, "U.N. Losing the Battle to Eliminate Sexual Abuse," *Los Angeles Times*, October 19, 2005.

16 "The Growing UN Scandal over Sex Abuse and 'Peacekeeper Babies,'" *Washington Post*, February 27, 2016.

17 "Kompass v. Secretary-General of the United Nations: Order on an Application for Suspension of Action," UN document UNDT/GVA/2015/126, May 5, 2015, www.un.org/en/oaj/files/undt/orders/gva-2015-099.pdf.

18 Obi Anyadike, "Top UN Whistleblower Resigns, Citing Impunity and Lack of Accountability," *IRIN*, June 7, 2016; www.irinnews.org/analy sis/2016/06/07/exclusive-top-un-whistleblower-resigns-citing-impunity-and-lack-accountability.

19 Warren Hoge, "Khartoum Expels U.N. Envoy Who Has Been Outspoken on Darfur Atrocities," *New York Times*, October 23, 2006.

20 Quoted in "Dodging Accountability at the U.N.," *New York Times*, August 22, 2016.

21 Thomas G. Weiss and David A. Korn, *Internal Displacement: Conceptualization and its Consequences* (London: Routledge, 2005).

22 David A. Korn, *Exodus within Borders* (Washington, DC: Brookings Institution Press, 1999).

23 UNHCR, *Global Trends, Forced Displacement 2015*, www.unhcr.org/en-us/statistics/country/556725e69/unhcr-global-trends-2015.html.

24 Erin D. Mooney, "The Concept of Internal Displacement and the Case for IDPs as a Category of Concern," *Refugee Survey Quarterly* 24(3) (2005): 9–26.

25 Roberta Cohen and Francis M. Deng, *Masses in Flight: The Global Crisis of Internal Displacement* (Washington, DC: Brookings Institution Press, 1998), p. 3.

26 Donald Steinberg, *Orphans of Conflict: Caring for the Internally Displaced* (Washington, DC: US Institute of Peace Press, 2005), Special Report #148.

27 Centers for Disease Control, "Famine-Affected, Refugee, and Displaced Populations: Recommendations for Public Health Issues," *Morbidity and Mortality Weekly Report* 41, RR-13 (1992). Later estimates are comparable in Peter Salama, Paul Spiegel, and Richard Brennan, "Refugees – No Less Vulnerable: The Internally Displaced in Humanitarian Emergencies," *The Lancet* 357(9266) (2001): 1430–1.

28 Roberta Cohen and Francis M. Deng (eds), *The Forsaken People: Case Studies of the Internally Displaced* (Washington, DC: Brookings Institution Press, 1998), pp. 128–9.

29 Cécile Dubernet, *The International Containment of Displaced Persons: Humanitarian Spaces without Exit* (Aldershot, UK: Ashgate, 2001) is rebutted by Erin D. Mooney, "In-country Protection: Out of Bounds for UNHCR?" in *Refugee Rights and Realities: Evolving International Concepts and Regimes*, ed. Frances Nicholson and Patrick Twomey (Cambridge: Cambridge University Press, 1999), pp. 200–19.

30 Gil Loescher, Alexander Betts, and James Milner, *UNHCR: The Politics and Practice of Refugee Protection into the Twenty-First Century*, 3rd edn (London: Routledge, 2017).

31 UN, *New York Declaration for Refugees and Migrants, Outcome Document*

for 19 September 2016 High-Level Meeting to Address Large Movements of Refugees and Migrants, UN document A/RES/71/1.

32 Stephen Browne and Thomas G. Weiss (eds), *Peacebuilding Challenges for the UN Development System* (New York: Future UN Development System Project, 2015).

33 Nicola Reindorp and Peter Wiles, *Humanitarian Coordination: Lessons from Recent Field Experience* (London: ODI, 2001), p. 8.

34 *Global Humanitarian Assistance Report 2016* (Somerset, UK: Development Initiatives, 2014), hereafter GHA, pp. 4–5; http://devinit.org/wp-content/uploads/2016/06/GHA-Report-2016_Executive-summary.pdf.

35 Ibid.

36 Naomi Klein, *The Shock Doctrine: The Rise of Disaster Capitalism* (New York: Metropolitan Books, 2007).

37 Alexander Cooley and James Ron, "The NGO Scramble: Organizational Insecurity and the Political Economy of Transnational Action," *International Security* 27(1) (2002): 13.

38 Kofi Annan, *Renewing the United Nations: A Programme for Reform* (New York: UN, 1997); and Thomas G. Weiss, "Humanitarian Shell Games: Whither UN Reform?" *Security Dialogue* 29(1) (1998): 9–23. See also James C. Ingram, *The Future Architecture for International Humanitarian Assistance* (Canberra: Peace Research Centre, 1993).

39 Alexander Betts et al., *Refugee Economies: Forced Displacement and Development* (Oxford: Oxford University Press, 2017).

40 Anna Powles, Negar Partow, and Nick Nelson (eds), *United Nations Peacekeeping Challenge: The Importance of the Integrated Approach* (Farnham, UK: Ashgate, 2015).

41 Humanitarian Policy Group, Tufts Feinstein International Center, and King's College London, *Planning from the Future: Is the Humanitarian System Fit for Purpose?* November 2016, p. 55; www.planningfromthefuture.org.

42 Laura Shepherd, "Power and Authority in the Production of the United Nations Security Council Resolution 1325," *International Studies Quarterly* 52(2) (2008): 383–404.

43 UN Women, *Preventing Conflict, Transforming Justice, Securing the Peace: A Global Study on the Implementation of Security Council Resolution 1325* (New York: UN, 2015), p. 14.

44 Melissa Labonte and Gaynel Curry, "Women, Peace, and Security: Are We There Yet?" *Global Governance* 22(3) (2016): 311–19.

45 UN, *Delivering as One* (New York: UN, 2006).

46 UN, *2005 World Summit Outcome,* General Assembly resolution A/RES/60/1, October 24, 2005.

47 Dan Plesch, Thomas G. Weiss, and Leah Owen, "UN War Crimes Commission and International Law: Revisiting World War II Precedents and Practice," in *Global Community Yearbook of International Law and Jurisprudence 2015* (Oxford: Oxford University Press, 2016), pp. 71–109; and Dan Plesch, *Human Rights after Hitler: The Lost History of Prosecuting Axis War Crimes* (Washington, DC: Georgetown University Press, 2017).

48 Fanny Benedetti and John L. Washburn, "Drafting the International Criminal Court Treaty," *Global Governance* 5(1) (1999): 1–38.

49 Richard Goldstone, "Foreword," *The United Nations War Crimes Commission Symposium, Criminal Law Forum* 25(1) (2014): 9–15.

50 Andrew Hurrell, "Foreword to the Third Edition," in Hedley Bull, *The Anarchical Society* (London: Macmillan, 2002), p. xiii.
51 Dan Plesch and Thomas G. Weiss, "1945's Lesson: 'Good-enough' Global Governance Ain't Good Enough," *Global Governance* 21(2) (2015): 197–204.
52 *Informal Expert Paper: The Principle of Complementarity in Practice*, www.icc-cpi.int/NR/rdonlyres/20BB4494-70F9-4698-8E30-907F631453ED/2819 84/complementarity.pdf.
53 Ramesh Thakur, "Atrocity Crimes," in *Why Govern? Rethinking Demand and Progress in Global Governance*, ed. Amitav Acharya (Cambridge: Cambridge University Press, 2016), p. 31.
54 UN News Centre, "Interview," www.un.org/apps/news/story.asp?NewsID=52126#.V7xjSlsrJaQ.
55 Peter Gatrell, "World Wars and Population Displacement in Europe in the Twentieth Century," *Contemporary European History* 16(4) (2007): 415–26.
56 The compact that is supposed to emerge as a follow-up to the September 2016 UN Summit and the "New York Declaration for Refugees and Migrants," UN document A/71/1, September 19, 2016.

CHAPTER 8 A LESS IMPOVERISHED AND POLLUTED WORLD WITH ENHANCED DEVELOPMENT?

1 Kenneth Quinnell, "Executive PayWatch 2015: CEO Pay Continues to Skyrocket," *AFL-CIO*, May 13, 2016; www.aflcio.org/Blog/Corporate-Greed/Executive-PayWatch-2015-CEO-Pay-Continues-to-Skyrocket.
2 Institute for Policy Studies, "Income Inequality," http://inequality.org/income-inequality/; and "Global Inequality," http://inequality.org/global-inequality/.
3 Mahfuzur Rahman, *World Economic Issues at the United Nations: Half a Century of Debate* (Dordrecht: Kluwer, 2002), p. 145.
4 Johan Kaufmann, *United Nations Decision Making* (Alphen aan den Rijn, Netherlands: Sijthoff & Noordhoff, 1980).
5 "Poverty and Inequality," www.fao.org/docrep/015/i2490e/i2490e02c.pdf.
6 Stephen Browne and Thomas G. Weiss, "The UN's Post-2015 Development Agenda – New Goals, New Leadership," in *Great Decisions 2016* (New York: Foreign Policy Association, 2016), pp. 63–74.
7 *Development Aid in 2015 Continues to Grow Despite Costs for In-Donor Refugees*, OECD, April 13, 2016.
8 "Unsustainable Goals," *The Economist*, March 28, 2015.
9 Nate Silver, *The Noise and the Signal* (New York: Penguin, 2013).
10 Roberto Bissio, "The 'A' Word: Monitoring the SDGs," *FUNDS Briefing* 26, February 2015; www.futureun.org/media/archive1/briefings/FUNDS_Brief26_Feb2015_Bissio.pdf.
11 Louis Emmerij, Richard Jolly, and Thomas G. Weiss, *Ahead of the Curve?* (Bloomington: Indiana University Press, 2001).
12 Roger Normand and Sarah Zaidi, *Human Rights at the UN: The Political History of Universal Justice* (Bloomington: Indiana University Press, 2008), pp. 301–2 and 309.

13 Ibid., p. 303.
14 Philip Alston, "Making Space for New Human Rights: The Case of the Right to Development," *Harvard Human Rights Yearbook* 1 (1988): 21.
15 Fantu Cheru, "Developing Countries and the Right to Development: A Retrospective and Prospective African View," *Third World Quarterly* 37(7) (2016): 1268–83.
16 Martin Khor, *Rethinking Globalization: Critical Issues and Policy Choice* (London: Zed Books, 2000), p. 37.
17 David Hulme, *Should Rich Nations Help the Poor?* (Cambridge: Polity, 2016), pp. 110–24.
18 Craig Murphy, *International Organization and Industrial Change: Global Governance since 1850* (Cambridge: Polity, 1994).
19 Sonia Shah, *Pandemic: Tracking Contagions, from Cholera to Ebola and Beyond* (New York: Farrar, Straus & Giroux, 2016).
20 UN AIDS, "AIDS Fact Sheet," 2013.
21 World Bank, "Prevalence of HIV, Total (% of Population Ages 15–49)," http://data.worldbank.org/indicator/SH.DYN.AIDS.ZS.
22 UNAIDS, "Fact Sheet 2016: Global Statistics – 2015," www.unaids.org/sites/default/files/media_asset/UNAIDS_FactSheet_en.pdf.
23 Leon Gordenker, Roger A. Coate, Christer Jönsson, and Peter Söderholm, *International Cooperation in Response to AIDS* (London: Pinter, 1995).
24 WHO, *World Health Report 1998* (Geneva: WHO, 1998) and *World Health Report 1999* (Geneva: WHO, 1999).
25 Quoted in *Washington Post*, July 5, 2000.
26 "Will Ebola Change the Game? Ten Essential Reforms before the Next Pandemic," *The Lancet* 386 (10009) (2015): 2204–21.
27 Martin I. Meltzer et al., "Estimating the Future Number of Cases in the Ebola Epidemic – Liberia and Sierra Leone, 2014–2015," *Morbidity and Mortality Weekly Report*, September 26, 2014, US Centers for Disease Control and Prevention.
28 Sheri Fink, "Panels Advise Bolstering W.H.O. for Crises Like Ebola," *New York Times*, November 23, 2015.
29 "U.N. Health Agency Dismisses Call to Move Olympics over Zika Virus in Brazil," *New York Times*, May 29, 2016.
30 Sidney Dell, "Economics in the United Nations," in *Economists in International Agencies*, ed. A. W. Coats (New York: Praeger, 1986), pp. 44–5.
31 Devesh Kapur, John P. Lewis, and Richard Webb, *The World Bank: Its First Half Century* (Washington, DC: Brookings Institution Press, 1997), Vol. 1: *History*, p. 154. See Richard Jolly, Louis Emmerij, Dharam Ghai, and Frédéric Lapeyre, *UN Contributions to Development Theory and Practice* (Bloomington: Indiana University Press, 2004), ch. 3; and Olav Stokke, *International Development Assistance* (Bloomington: Indiana University Press, 2010).
32 Quoted by Thomas G. Weiss, Tatiana Carayannis, Louis Emmerij, and Richard Jolly, *UN Voices: The Struggle for Development and Social Justice* (Bloomington: Indiana University Press, 2005), p. 202.
33 UN, *A Study of the Capacity of the United Nations Development System* (Geneva: United Nations, 1969), UN document DP/5.
34 Quoted by Weiss et al., *UN Voices*, p. 206.

35 ECOSOC Independent Team of Advisors, "The Future We Want – the UN We Need," informal document dated June 21, 2016, for ECOSOC Dialogue Workshop, p. 1.
36 High-Level Panel on UN System-Wide Coherence in the Fields of Development, Humanitarian Assistance and Environment, *Delivering as One* (New York: UN, 2006).
37 Ibid., p. 44.
38 Stephen Browne and Thomas G. Weiss, *Supporting the 2030 Sustainable Development Agenda: Lessons from the MDG Fund Experience* (New York: FUNDS, 2016).
39 Sally Fegan-Wyles, "Delivering as One: Could It Help the 2030 SDG Agenda?" *FUNDS Briefing 38*, February 2016; www.futureun.org/en/Publications-Surveys/Article?newsid=85.
40 UN, *Independent Evaluation of Delivering as One* (New York: UN, 2012), pp. 74–5.
41 Silke Weinlich, *Reforming Development Cooperation at the United Nations: An Analysis of Policy Position and Actions of Key States on Reform Options* (Bonn: German Development Institute, 2011), p. 27.
42 UNDG, "Delivering as One: The United Nations We Want – Our Commitment to the Way Forward," June 2012; https://un.org.al/subindex.php?faqe=details&id=112&mnu=36.
43 *Independent Evaluation of Delivering as One*, p. 307.
44 Silke Weinlich and Urs Zollinger, *Lessons from Delivering as One: Options for UN Member States* (Bonn: German Development Institute, 2012).
45 Bruce Jenks and Bruce Jones, *United Nations Development at a Crossroads* (New York: Center for International Cooperation, 2013).
46 Available at www.futureun.org.
47 Catherine Weaver, *The Hypocrisy Trap: The World Bank and the Poverty of Reform* (Princeton, NJ: Princeton University Press, 2008).
48 UN, *A Study of the Capacity*, p. iii.

CHAPTER 9 LET'S BE SERIOUS – THE UN WE WANT (AND NEED) FOR THE WORLD WE WANT

1 "Master, Mistress or Mouse?" *The Economist*, May 21, 2016. For an account of what changed in 2016, see Yvonne Terlinghen, "A Better Process, a Stronger UN Secretary-General: How Historic Change Was Forged and What Comes Next," *Ethics and International Affairs* 31(2) (2017): forthcoming.
2 Kjell Enkelbrekt, *High-Table Diplomacy: The Reshaping of International Security Institutions* (Washington, DC: Georgetown University Press, 2016); and Vincent Pouliot, *International Pecking Orders: The Politics and Practice of Multilateral Diplomacy* (Cambridge: Cambridge University Press, 2016).
3 Peter Nardin, *UN Security Council Reform* (London: Routledge, 2016).
4 Secretary General's High-Level Panel on Threats, Challenges and Change, *A More Secure World: A Shared Responsibility* (New York: UN, 2004), paras. 247–60.
5 UN, *2005 World Summit Outcome*, General Assembly resolution A/RES/60/1, October 24, 2005, para. 154.

6 Thomas G. Weiss, *Overcoming the Security Council Impasse: Envisioning Reform*, United Nations Occasional Paper no. 14 (Berlin: Friedrich Ebert Stiftung, 2005).

7 Georg Kell, "Relations with the Private Sector," in *The Oxford Handbook of International Organizations*, ed. Jacob Katz Cogan, Ian Hurd, and Ian Johnstone (Oxford: Oxford University Press, 2016), pp. 730–73. See also Catia Gregoratti, *The UN Global Compact* (London: Routledge, forthcoming).

8 John Gerard Ruggie, "global_governance.net: The Global Compact as Learning Network," *Global Governance* 7(4) (2001): 371–8. See also Jean-Philippe Thérien and Vincent Pouliot, "The Global Compact: Shifting the Politics of International Development?" *Global Governance* 12(1) (2006): 55–75; and Klaus Schwab, "Global Corporate Citizenship: Working with Governments and Civil Society," *Foreign Affairs* 87(1) (2008): 107–18.

9 Tagi Sagafi-Nejad with John Dunning, *The UN and Transnational Corporations* (Bloomington: Indiana University Press, 2008), pp. 41–54.

10 Oliver F. Williams, *Corporate Social Responsibility: The Role of Business in Sustainable Development* (London: Routledge, 2014).

11 John Gerard Ruggie, "Business and Human Rights: The Evolving International Agenda," *American Journal of International Law* 101 (October 2007): 819–40, at 819; and *Promotion and Protection of all Human Rights, Civil, Political, Economic, Social and Cultural Rights, Including the Right to Development*, UN document A/HRC/8/5, April 7, 2008.

12 Michael Mandelbaum, "The Reluctance to Intervene," *Foreign Policy* 95 (Summer 1994): 11.

13 John Mackinlay, "The Requirement for a Multinational Enforcement Capability," in *Collective Security in a Changing World*, ed. Thomas G. Weiss (Boulder, CO: Lynne Rienner, 1993), pp. 139–52.

14 Mateja Peter, "Between Doctrine and Practice: The UN Peacekeeping Dilemma," *Global Governance* 21(3) (2015): 351–70.

15 Anna Powles, Negar Partow, and Nick Nelson (eds), *United Nations Peacekeeping Challenge: The Importance of the Integrated Approach* (Farnham, UK: Ashgate, 2015).

16 Thomas G. Weiss and Martin Welz, "The UN and the African Union in Mali and Beyond: A Shotgun Wedding?" *International Affairs* 90(4) (2014): 889–905.

17 Somini Sengupta, "Beleaguered Blue Helmets: What Is the Role of U.N. Peacekeepers?" *New York Times*, July 12, 2014.

18 "Contributors to United Nations Peacekeeping Operations as of 31 July 2016," www.un.org/en/peacekeeping/contributors/2016/jul16_1.pdf.

19 UN, *Uniting Our Strengths for Peace – Politics, Partnership and People*, Report of the High-Level Independent Panel on Peace Operations, June 16, 2015; www.globalr2p.org/media/files/n1518145.pdf.

20 Lisa Hultman, Jacob Kathman, and Megan Shannon, "United Nations and Civilian Protection in Civil War," *American Journal of Political Science* 57(4) (2013): 875–91.

21 Thomas G. Weiss and Tatiana Carayannis, "Windows of Opportunity for UN Reform: Historical Lessons for the Next Secretary-General," *International Affairs* 92(2) (2017): 1–18; and Ramesh Thakur, "Choosing the Ninth United Nations Secretary-General: Looking Back, Looking Ahead," *Global Governance* 23(1) (2017): 1–13.

22 Kofi Annan, "The Quiet Revolution," *Global Governance* 4(2) (1998): 123–38.
23 Christine Chinkin and Hilary Charlesworth, *The Boundaries of International Law: A Feminist Analysis* (New York: Juris, 2000).
24 Karin Landgren, "The Lost Agenda: Gender Parity in Senior UN Appointments," *Global Peace Operations Review*, December 14, 2015; http://peaceoperationsreview.org/commentary/the-lost-agenda-gender-pari ty-in-senior-un-appointments.
25 Paul A. Volcker, Richard J. Goldstone, and Mark Pieth, *The Management of the United Nations Oil-for-Food Programme*, vol. 1: *The Report of the Committee*, September 7, 2005, p. 4; http://news.bbc.co.uk/2/shared/bsp/hi/ pdfs/08_09_05_volume1.pdf.
26 Kevin Rudd, "My 10 Principles to Reform the United Nations, before it's Too Late," *The Guardian*, August 8, 2016.
27 Franz Baumann, "United Nations Management– an Oxymoron?" *Global Governance* 22(4) (2016): 453–60.
28 Quoted by Somini Sengupta, "After Years of Negotiations, U.N. Sets Development Goals to Guide All Countries," *New York Times*, September 26, 2015.
29 William Easterly, "The SDGs Should Stand for Senseless, Dreamy, Garbled," *Foreign Policy* blog, September 28, 2015; http://foreignpolicy. com/2015/09/28/the-sdgs-are-utopian-and-worthless-mdgs-development-ri se-of-the-rest/.
30 UNHCR, *2006–2015, Ten Years of Reforms: Structural Impact* (Geneva: UNHCR, 2016), p. 7.
31 Brian Urquhart, *Hammarskjöld* (New York: W. W. Norton, 1994).
32 Thomas Hale, David Held, and Kevin Young, *Gridlock: Why Global Cooperation Is Failing When We Need it Most* (Cambridge: Polity, 2013).
33 Brian Urquhart, "The New American Century," *New York Review of Books*, August 11, 2005, p. 42.
34 Moisés Naim, "Minilateralism: The Magic Number to Get Real International Action," *Foreign Policy* 173 (July–August 2009): 135–6.
35 Anne-Marie Slaughter, *A New World Order* (Princeton, NJ: Princeton University Press, 2004).
36 Daniel W. Drezner, "'Good Enough' Global Governance and International Finance," *Foreign Policy* blog, January 30, 2013; http://drezner.foreign policy.com/posts/2013/01/30/good_enough_global_governance_and_inter national_finance; and Stewart Patrick, "The Unruled World: The Case for Good Enough Global Governance," *Foreign Affairs* 93(1) (2014): 58–73.
37 Scott Barrett, *Why Cooperate? The Incentive to Supply Global Public Goods* (Oxford: Oxford University Press, 2013), p. 19.
38 Amitav Acharya, "The Future of Global Governance: Fragmentation May Be Inevitable and Creative," *Global Governance* 22(4) (2016): 461–72.
39 Dan Plesch and Thomas G. Weiss, "1945's Lesson: 'Good Enough' Global Governance Ain't Good Enough," *Global Governance* 21(2) (2015): 197–204.
40 John F. Kennedy, "Annual Message to the Congress on the State of the Union," January 11, 1962; www.presidency.ucsb.edu/ws/?pi.

INDEX